EDUCATION THROUGH PARTNERSHIP

EDUCATION THROUGH PARTNERSHIP

David S. Seeley

With a Foreword by Theodore Sizer

American Enterprise Institute for Public Policy Research
Washington, D.C.

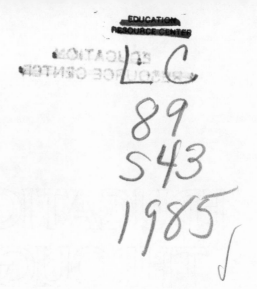
Library of Congress Cataloging-in-Publication Data
Seeley, David S.
    Education through partnership.

    Bibliography: p.
    Includes index.
    1. Education and state—United States. 2. Educational
equalization—United States. 3. Home and school—
United States. 4. School, Choice of—United States.
5. Social institutions—United States. I. Title.
LC89.S43 1985   379.73   85-11193
ISBN 0-8447-3579-5 (pbk. : alk. paper)

AEI Studies 417

1 3 5 7 9 10 8 6 4 2

 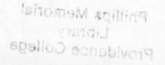
Printed in the United States of America

CONTENTS

PRESIDENT'S FOREWORD

The reissuance of this important book by David Seeley could not come at more auspicious time. Excellence in education is high on the nation's agenda, and Seeley provides a thoughtful and reasoned set of prescriptions to achieve that objective. When this book was originally commissioned—more than five years ago—the questions Seeley raised were still largely academic. A small group of education analysts and thinkers had begun to wrestle with these problems, but they did not yet figure in the national consciousness. Today they do.

Seeley's twin themes of choice and partnership are central to pioneering work that has become the hallmark of the American Enterprise Institute.

First is choice. As a people committed to democratic capitalism, choice is central to our definition of ourselves. The defining characteristic of a free people is their capacity—both as individuals and in association—to choose their destiny freely. For generations, the American people through their elected representatives have chosen to organize and run their schools locally. Schools emerged as small public monopolies. Students were compelled to attend school based on place of residence. In American public education, geography was destiny.

In a highly mobile society, with relatively low levels of education, the idea of mass education made it seem natural to standardize education and regularize the way people would receive its benefits. Since education was organized locally, and financed locally, patterns of neighborhood assignment were neither surprising nor irrational. But these patterns emerged from a much different society from the one in which we now find ourselves.

Today many parents know as much about the quality of schooling as the teacher or school board member. There is no longer any compelling reason to assume that compulsion needs to play its former role in American education. If a free people can choose their elected representatives, choose their neighborhood of residence, and select freely within the economic system among employment options and the supply of goods and services, why can they not choose among schools?

Indeed, if we believe that education is important, then the single most important decision a parent will ever make on his child's behalf is in which school to enroll him. Schools do more than impart skills—they transmit democratic and intellectual values, and parents should be active participants in selecting the school they consider congruent with those values. No school can be all things to all people. If it tries to be, it must of necessity fail. But every school can embody a coherent set of intellectual and pedagogical activities that will serve the interests of its teachers and students.

Choice then is a double-edged sword. It is not simply a matter of parents choosing from among a variety of passive service providers. Schools themselves are active partners in the process. If they are not, as Seeley points out, they will lose their capacity to respond to their constituency.

The issue is not one of dismantling the present system. To the contrary, we are confronted with an opportunity to evolve, through choice and partnership, an improved and more responsive system of public education.

There is a second dimension to Seeley's book that is also of the utmost importance today, the role of mediating structures in the modern world. Long an interest of scholars and analysts at AEI, mediating structures are those social institutions that stand between the individual and the larger society. They include but are not limited to family and friends, fraternal and benevolent associations, churches and synagogues, clubs and unions, and schools and colleges. Each has an institutional life apart from the state—they give individual and social life its richness, variety, and meaning. Public policy should at minimum make these institutions no worse off than they currently are; ideally, public policy should strengthen them. Seeley's fine book is a strategy to do just that.

As Seeley so aptly points out, we are not condemned to live with organizational forms that are no longer congruent with the needs and opportunities of the present. We too can choose the schools we think will best serve our children. *Education through Partnership*, a thoughtful and provocative book, moves us closer to that choice.

William J. Baroody, Jr.
President
American Enterprise Institute

FOREWORD

There is a nice *Garfield* cartoon strip that has the pudgy cat before a TV set, fingering the channel buttons. As Garfield's boredom visibly sets in, the show he is watching wails at him from the tube: "No, no! Don't change the channel! We need the ratings!" Garfield, heartless as always, punches the button for a new channel. The old station fades away with a moan, "Pleeeease! . . . Arrgh!" Garfield, in the final panel, turns to us, the readers: "Choice is a powerful thing."

Yes, choice is power. Citizens in a democracy try to have as much choice as possible, consistent with minimal public order. We want to decide where and how we live, where and how we work, what we believe. If we are, on a certain issue, in a minority, we want to know that we can voice our opinions and that they will be respected, indeed protected by the majority, on principle.

This book by David Seeley is about the richly varying voices and choices of individuals and groups in our American communities. It is about the necessary mediation which our society needs to protect both individuals and the legitimate claims of the larger community. It is about mediation between each one of us and the ever-increasing and powerful structures of modern society. Seeley writes of old-fashioned strengths such as trust and loyalty, and he casts them in intensely humanistic terms.

As current readers will be aware, Seeley's message runs counter to much current policy rhetoric about public education. The language in the air is full of bootcamp jargon: stiffen the program, toughen the curriculum, make people accountable—all with the assumption that these citizens will have no personal say in all this stiff toughness. The focus of policy is state government, and the results are regulation and direction, more standardized imposition from the central organs of government. Excellence, we are told, will evolve only when we (for which read, "central authorities") impose it, and insist on it.

One of the paradoxes of the current scene is that many of the people who favor more strictly regulated forms of public education—largely perceived to be on the neoconservative or conservative wing of American politics—are the same folk who are arguing for greater choice among schools. One marvels at this: if schooling is to have standardized ends and standardized means, why is *choice* at all necessary, indeed even desirable? At some point, the public is going to understand better than it does now the apparent contradiction between these two themes espoused by so many of the same people—the theme of centralized authority in education and the theme of the rights of families to have choices among their schools. The contradiction is frustrating, as there are strong claims on both sides. We need authority for education in the community-at-large, and we need real choices for families among significantly varied schools. David Seeley's book provides a way out, a compromise position, a pattern of partnerships which soften the edges both of ruthless regulation and of ruthless choice. Seeley creatively shows us a way to go that avoids both unbridled choice and autocracy.

Accordingly, Seeley's book is exceedingly important. It will be seen as fanciful and perhaps impractical by many, as he constantly reminds us about the subtleties of education and the need to honor these. American educational politicians abhor subtlety. While urging higher standards, he directly challenges the standardizers: "No system of education built on a service-delivery concept will achieve its goals because it cannot deal with human idiosyncracies." It is individual human contact that is important, a finding which is as revolutionary as it is obvious: "The fact that the student must be in partnership with whoever is immediately teaching him is the most fundamental element in any educational policy, one that is easily forgotten in bureaucratized and professionalized educational service-delivery systems. Successful learning partnerships are intense with emotional interaction."

It is in this intense human interaction that the mediation takes place. As Seeley points out, the world of the home and the world of the larger society are not the same and must not be treated the same. The values of one must understand and accommodate the values of the other: "Differing school and home values can ... be productive if properly blended. If schools were not different from homes, there would be no need for schools. Even bureaucratic values, usually missing at home, are important for inducting students into the more impersonal and abstract relationships of the public worlds of work, technology, law, and citizenship."

Very simply, David Seeley has given us a different—and necessarily more complicated—way of looking at schools and schooling than is the case in current educational policy. His suggestions will not appeal to those who are looking for the quick fix in educational "reform." Nor will it satisfy others who stridently argue the absolute claims for educational freedom on the part of any small subgroup, including a particular family. Those who claim that the state should decide what ideas are exposed to our children will certainly not like it. Seeley gives us a middle ground—a compromise—and like all middle grounds it is suffused with necessary ambiguity. It involves give and take, a sharing of power, a balance of competing claims. Above all, it calls for a *partnership*. And partnerships require trust and respect and toleration.

Is American politics patient enough and generous enough to take Seeley's message seriously? Can we have standards in American education and variety too, community authority on behalf of excellent education as well as personal freedom?

One fervently hopes so. Seeley points the way.

Theodore R. Sizer

PREFACE

The mediating structures project, of which this book is a part, had an ambitious purpose. Directed by Peter L. Berger and Richard John Neuhaus, with funding from the National Endowment for the Humanities and sponsorship of the American Enterprise Institute, it was designed to stimulate significant reconceptualization of public policy in five important areas—health, education, welfare, criminal justice, and housing. It hoped also to build a bridge between conservatives and liberals whose ideological battles over the role of government have become increasingly sterile and unproductive.

When Peter Berger asked me to undertake the volume on education policy, I was somewhat stunned. I was not in the business of writing books. As a lawyer, activist, and sometime government education official, I was busy trying to reform education in other ways. It seemed to me there were already too many books; I barely had time to read them, let alone write one. Nevertheless, I was immensely pleased and challenged by the invitation. I had spent over twenty years trying to figure out why public education in the United States was so much less effective than it could or should be, and I had finally begun to arrive at some answers.

In line with the assumptions of the project, I too felt that much of the current debate over educational policy was misdirected. Neither the attacks on the present system nor the arguments of its defenders were getting us very far. Both liberals and conservatives had a right to be dissatisfied with what the schools were doing, but neither seemed to have a handle on moving us toward something better. Nor did the answer seem to lie just with specific projects and policies that might produce improvement here and there. I had been involved with such efforts since the mid-1950s. I was beginning to understand why so many of these reforms failed in the end to accomplish very much, why the energies and efforts of so many dedicated school and community people so often ended in frustration, and why, finally, the richest society in human history continues, even as it races toward the 21st century, to provide such inadequate education for so many of its children.

The opportunity to write this book gave me the chance to think through those answers and see if they indeed made sense. In the process of writing the book, my thinking, of course, changed in many ways. What seemed to be sound ideas to begin with melted away on more careful reflection or were transformed into what I hope are better ideas. And as work on the book progressed, some new ideas derived from research on the project played a major role in shaping its structure.

The end product is by no means a final answer. In many ways the book is just a beginning for me—as I hope it will be for many of its readers—of a process of testing and perfecting a new conceptual framework for educational policy, which itself will undoubtedly continue to be modified and transformed as it comes up against the ever-changing issues and problems in the drama of American public education.

It is, however, a beginning I profoundly believe worth making. Indeed, the project "worked" for me—it helped me reconceptualize public education policy, even though in the end my analysis did not always agree with that of Berger and Neuhaus. I hope it will likewise work in the same way for its readers, whether or not they agree with my conclusions. I am very grateful to Berger and Neuhaus for getting me to do the book and for their patience and forebearance in helping me think through its thesis and letting my analysis carry me where it would. I am also grateful to the American Enterprise Institute; never in the course of the study did it try to impose any ideological constraints upon me.

I am grateful above all to Kathy Kenyon, the research assistant provided by the project, who steered me to significant research, argued with me brilliantly and tenaciously when she felt my analysis was fuzzy or off-base, and worked laboriously and loyally long after her stipend ran out to finish up the work on the project.

The scholar who above all others influenced the structure of this book is the political economist Albert O. Hirschman, whose brilliant essay, *Exit, Voice and Loyalty* suggested the concepts of voice, choice, and loyalty around which the heart of my proposed reconceptualization of public education policy is built (see Chapters 8–11). The number of others to whom I owe a debt of gratitude is too long to list, but those who come to mind whose books and thoughts helped to jog me into new thinking or who read parts of the manuscript and made suggestions include David Rogers, Don Davies, Mario Fantini, Jacob Michaelsen, Lloyd Nielsen, Francis Keppel, Roberta Knowlton, James Comer, Ray Rist, David Tyack, Larry Cremin, Theodore Sizer, Henry Perkinson, Sara Lawrence Lightfoot, Jack Coons, Ivan Illich, and Jonathan Kozol. Needless to say, I did not always agree with these writers and critics, and they should in no sense be held responsible for the conclusions I have reached.

Lastly, I want to thank the Trustees of the Public Education Association who permitted me to write the book even while working full time for the Association; the staff of the Association, especially Judy Baum and Aisha Abdul-Aziz, who helped so much in so many ways; Pauline Hill and Catherine Meyer, who typed much of the manuscript and put up with endless corrections and retyping; and my family who put up with many nights and weekends when I was unavailable for the ordinary duties of my own immediate mediating structure. It is a formidable task to write a book while still engaged to the hilt in efforts to reform public education in New York City. There is no way this book could have been written without the help of all these people.

David Seeley

THE PROBLEM

1 INTRODUCTION

What H.G. Wells called the "race between education and catastrophe" is in full stride, and in the last quarter of the twentieth century, education is losing that race in the United States of America. The massive, once unsurpassed system of publicly administered schools is failing—failing individual students, failing families and communities, and failing the nation and its future.

The problem with public education is not that the system is a little rusty; the solution is not a can of oil and a few new parts. The problem is that the United States has the wrong kind of system; the solution will require fundamental changes in both philosophy and technique. As it exists, the public education system is built on noble motives gone awry.

For a century after the Civil War, public education in America experienced unprecedented expansion, accomplishment, and public support. It became prima facie evidence of American success. Somewhere along the way, however, the system began to stumble, so badly that the trouble today cannot be countered by public relations campaigns, innovations, coalitions of special interests, or that supposed cure-all, full funding.

Educational officials themselves speak of the problems: disorderly or violent pupils, low teacher morale, public apathy, and fiscal crises. Parents complain of poor discipline, falling achievement scores, and

3

illiterate graduates. These complaints are only symptoms of the essential trouble causing increasing disaffection with the system.

The essential trouble is the nature of the system itself, a system that has become beguiled by a "delivery system" mentality. Public education is today a professionalized, bureaucratized, governmental enterprise attempting to deliver education as a service. The system is faulty because it is designed to deliver something that cannot be delivered. The system is failing and will continue to fail until education is rediscovered as a dimension of human development dependent on personal motivation, initiative, and relationships, not on systems and "service delivery."

This book is about changing a system that is losing momentum. The tone is neither that of Cassandra nor that of Pollyanna. The present system is doomed—has doomed itself—but the nation can meet the challenge of changing it. A successful educational system is a necessity in any society, but especially in one that wants to preserve democratic values; without it catastrophe is certain. The race need not be lost, indeed, dare not be lost if America is to have a future.

Ivan Illich was one of the first of recent educational critics to recognize that the system itself is bankrupt.[1] His prescription, however, was to abolish schools—a solution that has the virtue of facing the seriousness of the problem, but one that is out of touch with social realities and public expectations about education. Illich is, nevertheless, right in understanding that the present school system kills the initiative and motivation essential for successful learning.

This book champions the cause of successful learning—learning at far higher levels than we are now achieving—but it will not offer simple solutions. Its aim is to stimulate thought. What follows grows out of a thesis set forth by sociologist Peter L. Berger and theologian Richard John Neuhaus in a project designed to foster greater focus on "mediating structures" in public policy.[2] Berger and Neuhaus theorize that many sectors of American society, including the educational sector, have surrendered too much responsibility for human affairs to governmental bureaucracies and professionalized institutions. This surrender has resulted in the neglect of the more human-sized groups, such as families, communities, voluntary associations, and religious groups: the "mediating structures" of society, which generate and communicate meaning and values and which nurture initiative and motivation.

The Berger-Neuhaus thesis by itself prescribes no single set of policies for correcting the imbalance between society's megastructures and its mediating structures. This book, like companion studies in health, welfare, housing, and criminal justice, is an exploration of the policy implications of the mediating structures concept. Within the context of education, it looks at the balance between large-scale government bureaucracies and the human-sized concerns of people. It makes proposals for changing public educational policy in order to create relationships between schools and communities, and between teachers and learners, in which more learning can take place and in which both school and nonschool resources can be more effectively used to promote learning.

The needed reconstruction of educational policy will not cure all social ills. Successful learning does not necessarily correct poverty or heal social pathologies. Social, political, and economic trends, particularly those that affect employment and social alienation, create difficult problems for education. A rebuilt educational system will not be immune to such forces, but it can establish an integrity of its own, and its success, which is possible despite serious social problems, can provide a firm base from which society can deal with its other problems.

The United States is at an educational juncture where basic values must be affirmed with open minds. Questions must be raised about how values relate to institutions and how individuals' interests can be realized in a complex, pluralistic, technological society. The achievement of successful learning requires inventive thinking and new institutional forms that can help education regain its stride.

This book is a partisan of education in the race with catastrophe. It criticizes a failing system in the hope of helping it win the race.

There are three parts to the book: Part 1 shows how the current overemphasis on governmentalization, bureaucratization, and professionalization has undermined the effectiveness and legitimacy of public education. Part 2 proposes an alternative policy framework, based on the concept of partnership and the voice, choice, and loyalty of those involved in the educational process. Part 3 applies the proposed alternative framework to a number of policy concerns facing education today—equality, the role of communities and families, decentralization, and accountability. The last chapter applies the framework to some of the most troublesome current policy controversies, such as busing, bilingual education, and book censorship.

2 THE ROOTS OF EDUCATIONAL FAILURE

The way the educational bureaucracy is organized and the values it espouses are nearly antithetical to the goals of free inquiry and social mobility.

Ray Rist, *Restructuring American Education*

Educational statistics have poured forth in recent years to prove the success or failure of American public schools. They seem only to confuse people. On the one hand, we are told that levels of literacy are higher than ever before in history and that the United States is doing a remarkable job of educating its children. On the other hand, we hear that the percentage of adult illiterates in the United States is three times as high as in the Soviet Union and that four-fifths of the students in Japan do better in mathematics than the top one-fifth in the United States.[1]

Perhaps it means more to think in terms of children than of statistics. We like to think of the successes—of Billy Smith of Hometown, U.S.A., whose education was quite good enough to get him through college and into a successful business career, or of Carmen Rodrigues of the South Bronx, who was identified as gifted in the fourth grade and went through special classes in elementary school, the Bronx High School of Science, and Harvard to become a successful physicist.

What of Carmen's classmates, however, who have not been identified as gifted? Most of them will drop far behind by the time they reach the sixth grade. Seventy percent will never graduate from high school—and not because they have alternative ways to prepare themselves for a productive life. Even many of those who do graduate will not fulfill minimal goals of literacy and competence.

And what of Billy Smith's classmates? Many of them, though literate, will have the most meager education. Twenty percent will drop out, and many of those who remain in school will not be able to write a coherent paragraph. Few will be able to read, or will be interested in reading, a thoughtful newspaper.

Billy and Carmen themselves may not be such a cause for comfort when we look at them more closely. Billy will become a successful businessman, but he will have only the vaguest understanding of science and almost no appreciation of the art, music, poetry, and literature of Western or any other civilization. He will never have had a serious conversation with a black American. Carmen, though well trained in science, will probably be weak in literature, music, and art and, because of the lack of programs in her elementary and junior high schools, may never enjoy sports.

Some critics say that public education has always failed, that it never attained Horace Mann's goal of providing for every citizen an education "the equivalent in quality of any comparable private institution," so that all could participate on an equal basis and fulfill their role as responsible citizens in a self-governing society.[2] That may be true; the important question, however, is not the achievements of the past but the education needed for the present and the future. In the race with catastrophe, the goals of education keep escalating. The failure of American schooling comes from measuring present achievement against the educational needs of children who will spend most of their lives in the complex and changing world of the twenty-first century. The important issues are why, in the most affluent society the world has ever known, educational achievement is so much lower than it need be for so many children—and what can be done about it?

One reason we have not found the answers is that we have been looking in the wrong places both for the causes of failure and for the needed solutions. Preconceptions about education and the organization of schools stand in the way of our seeing why schools fail to reach many students and why they obstruct successful learning.

SCHOOL FACTORS OR HOME FACTORS?

Much recent discussion in education has revolved around the question of whether "the school" or "the home" is at fault in the system of failure. Although dressed up with the jargon of social science, this debate is primarily political: those who advocate changes in school policy emphasize school factors as the culprit; those who defend the present school system emphasize home factors. Seldom has there been a grosser misuse of social science.

An example of this misguided debate is the public discussion of the famous Coleman Report and related studies correlating home and school factors with educational achievement. In simple outline, James Coleman and his team of statisticians and social scientists, carrying out a congressional mandate to explore "the lack of availability of equal educational opportunity in American public schools," collected data on the home backgrounds and school achievement of 645,000 public school children across the United States. The report confirmed what everyone knew: poor and minority children generally do poorly in school. The researchers also found that the kinds of "school factors" they measured, such as the age of the buildings and the percentage of teachers with master's degrees, seemed to make little difference in school achievement.[3]

Since the study was published in 1966, educational policy makers have cited Coleman's massive government study to support a number of totally unsubstantiated policy assumptions—most perniciously, that schools can make little difference in education, that school failure is caused primarily by factors outside the school, and that family background is the prime cause of school failure. Although scholars have repeatedly warned that such conclusions are neither statistically nor scientifically legitimate, the mistaken assumptions extrapolated from the Coleman Report have become Holy Writ. School officials find comfort in believing that they are doing all that can be done and that society must change home life and families if it wants to improve school achievement. Many members of the public meanwhile seem equally satisfied with the conclusion that those who are not learning in school have only themselves, their families, or their social conditions to blame.

Why are the conclusions illegitimate? The main reasons are easy to grasp. The elementary rule of statistical studies is that *correla-*

tion does not mean causation. If poor children usually do poorly in school, the statistics can just as easily mean that schools do a poorer job of teaching poor children as that poor children cannot learn. As Good, Biddle, and Brophy point out, "school quality is so tied up with both community and pupil characteristics that independent measure of it cannot be obtained."[4] Those who want to know whether to blame schools or homes for poor learning can get no comfort either way from the Coleman Report or the other statistical studies linking poor performance with children of low-income families and minority groups.

In any process in which there are many causes (and education is surely one), the choice of which cause to highlight is a question not primarily of science but of policy. Let me illustrate: A child is killed in a tenement fire. Investigation shows that the victim had been left alone by his parents and that the fire was set by a juvenile delinquent in a pile of hallway rubbish. Which of the various contributing factors was the "real cause" of the child's death? Science will not provide the answer. The relevant cause for the fire inspectors is the pile of rubbish. The relevant cause for the police and the local youth organizations is the juvenile delinquent. The relevant cause for the welfare and family services agencies is the parents' neglect.

When it is known that many children are not learning, it is not productive for school officials to spend time blaming the childrens' poverty, unstable homes, or bad neighborhoods. And when "scientific studies" are brought forth to show that the "real causes" of failure are in the home and families, this is just a professional way of saying, "Leave me alone; I'm doing my job as well as can be expected; I can't or don't want to change."

SCHOOL-HOME FACTORS

Given widespread low academic achievement, the relevant question for school policy is, What can we do about it? The goal of practical educational research should be to find those causes of failure that educational policy and practice can address. Here the Coleman Report is again distressingly, and no doubt unintentionally, misleading. It did not measure the most important school elements that might make the difference between success and failure. It ignored the sense of mission, purpose, and commitment of the school staff, their ability to teach or manage schools (as opposed to their formal credentials), the presence or absence of a systematic learning strategy, the success of the school in gaining parent and student support. While the data on these factors are not readily available, studies that have attempted to look at them confirm their importance for successful learning.[5]

An even more serious problem with Coleman-type studies is their tendency to separate school and home factors as if they were independent variables. This has obscured what successful educators have always known and what sensitive analysis again confirms: the crucial issue in successful learning is not home or school—teacher or student —but the relationship between them. Learning takes place where there is a *productive learning relationship.*[6]

Research confirms that successful learning depends almost entirely on two factors: student motivation and good teaching. If a student wants to learn and is taught competently, the results are virtually bound to be successful, regardless of almost any other factors.[7]

Is this a truth too simple to be useful? It is always dangerous to ignore simple truths because they are simple. If we want to know, for instance, why millions of dollars of federal money have been wasted on ineffective programs, it is worth noting that it was never required that these programs improve either student motivation or teaching performance. Often, special classes, equipment, or personnel were simply added to situations in which one or the other of these two essential elements was missing.

It is not too simple to look at the problem of educational failure within a framework that takes these two basic elements of the learning process into account. It is, however, too simple, to think that student motivation and good teaching are independent factors that students and teachers bring separately to the educational process. One reason why educational policy is in a state of paralysis is that the present policy framework and institutional arrangements tend to separate these two factors. To a large extent both student motivation and good teaching are the products of a relationship—a productive learning relationship between students and teachers and between home and school. In this relationship will be found the prime roots of educational success. And, as the next three chapters attempt to show, the prime roots of educational failure are found in the neglect and obstruction of this relationship in present school policy and practice.

3 GOVERNMENTAL SCHOOLING

Public control . . . was at the very center of the common school ideal.

Lawrence A. Cremin, *Horace Mann on the Education of Free Men*

Today we take government-run schooling for granted; it is an established part of American society. It was not always so, however. Until the middle of the nineteenth century, "there were few sharp lines between 'public' and 'private' education. States liberally subsidized 'private' academies and colleges while towns and cities helped to support 'private' charity schools."[1] The hundreds of private and church-related schools scattered across the country were typically run by independent boards of trustees who, although they were often thought of as carrying out public purposes, were not part of the government; they were not elected and were usually not appointed by public officials. Nor was government control of schools accepted without a struggle. It seemed to many an invasion of individualism and independence, to others a dangerous step toward the establishment of orthodoxy by controlling groups.

Once the common school movement had gained momentum, however, the logic of government control over the burgeoning system of public schools seemed inexorable. As Lawrence Cremin has pointed out, the rationale was obvious: "Public control followed from public support; the public was simply interested in how its tax dollars would be spent." Furthermore, public control would ensure that "the 'commonness' of the school would be preserved," and that the whole community could participate in defining the public goals to be achieved.[2]

The way this logic played itself out in New York City was interesting and illustrative of the changes that were taking place nationally. The first response to the growing need for schooling was the sprouting of many independent private and church-related schools in the eighteenth and early part of the nineteenth centuries. One of the independent groups, the Free School Society, which specialized in providing schooling for poor children, became increasingly successful in gaining public funding for its efforts. Gradually it began to take over many smaller independent schools until, by the middle of the nineteenth century, it was running a substantial system of schools that virtually monopolized public funding. In the process, significantly, it changed its name to the Public School Society, although it was still run by a private board of trustees. Finally, the legislature "legitimized the unitary system by making school officers elective."[3] Although it was with some bitterness, it was probably without hope of an alternative that the private trustees of the society turned their schools over to the new elective city board of education in 1853.

Although the specific history was different in different parts of the country, the process of establishing publicly accountable—that is, governmental—boards of education for public schools proceeded all across the country throughout the nineteenth century until the system of local school boards we now take for granted was in place. Gradually, the logic of increased state and federal governmental involvement also took hold, giving rise to our present multilayered educational system.[4]

What seemed so logical and practical a century ago, however, is today a governance system which is unresponsive to the people in many communities and which frequently betrays its intended purposes. Serious social, political, and educational problems inherent in government-run schooling, which some critics pointed out from the beginning, are becoming increasingly difficult to ignore. These include its potential for violating the interests of the politically weak, the contradictions involved in trying to be "value neutral," its tendency to become monopolistic and thus to displace individual accountability and weaken student-teacher, and home-school relationships, and, as will be seen in the next two chapters, its propensity to promote self-defeating professionalized bureaucracies.

THE POLITICALLY WEAK

In any political system the politically weak are less able to defend their interests and less likely to benefit from government than those who have the power to control its policies for their own benefit. Governmental education is no exception.

The most widespread example of this phenomenon is the pervasively low-quality schooling provided to poor children. Despite the rhetoric and even the good intentions of educators, the poor are typically subjected to educational conditions that would never be tolerated by the politically powerful. Research in the last twenty years has documented what many poor parents have known for years: teachers unconsciously favor middle-class children over lower-class children, and a complex web of social and political forces keep poor parents either unaware of the poor education their children receive, aware but accepting of the lower expectations for their children, or unaccepting but powerless to do anything about it.

There is irony in this. One of the main reasons for making education a governmental function was to spread its benefits more equally, and indeed government has been a major instrument for promoting educational equality. But since education can be provided with differential quality to different people, it ends up being provided on a much lower level to those who lack the political power to demand better. This is not to argue that the solution is to remove education from governmental involvement, but only to point out that making education a government function in no way guarantees equality and in some respects only translates unequal political power into unequal education.

The problem, furthermore, is not just one of inequities for poor people. Majority rule can result in injustices for all kinds of minorities; politically dominant forces can impose their will and values on those who fail to gain sufficient control over government policy to defend their interests. "You can't please all of the people all of the time," and public schools displease many people much of the time. This is inherent in collective governmental activities in a pluralistic society; decisions made on behalf of "all of the people" are bound to displease some. The sex education program decided on by a school board as good for the children of the community may seriously violate the values of some families. The curriculum seen as progressive and creative by some may be seen as so much watered-down hokum to others. The system of school discipline decided upon by the schools' governing body may completely undermine some parents' confidence in the schools.

The whole idea of the kind of public school system seen as logical, practical, and good for the people of New York City by the politically dominant forces of the mid-nineteenth century were seen as bad for his flock by Roman Catholic Archbishop John Hughes, and he fought vigorously for public funding for separate parochial schools. The prelate was offended by the none-too-well-concealed Protestant biases of the public schools, and when he lost his political battle, he set out to construct an extensive privately funded parochial school system in which Catholic values would be respected.[5] He could foresee only continuing violations of his group's interests in the government-run schools. Many other groups that did not take the course of separate schooling have had continuing problems with governmental schools that do not reflect the values they want for their children. The recent growth of the so-called Christian schools shows that the problem is by no means disappearing and that some groups still feel sufficiently alienated from governmental educational policies to set up their own schools at great expense and personal sacrifice.

"VALUE NEUTRAL" EDUCATION

One of the remedies that has been applied to reduce the injustice of enforcing "collective" educational policies upon a population with diverse values has been to try to make education "value neutral," or "value free."[6] In some respects the cure is worse than the disease. A value-free education is impossible. The attempt to make it value free often renders it valueless.

A standard result of a value-neutral outlook is the "lowest common denominator" among whatever array of educational aspirations exists in a community. Even if most of the families have high educational expectations for their children but their ideas about education differ, the collective school system tends to find a safe, homogeneous blend with no outstanding features to give offense to anyone. This is why public schools, though governed by 15,000 local school boards, show a surprising degree of bland similarity across the country. In isolated, culturally homogeneous communities, such as the Protestant communities of Appalachia or Catholic towns in northern Maine, one can find a strong and open value orientation in the schools, but in such cases, public school purists raise the question whether such schools are truly public.

To rise above the lowest common denominator, the government's educational agents sometimes try the "muddled middle," in which they usually get stuck. If half the community wants strict, traditional education with emphasis on the basics and half wants progressive, "open" education, with emphasis on creativity, the school system, in trying to reach a happy amalgam, may end up with a system having the benefits of neither approach. The teachers are likely to become as confused as the children, and they may end up teaching neither the basics nor creativity. Likewise with discipline: those who press for greater student freedom, with the goal of helping them learn to be responsible for their own actions, may succeed only in undermining a school's authority without establishing an alternative system for student responsibility. Rather than having a system where one group imposes its values on another, a system governed by the principle of the "muddled middle" manages to support the values of no one.

Most parents want some framework of values to be part of their children's education—and rightly so. Educators should be equally interested in strong values in their schools. In values are found the bonds that make learning relationships possible.[7] If the school tries to operate on a value-free basis, that is in itself a value system of sorts, and one that is out of phase with the values of most parents and most successful teaching and learning relationships.

The philosophical fashions of pragmatism and positivism at the turn of the century helped to provide an easy way out for public school officials beleaguered by value conflicts. In their popularized form they implied that no human values are inherently superior to any others; only personal preferences can define the "good" and the "valuable." Relativism became widespread in public education, and the "old-fashioned" professional standards of academic excellence and conduct gave way to personal development and creativity. "We teach children, not subjects" became the cry of those who saw the induction of children into the traditional academic disciplines as a form of authoritarian oppression. In more recent years, "Doing your own thing" became the answer for those who did not want to "impose" standards of behavior on children.

No doubt much bad teaching and boneheaded authoritarianism was swept out by those trends, and some good individual attention to children and their problems was introduced. But the final result left many teachers and school administrators with no clear idea of their mission. The "old-fashioned" moral and intellectual certainty that was so infuriating to modern relativists provided the value base for strong student-teacher relationships for thousands of students, including many of those who succeeded in schools despite disadvantaged backgrounds. The old truths are not the only possible basis for a sound home-school relationship, but when they were swept away there was often nothing provided to replace them.

Several decades of efforts to make schools value neutral in order to avoid imposing values on a culturally pluralistic clientele has created the worst of both worlds: a hidden value structure that is often at odds with the values of many families and students and a reluctance to make any commitment to academic or social values that might establish the basis for a strong bond between home and school.

THE DISPLACEMENT OF HOME-SCHOOL ACCOUNTABILITY

Closely related to the problems of value neutrality is the propensity of governmental education to be monopolistic, that is, its tendency not only to ignore the individual values and initiatives of its clients but to displace them in favor of the "collective will" of the community.

Government has many types of agencies. Some, like the Pentagon, necessarily implement a collective political will. Whether one approves or disapproves of its actions, there is no choice but to work through the political process to affect the way it provides for the common defense of the nation. The public is a collective client of such agencies, which are not expected to be accountable to individual citizens. They are sometimes called "commonweal" agencies to signify their responsibility to the society as a whole. A "service" agency, on the other hand, has been defined as one "whose prime beneficiary is the part of the public in direct contact with the organization, with whom and on whom its members work—in short, an organization whose basic function is to serve clients."[8] Some service agencies, such as a legal aid bureau whose lawyers are instructed to serve individual clients, at their option and in accordance with their stated interests, might provide a high degree of direct accountability to the clients served. In contrast, a state mental hospital, to which patients are committed against their will and to whom the organization's staff provides services according to organizational policies and procedures, presents quite a different picture. In such service institutions, as in the commonweal agency, formal accountability is to the public as a whole, often with little accountability to individual clients.

What kind of agencies are public schools? Viewed objectively, one must conclude that they typically operate to a large degree as service organizations of the commonweal type.[9] Although they "serve" a particular clientele, their accountability is not primarily to individual students and parents but to the public at large through a central, professional school administration and governing school board. This kind of governmental accountability tends to sap the initiative and responsibility of those "served." Both the accountability of the school to individual students and parents and the accountability of parents and students to the schools is weakened by the sense that the job of education has been delegated to government. Since "we" have provided for education collectively, "I" am no longer responsible individually.

If government provided no schooling, it would be clear that parents would be responsible for their children's education. It is not suggested that parents could or should by themselves meet this responsibility in modern society; the point is that the psychological orientation would be quite different from what it is today for the vast majority of parents whose children's education is "provided" by government schools. The sense of mutual responsibility of student and teacher, home and school, that is required for successful education is often missing. School officials complain about the irresponsibility of parents and students, but the idea that education has been delegated to government tends to encourage this kind of irresponsibility.

Needless to say, many individual principals, teachers, parents, and students do not accept the idea of education as only a generalized governmental responsibility; they accept professional or personal responsibilities and commitments that are not part of the formal system of government. Indeed, there is growing evidence that the official system of educational governance in the United States is more myth than reality—important myth perhaps, but myth nonetheless. Superintendents, for instance, tend to make more policy than the policy boards that employ them. And superintendents' own policy initiatives turn out to be not so much the product of their professional expertise as a complex reaction to the political forces playing upon them, both from within the system and from the outside community. This explains not only why school systems often fail to reflect the interests and values of the communities they supposedly serve but also why they are sometimes surprisingly effective and humane despite the problems inherent in having the government try to run schools in a pluralistic, democratic society.[10]

If the governmental structure of American public education is a myth, one might ask why it is a serious problem. The problem arises because the myth is powerful, and while it does not completely control behavior, it strongly influences it. More important, it helps to define the framework for educational policy. It also reinforces two other serious problems of contemporary public education: educational bureaucratization and professionalization, to which we now turn. Whatever tendencies there are to establish effective educational relationships in government-run schools are often stifled by the bureaucracy and misguided professionalism that has accompanied the governmentalization of schooling.

4 BUREAUCRATIZED EDUCATION

> The chief merit of bureaucracy is its technical efficiency, with a premium placed on precision, speed, expert control, continuity, discretion, and optimal returns on input. The structure is one which approaches the complete elimination of personalized relationships and nonrational considerations (hostility, anxiety, affectual involvements, etc.).
>
> Robert Merton, "Bureaucratic Structure and Personality"

Bureaucracy is everyone's whipping boy in education: teachers rail at it; parents demonstrate against it; taxpayers denounce it. Even bureaucrats themselves complain about it. It has been so unmercifully denounced that people, in fairness, are beginning to come to its defense, hailing its virtues of efficiency and impartiality. The critics, however, come closer to the truth. Bureaucracy and education are like oil and water—they do not mix.

The bureaucratic organization of schooling became widespread mostly because, like governmental control, it seemed to be the most practical way to solve the problems of rapidly growing school systems in the nineteenth century: "Year after year, common sense led to the consolidation of schools for economy and efficiency, and the pressure of numbers led to standardization."[1]

Some of the early forms of school bureaucracy were even more machinelike than modern schools. The Lancastrian system, for instance, used in some areas in the nineteenth century, had features such as "detailed procedures, prescribed content, authoritarian pedagogy, hierarchical teaching structure." The students themselves were highly bureaucratized in this system—required to sit in fixed rows of benches with monitors for each row and a carefully worked out system of progression from one set of skills to the next until the entire curriculum had been mastered. The managers of the Free School Society in New York found that this method enabled it not only to organize each school with maximum efficiency but also to operate a growing system of schools, so that new ones could be opened by a simple process of "replication," with minimal high-level professional staff and only one board of trustees to make decisions, "rather than dozens of groups which ran one or two schools" each.

If the results looked somewhat mechanical, so much the better for a culture in the first blushes of its love affair with the machine. Governor De Witt Clinton waxed eloquent on how the "system operated with the same efficiency in education as labor-saving machinery," with children "marching, with unexampled rapidity and with perfect discipline, to the goal of knowledge."[2]

Although the highly mechanical Lancastrian system later lost favor, a standardized system of schools with uniform policies and a hierarchy of authority—that is, a classic bureaucratic organization—seemed the most practical and efficient way to meet the needs for expansion, and it gradually became established throughout the country. As David Tyack has described it, bureaucratic organization came to be viewed as "the one best system."[3]

During the intervening decades, educational bureaucracy has come less and less to mean "efficient" and more and more to mean "bumbling" and "unresponsive." It has earned this reputation through insensitive management, the loss of internal incentives, and the growth of crippling vested interests. Stories abound of teachers who can order supplies more quickly and cheaply from the local stationery store than through the central purchasing department.

"Bumbling bureaucracy," however, only connotes the annoyances of our present system. What is more important is the culture of bureaucracy—its fundamental values and the behavior they engender, which hinder effective learning relationships between students and teachers.[4] The need of a bureaucracy to be impartial, its tendencies to standardization and "interchangeable parts," its inflexibility, and its hierarchical structure, while all serving useful purposes, also help create barriers to effective parent-teacher-student relationships.

IMPARTIALITY

One of the prime and intrinsic characteristics of a bureaucracy, and one source of its supposed efficiency, is standardization. Uniform policies and procedures enable a large system to be governed by "one board of trustees rather than dozens of groups." Standardization enables schools to be "replicated" with minimal confusion. It is standardization that also supposedly guarantees fairness and prevents favoritism.

But standardization always has its price. Skirting for a moment schools' almost daily violations of the ideal of impartiality, the ideal itself presents problems. Kaestle describes this well in his analysis of the growth of bureaucracy:

> The dilemma of standardized impartiality and quality control through systemization is that the decision-making processes are taken out of the hands of the person who deals directly with the system's clients—the children—and therefore tends to depersonalize the relationship. The teacher becomes more a part of the apparatus and less able to be flexible. Also to the extent that the system intentionally masks the identity of the student to ensure impartiality, the student loses part of his individuality. Formalized impartiality leads to anonymity.[5]

Berger, Berger, and Kellner cite a similar effect in *The Homeless Mind:* the "justice" expected from a bureaucracy "entails a depersonalization of each individual case," the treating of the individual "as a number."[6]

The relationship between teacher and student must be personal to be effective. This does not mean it must be chummy. It does mean, however, that the student must sense the teacher as a flesh-and-blood human being who cares, rather than as a cog in some distantly controlled machine. Furthermore, the students themselves must also feel they are respected as human beings, rather than regarded as raw material being processed. When a fourth grader who has not yet mastered the fundamentals of reading or math is pushed along to fifth grade and branded "dumb" because he cannot do fourth-grade work, he is being dealt with as a thing and not as a person. As Bloom observes and others have confirmed, virtually every child can learn what schools have to teach as long as each one is taught in relation to his prior learning history and is engaged in the learning task.[7] Good teachers know this and act accordingly, but the pull of the bureaucratic system is to ignore these idiosyncratic differences and treat everyone "the same," both because it is simpler and because it is "fairer" in mechanistic terms.

Even when the system tries to provide differential treatment to students, the bureaucratic method is to use "objective," standardized tests to sort and classify them.[8] Since it is clear that all do not perform the same, the bureaucratic solution is to grade and sort the products by their achievement, rather than to deal individually with students to ensure their success. This is seen as fair by the bureaucratic mind, because all are judged by the same standard. Tests have their uses, but they are limited. It is hard for the bureaucratic mentality to keep these limits in mind. In our schools, test scores take on an almost sacred quality. They overrule not only sensitive human responses but even common sense and professional judgment. As John Ogbu found in his field work in Stockton, California, test scores often did "not agree with . . . teachers' knowledge" of students, and yet they were still "used to classify students into various 'ability groups' which . . . often determine their future."[9] It is easy to see how this behavior is reinforced by the values of bureaucracy. After all, unless the "objective" test score is used, how can we ensure against favoritism by the teacher or principal?

INTERCHANGEABLE PARTS

Another advantage of a bureaucratic system, as with a machine, is its interchangeable parts. When a grade 3 bookkeeper at the Ajax Corporation retires, the personnel department can use a standard job description for filling the slot. Presumably any qualified grade 3 bookkeeper will do. This same mentality applies in our bureaucratic school system. A third-grade teacher is a third-grade teacher; if one departs, another can be plugged in. The fact that the previous incumbant had a special personality that helped hold the school together, that she or he was the spark plug of the school play or yearbook or was the mainstay of the PTA, are all irrelevant to the bureaucracy. These are factors that a good principal will take into account, but only unofficially, since they do not show up in the official job description or in the qualifications of replacements.

In New York City, where so many aspects of bureaucracy are carried to extremes, the interchangeable parts enterprise went beserk during the 1975 fiscal crisis, when thousands of teachers were laid off. In the name of fairness to staff, the system had developed an inflexible procedure for bumping staff of lower seniority from school to school so that "rational" seniority rules would prevail. The result, of course, was not at all rational for the educational process but chaotic, with some children having as many as eight teachers in a single term. Because of the standardized, "fair" rules, enormous damage was done to student-teacher relationships. It was clear where the priorities of the system lay, and the maintenance of productive learning relationships between students and teachers was not one of them.[10]

INFLEXIBILITY

Another virtue of the machine is that it proceeds steadily and pre-dictably, regardless of the moods and idiosyncrasies of the people who run it. Its virtue is a lack of variation or, in other words, a *lack of human response*. It should not be surprising that this characteristic has a detrimental effect on student-teacher relationships. When children find that they fail regardless of their efforts, they can easily conclude that what they do makes little difference, and they soon become "unmotivated."

Lack of motivation is often not a characteristic of the child but a direct result of inflexible and nonresponsive bureaucratic relation-ships. A teacher who persists in following the prescribed curriculum, whether children learn or not, is likely to produce unmotivated youngsters. Such teachers may well be doing their formal jobs—they may report to work every day and follow their lesson plans duti-fully—but they fail to help students learn and at the same time create a sense of defeat in the students that will hamper all their future attempts at learning.[11]

REMOTENESS FROM THE LEARNER

The hierarchical aspects of bureaucracy increase its impersonality and ineffectiveness for education. Decisions made on high can be-come, and remain, out of touch with the realities of classroom rela-tionships. This aspect of bureaucratic impersonalism helps to explain why today's top school officials often operate with illusions never corrected by the realities faced by students and teachers. To cite but one example, the eloquent speeches of school officials about the economic advantages of having a diploma overlook the fact that no jobs exist for many teen-agers regardless of whether they finish high school. The students are realistic about structural unemployment even if their superiors in the school system are not. If the superintendents and board members had to deal directly with the students who have little hope of employment, they might develop other strategies for motivating students. They might even hit upon the idea of developing an interest in learning for its own sake—because it is fun, and gives students a sense of self-confidence, competence, and power.

More generally, the tendency to cling to assumptions that are out of touch with reality explains why some school systems, particularly the larger ones, perpetuate patently ineffective education and demonstrate little or no will to do anything about it. The managers at the top can successfully maintain their illusions. Their jobs have little to do with ensuring productive learning relationships between teachers and learners.

THE FAILURE OF BUREAUCRATIC REFORMS

An indication of the inappropriateness of bureaucratic structures for education is found in the pointlessness of many efforts to reform them. Reform seems only to compound their flaws and increase their violation of healthy educational relationships. Just as with the scientific management movement at the turn of the century, so now with some of the efforts to apply the more recent "systems" approaches, the tendency of bureaucracies is to circumscribe their boundaries so that internal operations can be "rationalized."[12] Teachers become defined as workers, and policies are devised to increase their efficiency in delivering services. Teachers, however, are *not* the prime workers in the educational process; the students are, and they produce learning by their own efforts, not by having it "delivered" to them. Yet students are not part of the "system"; they are not employees subject to bureaucratic control. The bureaucratic mind, therefore, finds it hard to see students as key actors in the learning process.

The more the bureaucratic attitude takes over as a result of rationalizing the processes within the system, the greater become the barriers to relating to those "outside" the system—students and parents. The more the system concentrates on how it can make its operations more effective and efficient, the less is asked of those to whom it is "delivering its services." The more inert students are, the more comfortable it is for the bureaucrat, since any action or reaction from those being served is unpredictable and, therefore, threatening to the standardized procedures of the bureaucracy. Just as the patient undergoing surgery is made unconscious so that he can be operated upon, so the ideal client of the bureaucracy is never an active participant. As Peter Berger has pointed out, "a client of bureaucracy . . . is always passively involved."[13] Under such a system there is clearly little room for the active learner.

The tendency to focus on factors within the system and under its control also blinds the school to the relationship of the educational process to other institutions. As Lawrence Cremin and other perceptive educators have realized, schooling constitutes only a small part of the total process of education, which goes on before and after school as well as throughout the school years, through the family, peers, the community, employment, and the media. A successful learning relationship in school requires the school to relate positively to this total context. The bureaucratic mentality within the school, however, works in the opposite direction, closing off the disorderly, uncontrollable, outside world and seeking to build a rationalized world in which these factors will be irrelevant—an endeavor that cannot of course, be successful except to the extent that the school loses sight of its mission, which is just what it all too often does.

BUREAUCRACY IN SMALLER SYSTEMS

Are the problems of bureaucracy and their baleful influence on the learning process characteristic only of very large systems? Sadly for the smaller systems, the answer seems to be no. The problems are often more severe in the large city systems, but many of the same dynamics prevail in even relatively small systems.

Ironically in the early part of this century the "modern" management practices of large city systems became the pattern for the smaller systems, and the big city superintendents became the professional role models for those aspiring to climb the career ladder of ever larger superintendencies. Organizational charts (increasingly filled in with deputy and assistant superintendents), lines of authority, spans of control, rationalized bylaws, and reams of written circulars and memorandums became the trappings of even modest-sized systems. Too few knew or cared to know what this did to the lives of students and their teachers.

It is to the effects of bureaucracy on teachers that we now turn, for, in addition to governmentalization and bureaucratic structure, the way in which the teaching profession has been conceived provides a third major element of the present misguided public education policy framework.

5 PATHOLOGICAL PROFESSIONALISM

These are technical matters, as much as the construction of an efficient engine, to be settled by inquiry into facts; and as the inquiry can be carried on only by those especially equipped, so the results of inquiry can be utilized only by trained technicians. What has the counting of heads, decision by majority, and the whole apparatus of traditional government to do with such things?"

John Dewey, *The Public and Its Problems*

The antieducational effects of bureaucratized governmental schooling might have been counteracted by the development of an education profession that emphasized the mission of teaching and the importance of relationships between teachers and learners. That, sadly, did not happen. Instead, the public school teaching profession has been shaped by, and tends to reinforce, the harmful effects of the political-bureaucratic structure of American public education.

Professionalization of public school teachers has followed two main courses, both unfortunate: one has attempted to define professionalism in terms of the possession of expert *knowledge about* education; the other has attempted to enhance the status and prestige of the profession by increasing its collective power. Expert knowledge and professional power are classic hallmarks of professions and, like bureaucratic organization and collective accountability, have their legitimate and useful place. As the dominant elements of the teaching profession, however, they jeopardize successful learning relationships; they drive wedges between student and teacher and between home and school. They have proved to be false paths to true professionalism in teaching, and they contribute to the systematic miseducation of American children.

PROFESSIONAL KNOWLEDGE

Expert technical knowledge is intimately connected with bureaucracy, since one of bureaucracy's functions is to organize human behavior according to rational categories and guide it by rationally determined procedures. When the rationalizing process is complex, as it certainly is in school systems, it takes on an increasingly specialized and expert character. It is not surprising, then, that a bureaucratized teaching profession should have seized upon expert knowledge about education as a foundation for its professional identity. A typical example of the justification for this approach is found in the report of a New York State educational task force, which, after deliberating on the question of teaching as a profession, pronounced that "profession is defined as such by the degree of intellectualism it achieves. Teaching has a body of knowledge which is limited, but which allows aspects of the teaching act to be subjected to theoretical analyses. These knowledge bases are what is or should be taught in professional education programs and what can be tested for in examinations."[1] The task force report makes this knowledge base the foundation of the teaching profession's identity.

There is nothing wrong with subjecting "aspects of the teaching act . . . to theoretical analysis." Much can be said for social scientists studying the teaching-learning process. The problem comes in placing this "body of knowledge" at the heart of the teacher's professional identity.

Nothing sensible supports the contention that teachers' theoretical knowledge of education improves their teaching performance. Does knowledge of sound waves help a violinist play more beautifully? A physicist may devise improvements in the construction of a violin or even in the technique for playing it, but to base the professional identity of the musician on the "knowledge bases" of physics would be absurd. Teaching might appear closer to the social sciences than violin playing to physics, but the appearance is deceptive. The *practice* of teaching is very different from *theorizing* about teaching.

It should be noted that the intellectualism called for in the professional manifesto of the New York State task force quoted above is not an increase in knowledge of history, art, or science or an increased emphasis on the excitement of ideas and learning. Rather, it is an increased emphasis on "theoretical analysis" of teaching. In other words, it is part of the effort to define the teacher as an applied scientist or a technician—a role compatible with that of a bureaucratic functionary whose job is to deliver educational services in accordance with scientifically designed procedures, but not compatible with successful teaching. As Dan Lortie has pointed out in his masterly study of the teaching profession, most teachers consider teaching more of an art than a science.[2] Their instincts are correct, despite several generations of efforts to persuade them to the contrary. The human interaction between teacher and student that stimulates, encourages, inspires, and assists learning can be studied and analyzed, but the study of this process (which can be scientific) should not be confused with teaching itself. Nor should the role of the scientist who does the studying be confused with the role of the teacher. The attempt to base the professional identity of teachers on a body of knowledge *about* teaching has a deadening effect on creative thinking and on the love of learning that should be at the heart of the teacher's professional identity.

The scientific approach may explain why so many education courses misfire. Few teachers have much respect for them, and these courses have such a low reputation in universities that the requirement to take them dissuades many talented people from even considering the teaching profession. The intellectual excitement involved in the original social science research and scholarship gets lost in the translation into professional preparation programs. As a result, instead of increasing teachers' intellectualism, the misguided effort contributes to anti-intellectualism in the education professions.

The emphasis on the theoretical base for teaching also diverts attention from the importance of skill in teaching. It takes real skill to gain the attention and interest of a group of students, to explain complex ideas, to give students a sense of the excitement of learning, to deal with disruptive behavior so that it does not interfere with learning, to identify and work with a variety of learning styles, to build on students' strengths and correct or sidestep weaknesses, to encourage a sense of partnership with students and parents in the learning process.[3] Professionalism in teaching should mean the possession of these skills and the special commitment it takes to apply them. The emphasis on a specialized scientific "body of knowledge" has served as a poor substitute.

BARRIERS TO STUDENT-TEACHER RELATIONSHIPS

In addition to neglecting the art and skill of teaching, the emphasis on expert scientific knowledge tends to create barriers between teachers and students and their families, to disempower them in learning relationships, and to foster a "weakness" and "therapy" approach to teaching instead of a "strength" and "participation" approach.[4]

One function of specialized professional knowledge is to separate professionals from their clients. Doctors, lawyers, and engineers all have their specialized knowledge and esoteric language, unintelligible to the layman, which presumably enhances not only their competence but also their prestige and earning power. Why should teachers be denied this classic technique of professional enhancement? Because teaching is a very special kind of process, in which this type of separation obstructs successful learning, which is the prime mission of the profession.

The professional "distance" involved is not caused by the teacher's superior knowledge of biology or literature or superior skill in teaching it. That kind of knowledge and skill can enhance the teaching-learning relationship. But the mystique of specialized scientific knowledge *about education* can have the opposite effect. John Ogbu, for instance, found that productive parent-teacher conferences are obstructed when teachers do not listen to parents because "they believe that parents are not 'experts' in educational matters."[5] In a National Committee for Citizens in Education publication listing the "six reasons parents give for not becoming involved in public schools," three of the reasons given relate to the parents' sense of inferiority in relation to the professional expertise of the school: "I do not have enough education to approach the schools with my ideas." "I don't understand the system and don't think it works anyway." "I don't feel confident enough to speak up in a group."[6]

If learning did not require the active participation of students—if teachers could, for instance, produce learning by operating upon students the way a surgeon operates upon an anesthetized patient—then a professional orientation dominated by expert knowledge would not be so harmful. But teaching is not like surgery; a teacher is not like a surgeon, nor like an engineer building a bridge out of inert steel and concrete. Teaching involves complex human interactions that vary from student to student, from classroom to classroom, and sometimes from moment to moment. The relationship with the learner is what counts, and a professional identity based primarily on expert scientific knowledge tends to obstruct direct human relationships.

Teaching is an intensely subjective process. The necessary learning relationship develops between student and teacher because the student senses the teacher's subjective involvement—the commitment to learning and to helping students learn. The scientific approach, on the contrary, tends to objectify the teaching process, asking teachers to become amateur sociologists and psychologists. They become *students of* teaching rather than *participants in* teaching-learning. As Gilbert Highet points out in *The Art of Teaching,* "a scientific relationship between human beings is bound to be inadequate and perhaps distorted. . . . Scientific teaching, even of scientific subjects, will be inadequate as long as both teachers and pupils are human beings."[7]

Gaps in understanding and trust are created by this professional orientation. The teacher who sees his job primarily as knowing and applying scientific knowledge about teaching tends to discount what the student brings to the learning process. After all, the student knows nothing about the "science" of education. Even if Jane is beginning to know a little mathematics or history, this does not open to her the mysteries of the teaching process. How, then, could she be a participant? It is more consistent with this vision of the profession to see students (and therefore to begin to treat them) as passive patients, to be processed and operated upon by the professional whose knowledge provides all the "input" needed. As Ray Rist points out, in bureaucratized, professionalized education, "children assume the role of client."[8]

When this does not work and the student rebels or dies intellectually, the next step for the professional who is a scientist-technician is to decide that the student was hopeless from the outset. This step is often taken with the most solicitous "professional" concern for the "problems" of the student, but with a built-in blindness to the possibility that the problems might be derived, in part at least, from the wrong professional approach. William Ryan calls this "blaming the victim," and he points out that "to continue to define the difficulty as inherent in the raw material—the children—is plainly to . . . acquiesce in the continuation of educational inequality in America."[9]

Textbooks for college education courses are full of theories about why children cannot learn because of the pathologies of home life and society. What could be more "rational" and "scientific" than to apply these theories to the student who is a nonlearner and thereby explain his failure? Teachers who have never heard that low achievement correlates with socioeconomic class may be better off than those trained to see this kind of "scientific knowledge" as the base of their profession. Defining professional status in terms of teachers' knowledge rather than students' learning encourages teachers to feel professional satisfaction because they "know" the scientific reasons why their students fail instead of professional dissatisfaction because their students are not succeeding.[10]

Many teachers, of course, reject this misdefinition of their role. They want to succeed, despite the excuses for failure provided by their professional mentors. But the directions suggested by the pseudoscientific approach are again often counterproductive. "Pupils' academic problems are often defined as clinical problems," and "therapy" is substituted for teaching.[11] As Riessmann points out, "Unfortunately, teachers too often behave like psychologists and social workers. They do not sufficiently stress learning processes."[12] Ogbu observed the same tendency among counselors in his field-work: "Because they define children's academic problems as those of personal adjustment to the school environment, counselors see therapy as the solution."[13] The main mission of the school—teaching —is forgotten in the name of scientific professionalism.

Let me make clear again that I am not arguing against developing scientific knowledge about the learning process or against teachers studying this knowledge. I am arguing that the attempt in recent decades to define the teaching profession in terms of this professional knowledge and to base teachers' professional training and identity upon it, is counterproductive. It obstructs rather than facilitates the basic learning relationships between students and teachers and between families and schools. Jacques Maritain analyzes this false direction of the profession as an emphasis of means over ends:

The child is so well tested and observed, his needs so well detailed, his psychology so clearly cut out, the methods for making it easy for him everywhere so perfected, that the end of all these commendable improvements runs the risk of being forgotten or disregarded. Hence the surprising weakness of education today, which proceeds from our attachment to the very perfection of our modern educational means and methods and our failure to bend them toward the end.[14]

TEACHER POWER

An obvious link exists between the claim to expert professional knowledge and the claim to professional power. If one group has a monopoly on knowledge about a function, why should it not be given control over that function without interference from those who are ignorant of this specialized knowledge and would only interfere? This has seemed all the more logical as schools and school systems have become more complicated and professional educators have been hired not only to teach in them but also to run them.

The logic and potential payoffs of this line of reasoning have been recognized for some years. In 1956 Myron Lieberman, then a leading mentor to teacher groups, wrote a full-length book called *Education as a Profession*, which strongly advocated this thesis, and the view has spread widely in professional organizations and teacher-training institutions.[15] The argument has a double-barreled appeal. On the one hand, if teachers want to gain respect and be recognized as true professionals, like doctors and lawyers, then, it is argued, like doctors and lawyers, they must have more power. On the other hand, the power of the professional staff to control education is obviously the most efficient way to put their expert knowledge to use for the public good. By either route, the answer seems clear: power for teachers is good for everyone.

In addition to these theoretical arguments, there were more down-to-earth motives for the drive for teacher power—most notably, the poor pay and shabby treatment that teachers received in many school systems. In a society that helps only those who help themselves, teachers found their salaries declining in comparison with salaries for other occupations. When the boards of education and state legislatures failed to respond adequately, teachers finally decided to "help themselves." Salary was not their only concern. Teachers were at the bottom of an increasingly elaborate bureaucratic ladder. They felt neglected; their concerns and interests were left out of the decision-making process as it became more concentrated in the hands of school administrators and central office staffs. Teachers often had the same complaint that parents and students were to raise a decade later: they got no "response" from the system. Even simple matters that might make their work easier or more pleasant, such as a prompt delivery of supplies or a rearrangement of the teachers' lounge, became entangled in the bureaucratic maze.

The self-respect as well as the working conditions of teachers were at stake. School administrators, not teachers, got the public credit for the achievements of the expanding public school systems. Dissatisfaction among teachers increased as they gained training and credentials and as they began to notice that superintendents were often bureaucratic politicians rather than educators. It seemed that only when blame was to be laid were the teachers remembered. As schools came under increasing criticism for failing to keep up with the public's expanding educational expectations, teachers began to feel they had to fight for their "psychic survival."[16]

Teachers' organizations fashioned two instruments to deal with their "bread and butter" and "psychic" concerns. One was the strike, and the other was political organization. Both of these weapons, in what has increasingly become a militant struggle, were originally resisted by teachers as unprofessional, but once they began to be used they were found to be irresistibly successful.[17] When school systems were shut down by a strike, intense pressures were brought to bear on school boards to capitulate, without looking too closely at the terms of settlement. The tactics as used by the American Federation of Teachers (AFT) were so successful that the more conservative National Education Association (NEA) soon followed suit, giving up its "professional" scruples against striking and becoming, in effect, another labor union.

The strike proved effective not only for winning monetary victories but also for enforcing other teacher interests, including, some have thought, "self-respect." As Albert Shanker, president of the AFT, pointed out in justifying a strike: "If teachers accept shabby treatment this time, they can expect the same treatment next time. If they stand fast now, it will alter not just this one set of negotiations, but all those which follow in the years to come—as well as their day-to-day relationships."[18]

The same progression toward increased militancy developed in the drive for political power. Teachers' organizations found that having publicly paid workers in close contact with parent and community leaders in every neighborhood put an incomparable political organization within their grasp if they chose to use it. And they did. Legislators, fearful of primary fights from the organized teachers, began to fall over like duckpins in the 1960s and 1970s on such issues as teachers' tenure, pension plans, and control by teachers of entry into the profession. As strikes by teachers have become less successful in the face of financial austerity, teachers' groups have increasingly shifted their efforts to political organizing, with considerable success. In short, teachers discovered and grasped *power.* Until recently their victories have been swift and sweet, after so many years of neglect and exploitation. What has seemed to make the whole situation even happier is the new ideology of teacher professionalism, which justifies the militancy not only in terms of teachers' self-interest but in terms of the public good. What has emerged is the most difficult kind of power to deal with: self-righteous power.

By the mid-1970s political power for teachers burst upon the national scene. Teachers' organizations already had strong lobbies in Washington, but in 1976, for the first time, the NEA endorsed a presidential candidate. Their candidate won, and in due course President Carter delivered on his campaign promise to establish a federal Department of Education. The NEA was riding high, and by the time of the 1980 Democratic Convention, it was able to field the largest single bloc of delegates—all committed to vote for Carter's renomination. Carter's defeat in the general election has discouraged some teachers, but they are discouraged for the wrong reasons. Their political accomplishment has been astonishing; their failure to hold back a landslide victory in no way detracts from their continued potential for political power, especially in less visible state and local politics.

What should bother teachers is not whether they are successfully building political power but whether this kind of power will help them be better teachers, for in the long run only their success in teaching can improve their professional status, and their organizational success in collective bargaining and politics puts their educational success in jeopardy.

THE NEGATIVES OF TEACHER POWER

Problems were bound to arise in the siege for teacher power. When the opponent is a rapacious corporation, organized employee power can add a healthy balance to the economic struggle. But when teachers strike a public school system, against whom are they fighting? Their employers are the public. Not surprisingly, the public often resents militant tactics directed against it by its own employees. Relationships with parents and students are often torn asunder. Many parents are angry because their children are used as pawns in the power struggle, and teachers in turn become hostile to what they view as parents' antiteacher reactions. Bitter feelings are compounded by the unions' use of their new-found political muscle to win their "battles."

In the early stages of teacher unionism, parents sometimes support the teachers because salaries are low and parent groups feel that raises might facilitate teacher recruitment and improve morale. Once salaries begin to catch up, however, parents wonder whether funds might not be better used to improve services for their children.

Before teacher unionism, both parents and teachers were losing power to increasingly centralized and bureaucratized school systems. The essential links between parents and teachers were being weakened by too much standardization, depersonalization, and collective, homogenized accountability. With collective bargaining and union political action, teachers are winning power at the expense of parents. Whatever slim lines of accountability parents have through their boards of education are being eroded through secretly negotiated teacher contracts and political deals made in state legislatures and city halls between powerful union leaders and political figures. When asked why decisions must be made against the interests of children, school officials often answer that they are mandated by the contract or by a state law written at union insistence.

Teacher unionism was a response to bureaucracy, not the cause of it.[19] Nevertheless, instead of helping to cure or correct the ills of the present structure, it has increased many of its antieducational aspects. The power won by the teachers has increased centralized power. As a stepchild of bureaucracy, teacher unionism has now become one of its strongest supports, since collective teacher power can most easily be exercised through centralized decision making. Furthermore, since it took collective strength for teachers to win their power, they are themselves more collectivized. It is not the individual teacher who has gained power, but teacher organizations.[20] The autonomy of the individual teacher is, if anything, weaker than ever. Teachers not only have to follow inane rules and procedures of school bureaucracies, which often at least have the virtue of being unenforceable; they now must also conform to the rules and standards of the union and its contracts, with the much more powerful enforcement of peer pressure and union loyalty to keep them in line. If a teacher wants to stay in during the lunch hour to work with a student, he risks being branded a "rate buster." If a teacher wants to visit a student's family, he feels negative pressure from both his peers and his bureaucratic superiors. If he sides with a student against the system, he might be ostracized. It is especially those actions that a teacher might take to strengthen the bond between student and teacher or between home and school that now become inhibited in the schoolhouse kept by government bureaucrats and union representatives.

THE IMAGE OF SELFISHNESS

Students can respond to many different styles of teaching, from the authoritarian to the "let's be pals" approach, as long as they sense that the teacher is working for them and with them. If they sense that the teacher is there just to earn a salary, however, they will not respond, and the crucial bond of learning will not be formed.

For their part, good teachers know that students' response to their commitment is not just a good feeling inside but an essential element of a successful learning relationship with students. That relationship is increasingly threatened by militant teacher power. The problem is not the justice of the claims for decent pay or status but the way in which these claims are fought for, through strikes and the aggressive use of political clout in a political arena in which parents and teachers are increasingly cast as enemies.

Albert Shanker facetiously tells the story of how, in the early days of organizing in New York City, Mayor Robert Wagner explained why millions of dollars could be found for hurricane and blizzard relief while none could be found to meet teachers' demands. "Al, those were disasters," the Mayor said. Shanker's answer: "That's when we decided to become a disaster."[21] People learn to "respect" earthquake, fire, and flood. They have even learned to "respect" human beings who have power over them, but it is not the kind of respect that promotes productive learning relationships.

To the already great handicaps of governmentalized, bureaucratic schooling and a teaching profession seeking its identity in esoteric professional knowledge, we now have the added "disaster" of militant teacher power breeding alienation and hostility in parents toward teachers and further eroding relationships between teachers and students and between homes and schools.[22]

It would be unfair, of course, to look only at these negative aspects of teacher power and the applied science approach to the teaching profession. One would hope that, when science discovers useful insights, they will be applied by teachers, and there are already signs that teachers' attitudes toward power may be changing as they come to understand the negative consequences of arrogance and militancy.[23] Nevertheless, the negative aspects of the professionalization of teachers in the present public education policy structure are a reality. Teachers are as much victimized by them as are children and families. The purpose of analyzing them is not to blame teachers for the ills of American public schooling but to shed light on why so much goes wrong in public school systems and why the present system is bad for teachers and children alike.

6 THE ONE WORST SYSTEM

Mann and his countless coworkers could not conceive of the possibility that those who would follow in their footsteps might actually build a suffocating and sometimes mindnumbing establishmentarian bureaucracy.

Jonathan Messerli, *Horace Mann*

As we have seen, three pervasive aspects of American public education—its governmentalization, bureaucratization, and professionalization—work against productive learning relationships. Even more devastating is the way these three factors interact to compound their individual effects. Their negative interaction is particularly destructive in the large urban school systems, but the same unfortunate dynamics operate in many smaller districts as well.

NEGATIVE REINFORCEMENT

One example of how the negative aspects of the present structure reinforce one another is the way in which governmental accountability increases the rigidities of bureaucracy. A single board of education in charge of all schools in a district necessarily becomes the focus of accountability and complaints from parents and the public. The board's typical response to public pressure is to turn to its chief

41

administrator, the superintendent of schools, who in turn acts through the bureaucratic hierarchy to deal with the problem. The result is likely to be new orders, rules, and procedures. If Billy Smith, had a bad experience on a visit to a museum, museum visits might be forbidden or allowed only if the trip is approved by superiors. If a child is harshly disciplined by a teacher, discretion for discipline may be withdrawn from teachers and put into the hands of principals and supervisors. If someone complains about the way Miss Jones teaches world history, new curriculum guidelines may be devised to prevent future problems. Much of the accumulation of rigid rules and procedures in school systems did not spring full blown from the heads of overzealous bureaucrats; it grew out of the natural governmental-bureaucratic response to public pressure.

As the system is now, the greater the demands for accountability, the more securely the links in the chain of command are tightened, putting more power into the hands of those at the top and stifling the initiative and responsibility of those at the "bottom"—especially individual teachers and parents and, in large systems, even principals. Ironically, in a top-down, politically controlled bureaucratic school system, the more "accountable" and "responsive" the system is to parental concerns, the more bureaucratic it may become, and the more the *direct* relationships between parents, schools, students, and teachers may be weakened. The same phenomenon applies when top-level decision makers respond to teachers' demands by establishing new rules and procedures that limit the decision-making capacities of those at the bottom—including the teachers themselves.

Bureaucracy, in turn, aggravates some of the worst problems of governmental accountability. When educational policy was settled in the informal politics of a small town, a majority might outvote a minority, but the face-to-face encounter most often produced workable compromises. When the system is a unitary bureaucracy, the tendency is to rationalize the organization through single, standardized policies, and in the event of disagreement over what that single policy should be, one side or the other must lose. When the issue is sex education, discipline, or suitable library books, there is particular danger of disaffecting those whose views are set aside. Professionalization makes the scenario even worse. Parents who disagree with a policy may not even get a chance to be outvoted, since the issue in question may be considered a professional matter and parents excluded from the decision. Expert knowledge is "scientifically grounded" and "objective" and, therefore, not amenable to the variations and idiosyncracies of democratic debate. The legitimacy of expert opinion reinforces and is reinforced by the bureaucratic values of uniformity and standardization. The values, concerns, and perspectives of individual parents, teachers, and students tend to be disregarded.[1]

When "expert knowledge" is linked to organized teacher union and political power, the problems are magnified still further. Teachers can be assigned only by seniority or rotation, regardless of their individual capacities to perform specific jobs in a school. School security problems are handled by elaborate codified procedures. In-service teacher training is so restricted by rules about what teachers can and cannot do outside their classroom hours as to make it meaningless and ineffective. The schools become ever more "centralized, uniform . . . factory-like"—and ineffective.[2]

Professionalization, even including the quest for expert knowledge and professional power, would not be such a travesty in public education if it were not for the system's bureaucratic, political, and supposedly value neutral structure. Since professionalism is defined in terms of accountability to the body politic as a whole rather than to individual clients and political accountability is exercised through the bureaucracy as the instrument of the public will, teachers are accountable to the bureaucracy and, increasingly over time, work out their relationships with bureaucratic officials, instead of with individual students and parents. Ineffective practices can be perpetuated under the combined labels of "professional expertise" and "official procedures," and if parents finally rebel, professional groups can apply their highly organized and well-funded power tactics to outgun them in the political accountability system. Professionalization, which always harbors a danger of undue control over clients, is given an extra edge of power in a bureaucratic governmental system.[3]

CONTRADICTIONS

The many contradictions in the relationships between democratic government, bureaucracy, and professionalism also help to explain some of the policy problems of the present educational system.

In rational terms the structure of the system sounds perfectly logical: the system is bureaucratic because bureaucracy is the most efficient way to organize large numbers of people and resources; the system is professionalized because expert work should be controlled by experts; and the system is politically accountable to the collective will of the people because we live in a democracy. But life seldom conforms to logic, and education is no exception. The realities of public education paint quite a different picture.

In the first place, there are historical contradictions between democracy and the professionalized bureaucratic structure. As the educational reformers at the end of the nineteenth century viewed the conditions of a rapidly expanding urban, industrial, immigrant society, they advocated professionalism and elitist boards of education, precisely to remove education from too much responsiveness to local politics.[4] Some of the antidemocratic aspects of our present educational bureaucracies were thus intentional—and they have been effective. Harmon Zeigler, one of the foremost students of public school governance, finds that boards of education have little real control over education and are very imperfectly accountable to the public. He concludes that the present structure "violates a fundamental principle of democratic institutions."[5] As economist Jacob Michaelsen points out, "Full tax support and compulsion firmly established the power of common school administrators and, in a different way, teachers over parents and children. Indeed, they created the essential conditions for insulating school management from citizens generally, namely the assurance of a budget independent of satisfied customers."[6]

Another contradiction is that the value-neutral ideology needed to justify collectively organized "common" education robs the bureaucracy of the coherent mission necessary for internal control. Without clear goals, bureaucracies inevitably become the victims of both internal and external special interests. But it is just such clear goals that tend to become blurred in trying to devise a common system for a diverse population. The more school systems are pressed to assure everyone of their value-neutrality, the more inefficient the bureaucracy is likely to become.

Democratic governance and professional-bureaucratic control of education also contradict each other in terms of the information the public needs for responsible public control. As Mario Fantini points out, the more parents and citizens find out about what is going on in schools, the more they join "school people in knowing that teachers do not really know how children learn, what knowledge is most valuable, how best to teach, how best to organize a school, how to evaluate learning."[7] The myth of expert professional knowledge is exposed, and with it the justification for professional control. If the professional staff closes off public knowledge, however, to protect itself in the name of professional prerogatives, then the first principle of democratic accountability—reliable information—is violated.

A further contradiction and irony is that, despite this uncomfortable bind of either being undemocratic or being professionally exposed and despite their great increase in political power through unionization, teachers end up with little real power over their professional work. As Lortie has shown, teachers never have gained control over the practice of teaching.[8] They have failed, in part, because their collective power has been directed at gaining control over the bureaucratic structure of the system, and this structure is inherently antieducational and antiprofessional. The bureaucracy makes rules; it does not educate children. Teachers gained power, therefore, over the rule-making machinery. As a result, they have ended up with influence over policies affecting such issues as salary scales, benefits, job security, and uniform work rules, all of which have little direct relation to the process of teaching and learning and, where they do, often work against it.

Thus the presumed efficiencies of bureaucracy are in many cases inefficient, the supposedly democratic governance of education turns out to be undemocratic, and professionalism produces unprofessional conditions. Each factor seems to bring out the worst in the others, resulting in educational systems that produce antieducation.

THE PROBLEM IN THE CITIES

Even defenders of the present public school system admit its clear failures in the large cities. The failure of urban schools is a matter of no little perplexity to educators, but there should be no mystery. All of the antieducational aspects of collective accountability, bureaucracy, and skewed professionalism are compounded by size.

Diseconomies of scale have been a subject of management notice for many years. The disabilities that often come with standardization, testing and sorting, interchangeable parts, inflexibility, remoteness from the learner, and the excesses of "systems" approaches become more excessive with larger systems.[9]

The problems of collective political accountability also increase with size. The larger and more varied the population, the more tenuous is the hold of the value-neutrality myth, and yet the more fiercely must it be maintained to keep contending groups from one another's throats. The fate of a "commonweal" organization when there is no common weal in the body politic is that the bureaucracy reigns supreme. It can play one interest off against another to ensure that there is no concerted public demand to which, and by which, it could be held accountable.

Again, the disenfranchisement of urban populations was not without intention. The architects of modern school bureaucracy were seriously concerned with the growing immigrant population in the cities; they feared that with a majority of Catholics, Italians, Slavs, or Jews in some school wards, "foreign" values might prevail. In the cities, therefore, even more than elsewhere, schools were intentionally put under the control of professional bureaucrats to be overseen by elite citywide boards of education that could be counted on to maintain the "common" American value system.[10] A modern example of the same political dynamic occurred when the boundaries of New York City's "community" school districts were drawn to eliminate the three experimental districts, where it was feared that blacks had gained too much local political momentum, and to split the black voters of Queens County among three separate local districts, thereby ensuring that they would control none of them.

Urban public education systems in which the disabilities of collective accountability, bureaucracy, and misguided professionalism have developed unchecked are travesties. To talk about the student-teacher and parent-school relationship being weakened by these forces is surely an understatement, which hardly begins to describe the lack of trust, hostility, and breakdown of anything that could be called a learning relationship in many city schools.

In middle-class urban schools, the antieducational forces of the system are often balanced by other, positive forces that allow education to proceed despite the system, including the greater options that middle-class parents have to escape from inferior schools if they are dissatisfied. But many ghetto schools are institutions of antieducation in which the prime lessons for all participants—students, teachers, and parents alike—are fear, defeat, and self-hatred. That they are allowed to continue as part of a public school system in the United States is an indictment of both the system that spawns them and the society that maintains them.

INSTITUTIONAL RACISM

If education in many inner city schools is pitiable, it is especially pitiable for minority students. The destruction of thousands of young black and Hispanic lives in urban public schools is a monstrous phenomenon that many Americans prefer not to face. Many who do see what is going on explain it with the one phrase: "institutional racism."

Institutional racism is systemic, or built-in, racism, often unintentional on the part of individuals. It is society's impersonal way of maintaining the racial status quo. While the extent of institutional racism in America and in American education can be debated, what actually happens in most urban minority schools—the massive failure of black and other minority children—is much the same as would result from an intentionally racist policy. It is important to realize that this result is facilitated and legitimized by the existing political, bureaucratic, professional structure of the system.

Most teachers, principals, superintendents, and school board members are not conscious of racist motivations, and the vast majority genuinely want to provide better education for minority students. And yet it does not happen. Why? Despite hundreds of innovative programs, thousands of special remedial classes, millions of dollars of increases in educational expenditures, the education being provided in most minority classrooms in America is so bad that it should not be called education at all. It is not just that the education provided is of somewhat poorer quality, as are most things for poor people, but that many of the school experiences are downright harmful: they produce incompetence instead of competence, alienation instead of socialization, and in some cases hostility and mental illness that lead directly to criminal and self-destructive behavior.[11]

The nation must look at the structure of the system to discover how it turns even good intentions into bad results. All of the anti-educational factors, which affect large systems more than small systems, affect minority education most of all. Minority children are routinely labeled slow learners and put into tracks or special remedial classes that provide little or no real education and in which students only confirm for themselves and for their parents the judgment the school has already made of them. Documentation about how these students fall further and further behind until they become "dropouts," "disruptive," and "delinquent" is overwhelming.[12] In some sections of our large cities, as many as 80 percent of the students follow these seemingly unavoidable paths to self-destruction and social disintegration. That these paths can be avoided is shown by those ʳchools that do educate minority children, in spite of the broken homes, unemployed parents, and all the pathologies that are supposed to make their education impossible—and in spite of the pervasively negative pressures of the system.[13]

Social and human destruction can occur along with perfect adherence to the rules and values of the professionalized, public bureaucracy, that is, to the real, operational values that are built into the structure of the institution. The labeling might be done with so-called fair and objective tests in which "all children are treated the same" and no favoritism is shown. If it turns out that most of those who test out as "slow" are minority students, that is no concern of a system that prides itself on being "color blind."

The tracks for "slow learners" are designed by professionals using the most up-to-date, expert knowledge as to what is "best" for this type of student. The teachers giving the tests may all have the proper credentials—established by the rules of the system—perhaps even credentials beyond those needed to teach "normal" children; because there is a "special" need, extra courses in "teaching the disadvantaged" may be required. Any effort to use teachers lacking the required professional credentials, such as teachers from the community, is resisted fiercely, and self-righteously, in the name of fairness and maintaining standards. Everything, in short, can be done according to the rules and can even be approved by the Board of Education to ensure public accountability to the community at large. But the children will not be learning.

It is important to understand that it does not take conscious racist intentions to produce racist results. Whether the society has racist intentions—or perhaps *had* racist intentions that are now diminished but are still embodied in our institutions—is an issue beyond the scope of this book. The point is that the structure of our educational institutions operates to bring about racist results. Charles Valentine describes the case of a foster care child that demonstrates how institutional racism works and how it involves the relationship between children and the other social institutions they must deal with: "As long as his early experiences with larger institutions were mediated by his guardians or other adults in the foster family, for example, in regular church attendance, everything went smoothly. When the boy was exposed alone to impersonal bureaucratic, mainstream institutional settings, problems arose immediately.[14] Valentine describes how the boy was excluded from school because of these "problems" and was "treated" by various state institutions for "retardation" and "pathology," which Valentine and the boy's foster family and neighborhood friends had never experienced and the reality of which they questioned. In these institutions no effort was made to understand the boy's background except in ways that reinforced the negative labels—ways that no doubt seemed properly scientific and professional. Valentine summarizes the case as follows:

> This youngster's problems can be understood primarily as a mainstream institutional failure. . . . In spite of a stressful and deprived early childhood, the patient succeeded in adapting sufficiently well to his Afro-American home and community. . . . The prognosis appears to be that a basically healthy child will end up being forced into one or more of the delinquent, mentally sick, or functionally illiterate roles defined by the society's major institutions.[15]

The only bright spot in all this for poor and minority people is that many middle-class schools are becoming infected by these same diseases—low morale, little sense of mission, poor standards of performance for both teachers and students, and drugs and violence that many people had assumed could be "contained" in the ghetto. The problems are indeed systemic, and as middle-class parents find that their children are not learning and are developing bad habits and attitudes, there is a chance that political forces will finally be generated to attack the problem.

With its built-in disabilities and contradictions, it is a wonder that the present system works as well as it does. That it does so is a tribute to the common sense and commitment of thousands of students, teachers, parents, and administrators who pay little attention to the formal structure and values of the school system and who develop their own constructive working relationships to carry out the goals of learning and teaching. Yet such common sense is getting less and less chance to operate, and people of good will, both professional and lay, are becoming discouraged. The "system" is closing in on them. "The one worst system" is not only losing its effectiveness; it is losing its legitimacy as well.

7 THE LOSS OF LEGITIMACY

> The schools are not then, ineffective simply because they are badly organized
> or ignorantly operated but because they lack legitimacy.
>
> Leonard J. Fein, "Community Schools and Social Theory"

Social and political systems are held together in large part by myths
that embody important social values. The public school system in the
United States is no exception. Its myths reflect some of history's
most noble commitments—to freedom, individualism, community,
equality, human progress, and democracy. Today, however, the
guardian institutions of the myths of public education are battered,
perhaps crumbling, and the values themselves are often not visible in
their operations. Public support for public education has waned as it
has lost its power to inspire confidence as the embodiment of important social myths.

Why has the public lost confidence? Some defenders of the
present system blame the unmerciful pillorying by critics and a hostile
press. Dissatisfaction with the public school system is, however, too
widespread to justify this explanation. Critics are not needed to call
attention to the system's failings. Parents whose concerns are ignored,
students who are bored and disaffected, and business officials who
must spend millions of dollars teaching high school graduates to read
and write know that something is drastically wrong. Many people in

51

the system tell horror stories even more devastating than those recounted by the critics and the press.

The reasons for the loss of faith in public schools go deeper than day-to-day annoyances and disappointments, however. They go deeper even than the disabilities and inefficiencies of a system that is failing to educate thousands of children. The public education system is in trouble primarily because of contradictions in the value structure of the system itself. In popular terms, for those who see public education dominated by bureaucratic and professional interests that serve themselves first and the children second, if at all, the question is, Who needs it? Public education is no longer either public in its original sense or effectively educational in the sense of meeting the needs of many of its students. As Mary Anne Raywid points out, "the educational criticism of today—in sharp contrast to that of 30 years ago—is approaching the dimensions of a legitimacy crisis" for the public school system.[1]

CHANGE FOR CHANGE'S SAKE

The fundamental nature of the problems confronting public education has been evident in at least vague outline for years and has motivated endless talk of educational change. Reform of the system has become a virtual industry, engaging experts, government agencies, and community associations. Millions of dollars have been spent on innovations in curriculum and school organization. The sad reality, however, is that little real change has taken place. Much of the purported revision, especially as it has come from the educational bureaucracies, has been public relations froth. Many classroom innovations have served only to divert teachers from old habits toward ill-conceived new ideas, either ideas that are worse than those they replaced or good ideas that have been executed so poorly that they brought bad results.

Educators today are frantically pursuing change for the sake of change. Such activity keeps the wheels turning in the bureaucracies, professional organizations, universities, foundations, and reform organizations, but change for change's sake leaves the serious problems of the system basically untouched. As a result, the contradictions in public educational ideology become ever more visible, and the formulas devised in past years to reconcile or accommodate to them are coming unstuck.

Society has seen significant changes since Horace Mann and his colleagues put forth the concept of the "common school" in the last century—changes in class segregation, educational goals, cultural pluralism, and faith in governmental schooling, among others. A review of several such areas of social change will show why educational change—real change in conception and practice—is imperative, for reasons that go beyond the inefficiencies of "the one worst system."

CLASS SEGREGATION

The ideology that underlays the founding of the public school included a kind of middle-class classlessness: "It was to be for rich and poor alike, not only free but equivalent in quality of any comparable private institution. In it would mix the children of all creeds, classes, and backgrounds, the warm association of childhood kindling a spirit of mutual amity and respect which the strains and cleavages of adult life could never destroy."[2]

The major social changes confronting the architects of the public school system were urbanization and industrialization—thousands of rural and foreign immigrants were flooding into the burgeoning towns and cities of nineteenth-century America, where the public school was seen as a way of creating a sense of community and at the same time inducting children of all backgrounds into solid middle-class values.

Since the Second World War the major demographic change in the social structure has been in the direction, not of urbanization, but of suburbanization. As middle-class families left cities in the 1950s and 1960s, they undercut the possibility of a classless common school. Today the socially and economically homogeneous suburbs and the poor cities, populated largely by minorities, are class segregated, a factor that adds to the racial controversies over busing. The idea of the common school no longer corresponds to social reality, except in a few small towns and rare urban or suburban situations. This creates a whole new set of social realities that educational policy makers must confront.

If Americans believe that such values as equality and fraternity should prevail in schools, we shall have to find something other than the classic common-school ideology to express them. Any system pretending that the ghost of Horace Mann presides benignly over both Scarsdale and the South Bronx is bound to fall on its face. Not even the dreamiest of planners can conceive of enough busing to recreate the conditions for Mann's common school.

SCHOOLS AS SORTING MACHINES

Although public schools were originally seen as classless in a certain sense, they were not seen as a means for making all people equal; American individualism did not permit that. Charles W. Eliot put the matter bluntly in an address to the National Society for the Promotion of Industrial Education in 1908. The schools, said Eliot, had come to have a new function of unparalleled importance: "The teachers of the elementary schools ought to sort the pupils and sort them by their evident or probable destinies."[3]

The idea of schools as social sorters was not as new in 1908 as Eliot may have thought. Thomas Jefferson's proposal for public education in the early days of the Republic set forth a plan in which "twenty of the best geniuses [would] be raked from the rubbish" in each county every year and given six years of education at public expense. Only ten of the twenty would be selected for secondary training.[4] While Jefferson's proposal was not accepted by the Virginia legislature, the idea that schools would help to select only a few students to be educated was old when mass public education was introduced. Nor was it seen as unacceptable by the general public, even as it celebrated the values of freedom and equality. Those who were not deemed suitable for advanced academic learning were not necessarily viewed as second-class citizens. In 1900 less than 10 percent of the population finished high school. The remaining 90 percent were not considered dropouts; they were seen as normal children with other routes to responsible adulthood.[5]

Revisionist historians point out that the 10 percent were drawn primarily from the privileged classes, with only enough academically talented lower-class children brought in to give the appearance of social mobility.[6] That may or may not be a fair reading of history. In coming to grips with contemporary educational problems, however, it matters little whether the founders intended to form a system to perpetuate a well-educated elite and a semiliterate general populace docilely turning the wheels of industry, or whether they genuinely believed public education was a reform movement opening opportunity to the masses. Whatever the motives, the system established was a sorting machine. Teachers were trained and supervised, curriculums planned and implemented, and tests developed and administered for the purpose of sorting people into their respective slots. The system assumed that a few students would be outstanding achievers, many would be average, and a large number would remain uneducated. That sorting system remains intact today; the only modification is that, because of race and class segregation, there are more schools where it is assumed that most or nearly all students will learn very little. The outstanding and average students are assumed to be in "better" schools.

To retain a system built on this kind of sorting mentality is socially suicidal in today's world. In contemporary society being a dropout is a serious problem, not just an alternative way of attaining adulthood. It is even a problem to be a graduate if, despite diploma in hand, you cannot read, write, or count. Today the 90 percent must have educational attainments equal to those of the 10 percent in 1900. People can no longer function socially, economically, or politically without at least the equivalent of a fairly good high school education. As John Gardner has pointed out, we have no choice but to provide *both* excellence and competent learning for all.[7]

Toward this goal of much higher levels of achievement for all children, Benjamin Bloom advances the possibility of "mastery learning." He argues that "what any person in the world can learn, almost all persons can learn" if provided with the proper learning conditions.[8] He says that we are selling our children short, that our normal assumptions about good learners and poor learners, or even about fast and slow learners, are fundamentally false—that if we organize education properly, all students can learn what they need to know. He argues persuasively not only that this can be done, but that it must be done.

Bloom is right. There has been a revolution in educational expectations. Our educational system, however, has not yet responded to it. Nor can it respond within its present policy framework. Bloom is talking about a fundamental change in the purpose of the system, from one in which a major function is sorting students into one in which a major purpose is the "mastery learning" by virtually all students. Whatever the intentions of educators, the reality is that the most fundamental habits, attitudes, and practices of the system are designed to sort children into academic winners and losers. It will take a fundamental reorientation and redesign of the system, including teacher training, parent expectations, and political accountability, to change it.

The changes do not require the elimination of competition or the diminution of people's desires to be winners. What is required is the elimination of the acceptance of losers, because in today's world losers in school are losers in life. The rhetoric of universal education now must become the reality. If one can talk about the "will" of an institution (as in "where there is a will there is a way"), then one can say that our present system of public education does not have the will to educate all its students. It was not set up for that purpose, and it cannot achieve it without fundamental changes.

CULTURAL PLURALISM

Horace Mann and his colleagues were not timid in their vision of the public school as an instrument for assimilating the children of immigrants and recruits from rural areas into a Protestant, Anglo-American, capitalistic culture. Professor E.P. Cubberly, one of the towering figures of public education at the turn of the century and for many years thereafter, characterized the new immigrants from southern and eastern Europe as "illiterate," "docile," "lacking in self-reliance and initiative." He pointed out that "these people settle in groups or settlements and set up their national manners, customs and observances." "Our task is to break up these groups and settlements to assimilate and amalgamate these people as part of our American race, and to implant in their children, as far as can be done, the Anglo-Saxon conception of righteousness, law and order, and our popular government."[9]

Such values are still strong in the United States; yet today cultural pluralism and ethnic diversity are also becoming acceptable values. Attitudes such as Cubberly's are no longer respectable.

Nathan Glazer has outlined how the ideal of cultural assimilation in education eroded from a peak of nationalism during the First World War, first into a concept of "intercultural education" and then into the "cultural pluralism" of the last two decades. He quotes a

1972 statement of the quasi-official American Association of Colleges of Teacher Education:

> Multicultural education rejects the view that schools should seek to melt away cultural differences or the view that schools should merely tolerate cultural pluralism. . . . Cultural pluralism is a concept that aims toward a heightened sense of being and a wholeness of the entire society based on the unique strengths of each of its parts. . . . Schools and colleges must assure that their total educational process and educational content reflect commitment to cultural pluralism.

Glazer also cites an authoritative statement of the National Council for Social Studies to the effect that "ethnic diversity should be recognized and respected at individual, group, and societal levels" and that "ethnic diversity provides a basis for societal cohesiveness and survival."[10]

Verbal rejections of old values and the affirmation of new ones do not mean, however, that the public school system has already responded to the change in values and has now been redesigned to foster cultural pluralism instead of cultural assimilation. Despite the new rhetoric, the practices, policies, and fundamental structure of the school system have changed little from the days when cultural assimilation was its avowed principle. Even at the level of policy and ideology, it is not clear that the "new" values have been accepted. The scattered bilingual programs in public schools are under severe ideological and political pressure not to extend beyond "transitional" bilingualism, which can be used only to help students get started in school until they learn enough English to be brought into the mainstream. Proposed federal regulations requiring even transitional bilingual instruction came under severe attack, causing both houses of Congress to pass resolutions to stop their enforcement.

The relative merits of assimilationist or pluralist positions form a serious and important debate that extends beyond educational policy. Whatever resolution may be found to this debate in future years, it is clear that our present public school system is still organized on the basis of resolutions worked out in the nineteenth century to meet the needs of a nation being flooded with immigrants from all over the world and trying to build a sense of national unity while constructing a modern industrial society. The needs and conditions of today and tomorrow are substantially different and call for new equations.[11]

Again, the changes cannot be dealt with merely through a few modifications in curriculum and teacher training. Some of the basic principles of the school system must be challenged and changed. A principal assumption of the assimilationist policy was that a common public school could be justified for all children because it was value neutral. It was thought that, unlike religious and private schools, where parents furthered parochial values, the common school embodied a common culture, neither promoting nor violating the values of any. This, of course, was and is a myth. Historians have laid bare the Protestant biases of the nineteenth-century public schools.[12] More to the point, as was pointed out in Chapter 3, it is literally impossible to have value-free education. Education always presupposes a value system, and efforts to deny this only make the biases involved more insidious.[13]

Value conflicts have occurred across the history of public education, but by and large the value-neutral ideology has held sway to legitimate a common school curriculum determined by government policy and provided to all "on an equal basis." Cultural pluralism in whatever form it takes questions the very idea of a single, politically determined, "official" value system. Fundamental conflicts of values put public school ideology in a dilemma: to argue that public education is truly value free only strengthens the claims of those who maintain a right to educate their children within a value framework. To counter this argument by claiming that public schools can and should teach moral and spiritual values only heightens the problems: Whose moral and spiritual values? Who decides which values to teach and how to teach them?

LOSS OF FAITH IN GOVERNMENT

Added to the contradictions in the ideology of public education that have become increasingly manifest over the years is a more recent cause for the present system's loss of legitimacy: the general decline of faith in government.

For many years after it had been successfully established, public education escaped the debates between liberals and conservatives as to whether it was desirable to have government take on a variety of tasks previously performed by individuals or private groups. This was partly because the public school system was an accepted part of the scene long before the modern growth of big government, partly because its architects succeeded in disguising it as a nongovernmental function, and partly because it was an integral part of our national pride, which placed it beyond the effective reach of conservative critics.

Now, however, the situation is changing. It is becoming clearer to liberals and conservatives alike that it is not so simple for government to "deliver" health, education, welfare, security, fire protection, and clean streets. Even with efficient management and hard-working professionals, government cannot keep streets clean if people litter them faster than they can be cleared; cannot give fire protection when arson reaches the level it has in the South Bronx; cannot provide security when so many people are committing crimes; cannot provide for the welfare of families and communities when the social fabric deteriorates too far; cannot deliver health when people insist on retaining unhealthy habits; and, finally, cannot deliver an educated citizenry just from the efforts of trained professionals working in expensive educational agencies.

The most that government can do is *assist* in producing these desired results. And what government is assisting is not a "what" but a "who," namely us—people, human beings—beings for whom motivation, meaning, loyalty, and a whole host of factors that have little to do with governmental efficiency are the determining elements. Any effort to deal with these persisting social problems only through governmental operations, without taking into account the preeminent importance of human motivation and behavior, is doomed to failure.

Public education is not escaping this new perception. When the issue was whether governmental action was desirable, the vote of the overwhelming majority of Americans on public education was affirmative. When the issue is whether government can by itself meet the needs of individuals and society, education becomes one of the governmental functions that makes it most obvious that "governmentalism" must fail. It is not just a conservative backlash that is catching public education in its first real life-or-death political crisis, but a whole rethinking of the governmental and political equation in American society. The concept of public education as a professionalized, bureaucratized governmental service-delivery system is doomed beyond recall. Its legitimacy is at an end. It will take a while for this fact to be fully recognized, but its impact is already being felt and will increasingly bring pressure for fundamental change.

CHANGE FOR THE SAKE OF SURVIVAL

If public education fails to respond to significant changes in American society, as it has in recent decades, it will be living with increasing contradictions that will sap its strength. It will continue to lose momentum and will eventually become extinct. Change for the sake of change is not needed; change for the sake of survival is.

One of the reasons why so many of the innovations have not worked is that, whether seriously intended to improve the system or only to quiet its critics, they have been literally superficial: they have dealt only with the surface, changing boxes on an organizational chart or adding a remedial program to an instructional program that is basically unworkable. Digging beneath the surface is far more difficult, and far more threatening to established habits and interests. But only such fundamental rethinking will meet the needs of survival for the society as a whole and for whatever system of education it adopts for its children.

II A SUGGESTED SOLUTION

8 EDUCATION AS PARTNERSHIP

My plea is to get teachers to break out of the "box" imposed by an obsolete structure by joining with students and parents in remaking the public schools.

Mario Fantini, *What's Best for the Children*

Part 1 concludes that the prevailing conception of public education in the United States is fundamentally faulty and that this faulty conception is at the heart of the policy problems confronting education today.

Education has been conceived as a governmental service-delivery system: we have set up government-run, professionally staffed bureaus to "deliver" education to our children. When the results are unsatisfactory, our service-delivery approach prompts us to try to solve the problem by delivering more services or by making the service-delivery machinery either more efficient, through improved technology, or more accountable, through political action or better management.

Attempts to reduce to a delivery system something that is by its nature not a service and not deliverable will not work. The effort withers the energy and commitment and obstructs the productive relationships of the key participants in the educational enterprise—students, teachers, parents, and citizens. To continue with the service-delivery approach can only perpetuate what John Holt calls "a failure and a disaster."[1]

What alternative conceptions are there? This is the most important question facing education in the United States today. The search for new approaches has begun and must not be abandoned until a new consensus is achieved, one that is appropriate to American social and political values and capable of producing the education wanted by individuals and society.

The following chapters suggest a framework to assist in the reconception of American education. Within the proposed framework, the concept of service delivery is replaced by the concept of partnership —partnership between learners and teachers, homes and schools, and communities and school systems. Government, bureaucracy, and professionalization are deemphasized to give greater attention to the voice, choice, and loyalty of the educational partners.

This refocusing does not imply that government, bureaucracy, or professionalism will disappear from education. Publicly accountable educational policy, organization, and expertise are necessary and useful, but they must be seen as instruments for promoting and sustaining learning partnerships, not as means of "delivering" education. Government, bureaucracy, and professionalization have become dominant concepts in educational policy, concepts that generate the controlling values of the system and guide the behavior of its participants. They have become ends in themselves, instead of means to achieve ends grounded in the values of the real parties at interest—parents, students, citizens, and teachers.[2]

Government, bureaucracy, and professionalization must be dethroned as the rulers of educational practice and policy. Partnership is more likely to promote policies and institutions that educate successfully in accordance with the values of a democratic society.

THE REALITY RATHER THAN THE RHETORIC OF PARTNERSHIP

School board and PTA meetings resonate with warm words about partnership, but the rhetoric often belies the reality. Successful educational partnerships indeed exist in many individual classrooms and schools, but genuine partnership is driven out of education as schools, parents, and students come to think of their relationships in terms of service delivery—of "provider" and "client," of "professionals" and "target populations."

The chief characteristic of partnership is common effort toward common goals. Partners may help one another in general or specific ways, but none is ever a client, because the relationship is mutual. Providers and clients can deal with one another at arm's length; partners share an enterprise, though their mutuality does not imply or require equality or similarity. Participants in effective partnerships may be strikingly different, each contributing to the common enterprise particular talents, experiences, and perspectives and sometimes having different status within the relationship and control over aspects of the work to be done.[3]

The concept of service delivery, unlike that of partnership, leads to conflict-producing ambiguities about whether provider or client wields more power in the relationship. "Client" is a word having two possible, contradictory meanings: in one, it means "slave," "dependent," "ward," "serf," "vassal." In the other, it is a synonym for "patron," "employer," "customer."[4] Education has instances of both kinds of client relationships—neither one healthy. In the first, parents and students are treated as powerless wards of professionalized bureaucracies; in the second, parents and students see themselves as customers purchasing services, either as taxpayers or private school patrons. Neither instance describes a productive educational relationship: The first disempowers students and their parents; the second disempowers teachers and professional staffs.

Horace Taft, headmaster of the Taft School, tells a story of the irate father with a "patron" or "customer" outlook coming into his office to object to his son's dismissal. "Mr. Taft," he said, "you seem to think you can run this school any way you damn please." Taft replied, "Sir, your manner is crude and your language is vulgar, but somehow you have gotten the idea."[5] The educational relationship envisioned by Taft obviously involved something more than the purchase and delivery of services. Likewise, the effective public school is something more than a dispenser of professional services paid for by taxpayers. For any kind of school, public or private, the concept of partnership comes closer to describing the necessary relationships conducive to successful learning. It builds policies on human relationships—on mutuality, which is the crux of education.[6]

These relationships are varied and complex, but when they are the focus of attention, education can avoid antieducational values, false professionalism, and impersonal bureaucracy.

RELATIONS AMONG THE PARTNERS

If the idea of partnership in education is to be taken beyond rhetoric, the relationships among the partners must be considered carefully. Political economist Albert O. Hirschman has suggested a theoretical model that is useful for this purpose.

Hirschman's perceptive essay *Exit, Voice, and Loyalty* focuses not just on education but on a wide range of political and economic activity in human affairs.[7] He notes two basic mechanisms through which individuals respond to problems in institutions: exit and voice. "Exit" is withdrawal from a product or an organization. "Voice" is an effort to improve the performance of an organization or the product of a company through complaint, argument, or political action. In either case, the individual is affected by his "loyalty" to the product or organization.

Hirschman sees an unhealthy dichotomy in contemporary American social policy between those who find correctives to institutional problems in exit, or market-type dynamics (the economics bias), and those who tend to emphasize voice as the proper response for dissatisfaction (the political bias). He suggests that *both* economics and politics would benefit by an acknowledgment that exit *and* voice are usually at work in human endeavor, often in complex combination.

The relevance of Hirschman's thesis to the current debates in public education is obvious: "voice" corresponds to the dominant way people in the United States have related to public education from the middle of the nineteenth century to the present; "exit" corresponds to the way many people are responding today to their dissatisfaction with the public schools, often after having despaired of achieving any change through voice—sometimes after their voices have grown hoarse trying.

To make Hirschman's thesis useful for educational policy, however, it must be expanded in two important respects: it must include affirmative as well as negative responses (that is, choice rather than merely exit); and it must include the reactions and motivations of educational staffs as well as consumers and citizens. Let us look more closely at each of these modifications.

CHOICE AS WELL AS EXIT

Hirschman's *Exit, Voice, and Loyalty* addresses only the issues of institutional malfunction and the human response of withdrawal when one is dissatisfied with an organization's products or policies. His essay is a litany of negatives on the "decay," "corruption," and "deterioration" of institutions.

Those who have experienced the frustrations of trying to improve public education may be tempted to seize on a framework for educational policy based on such negative concepts. That would be a mistake, however. Education is, and must be, a positive process. Every new generation starts afresh, full of hope and purpose. Education is a process of development, not deterioration. If the United States wants a policy framework for education, and not just for malfunctioning schools, we must account for voices and choices that are positive as well as negative, for entry as well as exit.

Fortunately, Hirschman's basic framework can be expanded to deal with positive situations. The concepts of voice and loyalty can be borrowed without change of terminology. The term "exit," however, which connotes only a negative response, is better changed to "choice," to accommodate both positive and negative responses.

SCHOOL STAFF AS WELL AS STUDENTS AND PARENTS

The other expansion of Hirschman's framework involves the inclusion of those who work for educational institutions as well as its members or customers.[8] Hirschman's main idea is that either through exit (switching to another product or resigning from an organization) or through voiced objection (seeking change through persuasion or political action), customers or members bring pressure on an organization to change its policies or practices. His essay does not discuss how those who work for the organization interact with these expressions of choice or voice, or how their values affect policy or product quality. An educational policy framework must take into account the interests and values of teachers, administrators, and school officials, as well as those of students, parents, and citizens. Educational relationships can be either enhanced or obstructed by the way staff members' values interact with those of students, parents, and citizens. Since school staff behavior is relatively uncontrolled by bureaucratic methods, it is important to develop policies that motivate teachers and administrators as well as parents and students in educationally productive ways.

With the change of "exit" to "choice" and the addition of organizational staff to the equation, we are ready to look at how partnership might replace service delivery as the primary framework for educational policy and how voice, choice, and loyalty can help to explain the relationships of educational partners.

9 VOICE

A crucial reason schools fail is that they neither recognize nor come to grips with the essential political nature of schooling in American society.

Ray Rist, *Restructuring American Education*

Voice is essential to partnership. Without voice, "I" am nothing. Without voice also, there is no communication; therefore, "we" are nothing as well. Since education must be based on "I" and "we," educational partners must have voice.

Voice has been a traditional component of American education. Education was a favorite topic of preachers and politicians in the early days of the Republic. The voices of Horace Mann, Henry Barnard, and other missionaries of the public school movement were heard up and down the land, in lecture halls and legislatures, as were the voices of their critics, such as Bishop Hughes, who thundered his opposition in New York, and Orestes Brownson, who warned of the dangers of governmental education in Massachusetts.

At the turn of the century, reformers who wanted to professionalize education and industrialists who wanted better vocational education were heard. In the 1920s and 1930s the progressives had a prominent voice, and in the 1950s the Admiral Rickovers and Rudolf Flesches voiced their complaints that "Johnny can't read."

While voice has been part of the American educational scene from

69

the beginning, the intensity and variety of voices increased significantly in the 1960s.[1] Teachers, who in the past had not felt it their role to speak out, not only voiced their concerns but organized unions to add power to their voice. Parents were heard from as never before—both those who accepted public schooling and tried to reform it and those who expressed their dissatisfaction by choosing an alternative and demanding public funding to pay for it. Students, whose rebellions in the past had seldom gone beyond overboisterous football rallies, began demanding a voice in policy making and governance.

Blacks found their voice first in the courtrooms and then, when they saw that court orders were not enough to guarantee their rights, they raised their voices in the streets and in the political arena. Hispanics joined in, challenging the hallowed goals of assimilation and Americanization. Indians came forth with reminders that they, after all, were the true "Native Americans," whose land had been stolen and whose culture had been brutally destroyed. These minority groups were no longer willing to accept the lie of a system that proclaimed principles of merit, fairness, equality, and uniform justice but practiced discrimination, oppression, and cultural imperialism.

The traditional minorities were not the only ones who raised their voices; the "unmeltable ethnics" were also beginning to speak out.[2] Even in the Anglo heartland—Iowa, Ohio, Kentucky—voices of religious minorities were lifted. And women: after years of being put "on a pedestal" and "worshiped" as in no other country in the world, they suddenly realized that these images were the creation of men's voices. When their own voices were heard, they said that they felt their own worth as individuals was being denied.

All these voices represented values that were being denied and repressed in a bureaucratized and homogenizing American school system. While the volume and shrillness of the voices have subsided, the landscape of American education has been permanently altered. Both consciousness and institutions have changed in fundamental ways. A younger generation of blacks will never accept discrimination as many of their elders did. They no longer *feel* like second-class citizens, even though they are still often treated as such. They increasingly feel like participants, not only in American society but in a human society in which a "third," nonwhite world is gaining prominence. Hispanics and other "ethnics" no longer feel ashamed of their cultural, religious, and genetic backgrounds. Women can no longer be satisfied with only the roles of housewife, mother, and obedient servant. Teachers will never again be just loyal and docile employees.

These are only a few examples of how consciousness has changed over the last twenty years, and the *voicing* of this consciousness has been essential to its reality.

THE LEGITIMACY OF VOICE

For many, the voices of the 1960s were unsettling, even frightening; and no doubt some of the causes for which they were raised will prove misguided and short-lived. Nevertheless, the *idea* of voice—the capacity of individuals or groups to speak out, to express their values, to call attention to their concerns and interests, and to demand changes—is a fundamental value of American democracy.[3]

What was discovered in the 1960s was not just that many people felt the need to voice their concerns but that established institutions were unresponsive or even hostile to the idea of voice. The shrillness of the voices was a sign both of the intensity of the feelings expressed and of the frustration of having concerns ignored and rejected.[4]

People were becoming aware that the professionalized educational bureaucracies that ran the schools were relatively immune to the voices of students, parents, teachers, and citizens. The relationships between the participants in the educational enterprise had become fixed and, whether satisfactory or not, were going to be hard to change.

As demands for change became stronger, however—sometimes underscored with civil disobedience—changes began to be made. Some changes, such as desegregation, bilingual education, open admissions, multicultural textbooks, affirmative action hiring, increased funding for "the disadvantaged," and increased pay for teachers, attempted to redress grievances. Other changes were procedural, intending to guarantee more opportunity for, and response to, voice in the future. Such changes included collective bargaining for teachers, parent councils, decentralization, and due process hearings for student suspensions.

Many of these changes are too new to be evaluated. Some are

merely the result of ad hoc tinkering within a bureaucratized service-delivery system. Nevertheless, they point in a common direction: educational policy for the future will have to take into account the legitimacy of voice throughout the educational enterprise.

In three areas in particular there is both more voice and more demand for voice—school governance, the courts, and the classroom.

VOICE IN SCHOOL GOVERNANCE

People lost voice in education when "education was taken out of politics."[5] There was good reason to remove education from the control of corrupt politicians, but when it was thought that education could be made apolitical, power was simply shifted from parents and citizens to educational bureaucrats.

The new undemocratic structure was quite consciously created, although one must hope that the sad consequences were unforeseen by its architects. A prime spokesmen for the shift, Nicholas Murray Butler, president of Columbia University, explained that it is as foolish to speak of "democratization of schools" as it is to speak of "democratization of the treatment of appendicitis. . . . The fundamental confusion is this: Democracy is a principle of government; the schools belong to the administration; and a democracy is as much entitled as a monarchy to have its business well done."[6]

Granted, it is often troublesome for people to assert voice in the governance of education in a pluralistic society with changing values. The voices are multiple and often conflicting. But to try to solve the problem by closing out voice undercuts the legitimacy of the whole system.

How much opportunity do parents or citizens feel they have these days to influence school policy? Very little. Some of the voluntary private schools set up by dissatisfied parents come closer to the democracy of the public schools in the days of Horace Mann than does the typical modern public school. Many parochial schools, as Donald Erickson has pointed out, are more "compatible with family and community values, and are responsive to parental wishes in a manner once more widely characteristic of the public schools."[7]

It is perhaps easier with hindsight to see the illegitimacy of what the bureaucratic reformers did when they shut out people's voices in the name of technocratic efficiency.[8] They were bedazzled by the thought that science made values irrelevant and that people were being excluded only from decisions for which they lacked the necessary expertise. Such reasoning was a colossal fallacy, of course, since education is, and must be, imbued throughout with values. To exclude people from decisions about education is to deny the most elementary aspects of democratic government. Democracy is not a matter of arbitrary definition. Democratic government must always embody the "will of the people," and government-run schools are illegitimate if based on anything except that will; when government does not follow the people's will, it follows its own will, and that is tyranny.

Efforts to reintroduce the voice of parents and citizens into education are now under way at every level of the public school system. Federal legislation, especially Title I of the Elementary and Secondary Education Act and the Head Start program, as well as local citizen action, have greatly increased participatory councils and advisory committees, whch today number more than 100,000 and involve over 1.2 million citizens and parents.[9]

But has anything really changed? The extensive survey of these various efforts conducted under a federal grant by the Institute for Responsive Education (IRE) concludes that "such participation has not resulted in practice in any substantial shift in power relations among school boards, administrators, and citizens. . . . Professional domination continues and school superintendents dominate school boards; both resist devolving power to parents and citizens." The survey expresses the fear that these efforts may be contributing to what former U.S. Representative Barbara Jordan has called "a network of illusions."[10]

The reasons for this may be explainable within the thesis of this book. Since much of the "participation" is government sponsored, it may, even when it is not designed as outright co-optation, actually *increase* rather than reduce bureaucratization. As Don Davies, who headed the IRE survey, points out, "This paradox can be most clearly seen in a program such as Title I, which promises participation for low-income people, but which, because of its size and complexity, presses school systems to centralized and bureaucratic management."[11] Furthermore, participation as a form of consumerism may only serve to reinforce the idea that schools are the "producers" of learning and parents and students are the "consumers." Since this service-delivery concept continues to dominate educational policy, encouraging parents to participate as consumers may merely enhance the psychological power of bureaucracy.[12]

Nonetheless, a new wind is blowing, even though it is not yet strong enough to blow down the walls of the entrenched educational bureaucracies. The discoveries made as people are given more voice in their own schools seem almost like revelations—as if old truths, long buried, are being unearthed, shined up, and found to be remarkably useful. In one local school council project, for instance, described in the press as "a radical plan" that "puts everybody in charge," a euphoric participant reported that "conflicts are settled with the participation of everyone involved . . . no one is frustrated because he can't get a hearing." The article went on to report that under the old system, "so often there was no response. Matters just disappeared into the bureaucracy." Under the new plan, "problems may not be settled to everyone's satisfaction, but no one is ignored."[13]

The "no one is ignored" is the secret of the democratic process. A person need not win to feel respected, but if his voice is not listened to, he feels worthless and irrelevant. It is ironic that modern public education, which is so full of rhetoric about the teaching of democratic values, has ended up making so many people feel worthless and irrelevant because their voices cannot, or will not, be heard.[14]

It remains to be seen whether legislative and citizens' action to reintroduce voice into education will prove to be mere lip service that leaves bureaucratic hegemony intact or will actually empower individuals and communities to give voice to their values. Voice can be effective only if the present educational tyrannies will yield to new relationships, attitudes, and behavior.

Yet voice in the governance of education is no simple matter. Before we examine (in part 3) recent efforts to gain voice through the political process, we must first see how voice can be expressed in other ways and how it relates to choice and loyalty.

VOICE THROUGH THE COURTS

When the parents of José P. voiced their concerns about the education of their multiply handicapped son to the New York City school authorities, they got no response. Like many parents before them, they took their story into court, where a judge listened to their pleas and ordered the school authorities to respond to them.[15]

This is only one of many cases where parents and citizens have had more success getting their voices heard effectively through the courts than through administrative or political processes. Litigation involving education has increased greatly in the last thirty years. For many years "school law" meant little more than the rules governing school bonds, contracts, and liability. School law today covers a vast number of issues concerning race discrimination, free speech, religious freedom, the rights of the handicapped, state aid formulas, due process for students, collective bargaining, and educational malpractice.[16]

Some people bitterly complain that by "intruding" into school affairs the courts are usurping democratic government, overturning the decisions of duly elected officials.[17] The most vehement objections, of course, were directed at the Supreme Court's 1954 desegregation decision outlawing the segregation statutes of seventeen states. But other less volatile decisions have also bred resentment: upholding the right of students to wear antiwar armbands, stopping school Christmas ceremonies, or requiring due process for a student "troublemaker" or a dismissed teacher.

In such cases it may seem that courts violate the "voice of the people." Yet in every case judges and juries are responding to the voice of a plaintiff or a whole class of plaintiffs seeking redress because their voices are ignored by the school system. They feel that their rights, interests, and values have been denied by the ordinary process of government.

A judicial decision is not the denial of voice, but the resolution of a conflict among voices—a procedure that is legitimate in a democracy in which the majority enjoys no right to suppress a minority and every citizen is entitled to his "day in court" if he feels his legal rights have been violated.

Some educators are troubled not only by decisions that may be controversial but also by the conflicting values introduced when educational problems are defined as legal issues. They complain that school discipline becomes a question of due process, that school rules and regulations become questions of the constitutionally protected rights of free speech or religious freedom, and that treatment of different children is reduced to a question of legally prohibited discrimination. The time-honored principle of *in loco parentis*—teachers or school administrators making discretionary judgments as though they were the parents of a child—has given way to detailed legalistic codes.[18] Guidance conferences, set up supposedly to help children or their parents deal constructively with problems, are replaced by formal proceedings, replete with lawyers and an adversarial atmosphere. The school, it is argued, becomes a place where family values cannot prevail, where participants must deal with one another at arm's length in accord with legally defined rights and responsibilities.[19]

These complaints of educators are ironic, since it is the increasing governmentalization and bureaucratization of education that have brought the courts and lawyers into the schools. The trend away from locally governed, community-oriented schools has frustrated efforts to resolve educational differences by face-to-face consultation among parents, teachers, and school administrators. When no one seems to be listening, the "clients" have turned to the courts as a place where their voices will be heard. If the result of the courts' intrusion is too often rigid and inflexible, professional educators might ponder whether they are only reaping the results of a system that closes its ears to parents and students.

Voicing concerns through the courts is indeed often unsatisfactory. It seldom rectifies the underlying problem of overbureaucratized and inhuman school systems and, in fact, often deepens the bureaucratic problem by increasing the rule-bound nature of the enterprise. But the courts may be the only place people can voice their concerns when the school system goes deaf. With voice so essential to the empowerment of individuals and groups and to effective human relationships, a forum in court is better than no forum at all. The question to be asked is why there is so little effective opportunity for voice in the educational process itself.

VOICE IN THE CLASSROOM

If education is to be conceived not as a service to be delivered but as a relationship between people, the voices of its participants must be heard not just in governmental decision making and in legal procedures to redress grievances, but in the very process of education itself—in classrooms and schools, in parent-teacher conferences and in one-on-one discussions between teachers and students.

Educators once knew this. Even in the days of "authoritarian" education, much of classroom instruction was carried on as recitation. Students had to speak, to respond, to express themselves in order to learn. They recited to be corrected, but at least there was awareness that Jane and Johnny had a part to play in producing learning.

Today, when the purported goal of education is to produce independent minds, the voice of the student is even more important. Students who cannot express themselves cannot learn, cannot find out who they are or what they think or what kind of independent minds they have. Education could be defined as the process of helping students find their own voice. Barnell Smith, head of a successful school for poor black students in Chicago, reports, "The majority of young people making up the underclass have the ability to read and write and do math, but what they don't have is the ability to articulate their feelings."[20] As one commentator said, unless children learn to speak, they "will spend their lives in the most awful silence, the silence in which, for lack of language, they will not even know that they think."[21]

Education has become a massive process for producing passive minds. A tutor of a New York high school senior who had failed a basic competency test asked, "What is half of fifty?" "Forty," the student answered. "Are you sure?" asked the tutor. "Thirty" was the next reply. The student was not thinking: she was guessing, as she had learned to guess during her twelve years of schooling. When she guessed wrong, she had perhaps been rewarded by letting another student, or the teacher, provide the answer. To have used her mind, to have said even "I don't know," might have run the risk of ridicule; but to have voiced honest ignorance would at least have provided an opportunity for learning. Never prompted to think, even about her ignorance, this student had a passive mind by the time she was a senior. She guessed in arithmetic because she had learned that guessers get by.[22]

When a student who is asked what half of fifty is answers "forty" and looks up to see if that is the answer the teacher wants, she is not only guessing but also trying to satisfy the wrong person. She has learned dependent thinking instead of independent thinking. She has not learned to satisfy herself that she has the right answer. This may seem like a trivial example, but it exemplifies the issue of voice in democratic education. If students cannot form judgments that first of all satisfy themselves, how can they speak with assurance? How can others know they are getting true judgments of the person speaking rather than the parroted views of others?

For a child to develop an independent voice, someone must be listening, for without a listener there is no relationship. A good teacher listens, and listens with respect even when the student is wrong, because teaching is concerned not merely with answers but also with emerging personalities trying to find their voice.

The value of one-to-one tutoring is the undivided attention the teacher can give to the student. Whereas a classroom teacher might "deliver educational services" to thirty students, whether they are participating or not, a tutor has little choice but to listen to the student, evoke his or her responses, and take part in genuine communication. An effective teacher does the same thing with a whole class.[23]

Voice is related to self-respect. It is also related to the "fate control" that research has linked to successful academic performance.[24] A sense of control over one's environment and one's future is both cause and effect of a thinking mind, a mind that can formulate thoughts and voice them to others. But voice in the learning relationship does not mean that students must control the curriculum or talk out at random. A good class is one in which all members feel that their values, aspirations, and personalities are respected and where they do not have to act out to get attention.

Writing is another way in which student voice can be expressed. Voice need not be oral. The great decline in the quantity and quality of writing expected of students is another aspect of the "passivication" of the intellect. Writing requires independent thought. Good writing requires competent independent thought. The process of writing down one's thoughts objectifies the personality in a way that allows the writer to see what he is saying and become more conscious of his own voice.

When we examine many classrooms today, we find that while there is often much noise, there is very little voice. The issue of voice, therefore, is one that must be thought of in terms not only of governance and lawsuits but also of the day-to-day relationships of teaching and learning, of keeping school and relating to parents.

VOICE, VOLUNTARISM, AND VOTING

Voice is related to volition. Consider two cases: in one, the twenty families of a small nineteenth-century American town got together and established a public school; in the other, twenty families in a twentieth-century city send their children to the local public school under the compulsory attendance laws. Both sets of families sent their children to public school, but in the first case the school was created and maintained by the voice of the families; in the other, the families have exercised no voice and no will. The city parents passively acquiesce in the will of a distant government. They may be happy or unhappy about their children's schooling, but, in either case, they have "no voice in the matter."

Respect for parental voice does not require that mom and dad march through the school halls issuing dictums; direct intervention may not be necessary at all. Ronald Edmonds, in his research on effective schools under a grant from the Carnegie Corporation, tells of a small school on Beaver Island, Michigan, where the children learn remarkably well with little direct parental participation. Parents neither attend PTA meetings nor swarm about the school during the day; they seem to leave teaching to the teachers and the running of the school to the school officials. Yet in such cases the voice of the parents and other citizens is very much involved. The teachers are aware that they are carrying out the will of the parents and the community. If they veer from that course they will hear about it—either through formal complaints or through the comments, attitudes, and body language they encounter at the local grocery store, gas station, or town picnic.

Closely related to volition is voluntarism. A person seeing a drowning man may shout, "Help that man!" Another may jump in to save him. Both are expressing their values and commitments, but in different ways. A school whose participants do only their assigned tasks is a school of automatons, in which there is no more expression of personal commitment than there is with puppets. A school, however, in which students, teachers, and parents reach out to one another, because they are concerned and want to express their concern to themselves and to one another, is a school in which there is voice.[25]

Even totalitarian Marxists have learned the value of voluntarism in education. Fidel Castro's campaign against illiteracy in Cuba bypassed the established education bureaucracy in favor of a program based on a hundred thousand volunteers, almost all students, who were recruited, trained, and dispatched to the rural villages for one-to-one tutoring using the principles developed by Paulo Freire in Brazil. Before they went forth, Castro advised the tutors not to assume a superior attitude, even though most of them, as city dwellers and students, had more education than those they would be tutoring. He urged them to listen as well as talk, telling them they would learn more than they taught. This effort to establish direct learning relationships between tutors and students was mounted as a highly visible, public campaign, with awards and banners for villages that succeeded in the battle against illiteracy. The idea was to get eveyone involved and to maximize peer pressure and support from every member of the community. It was a program with a great deal of voice. Although sponsored by a dictator, the values embodied in the project could not have been further from the bureaucratic model, and from all accounts the effort was remarkably successful.[26]

The true expression of voice involves a giving of the self—the exposure of beliefs and values to others. As with all volunteerism, the benefits are often greatest for the volunteer. Hirschman, who as an economist had focused in his earlier writings on the costs involved in voicing one's interests and concerns, came to realize that in some cases voice can be "a most sought after, fulfilling activity, in fact, the ultimate justification of human existence."[27]

VOICE OF TEACHERS AND SCHOOL OFFICIALS

The concentration of power in the hands of professionalized educational bureaucracies and unions might give the impression that school officials and teachers have too much voice already. Not so. What is excessive are the decisions of bureaucratic institutions, not the voices of individual teachers and administrators. How often has the beleaguered school official defended himself with the cry, "This is not my decision. I am only following board policy," or "This is required by state law." One of the characteristics of bureaucracies is the lack of personal responsibility on the part of its participants.

A great difference exists between teachers who relate to their students as human beings with feelings and values of their own and those who act only as the impersonal agents of a distant bureaucracy.[28] The point is not whether teachers are "authoritarian" or "democratic," but whether they are people who have personal values that are evident in their relationships with students and parents.

Teachers without voice may be able to deliver services, but they cannot participate in learning partnerships.

The voice of other school officials is important as well. In 1979 the New York State Board of Regents put Brooklyn's Boys and Girls High School on probation because of its poor academic quality, absenteeism, and overcrowding. Consternation greeted the decision. Resentment flared. Why had the regents "picked on" a predominantly black school? The regents held firm against the pressure, and Kenneth Clark, one of only two black regents, defended the probation decision as the only way the board could express its concern about the poor quality of the school. Even though the regents are the governing board of one of the most powerful state educational agencies in the country, Clark found that the normal bureaucratic channels were virtually useless in taking effective action to correct substandard education, especially in ghetto schools. The regents decided they had to take the route of public pronouncement to voice their concerns.

VOICE IN THE FUTURE OF EDUCATION

Voice is what created the American public school system in the first place, and voice is an essential characteristic of the active learner which should be the prime goal of the system. But voice is not what educational bureaucrats want to hear, either in the boardroom or in the classroom. Educational policy making and the delivery of educational services are now carried on in the context of bureaucracy and professional values, not voice.

Students, parents, teachers, and citizens are now demanding more voice and are, in some cases, getting it, if in haphazard forms. The governing structure, operating habits, and values of our public school system have not yet adjusted to these new demands for voice. To be successful, school policy in the years ahead must find ways to make the necessary changes to accommodate voice, but only within the context of two other key elements of educational partnership: choice and loyalty.

10 CHOICE

Choice was a device to reconnect students and schooling.

Denis Doyle, "The Politics of Choice"

If voice is one of the basic ways people express their values, choice is another, and quite different way. Choice is action, not words—deliberate selection among alternatives in an attempt to achieve a desired goal without argument or the persuasion of others.[1]

Personal choice to the degree common in America is relatively new in human history. Tribal and traditional societies make choice the exception rather than the rule. When mores, marriage customs, work, and beliefs are prescribed, individual choice plays a much smaller part in human existence.[2]

Americans, however, take choice for granted, assuming without question the right to choose among a wide array of consumer goods, careers, life styles, religions, mates, and neighborhoods. Choice is fundamental to both individualism and community in modern society.

Although not mentioned in the Constitution, the American system assumes only limited areas into which government may intrude, and outside these areas, one is "left to one's own choices." Indeed, as Hirschman points out, "the United States owes its very existence and growth to millions of decisions favoring exit [i.e., choice] over voice."[3]

Choice also provides the basis of most partnerships, whether in business, marriage, golf, or an evening of bridge. Choice, therefore, must be a key concept in any policy framework based on partnership.

CHOICE IN EDUCATION

If choice is so deep and pervasive in American culture, why has it only recently surfaced as an important concept in education?

Choice is indeed not at all new in American education. It was traditional until centralized, bureaucratic, and governmental schooling became dominant. As David Tyack has pointed out, "Prior to 1840, when the crusade for public education gained momentum, the typical attitude of the public toward education resembled a common attitude today toward religion: attend the school of your choice. There was an enormous variety of schools to choose from, as there are churches today."[4]

Nor did the advent of a public school system and compulsory attendance laws eliminate choice; it remains a major factor in education today, although its influence has been greatly diminished. Ever since the effort by Oregon to require all children to attend public schools was blocked by the Supreme Court in 1925, in *Pierce* v. *Society of Sisters*, no serious attempt has been made to challenge the legal right of parents to choose the schools their children will attend. Millions of parents exercise this right of choice by sending their children to private or parochial schools, and millions more have made a choice about schooling when they selected their place of residence. Violent objection could be expected if this right were taken away.

Interestingly, however, although it has been an integral part of American education from the beginning, choice played little part in discussions of public educational policy until recently. Choice may have been deemphasized because public policy was preoccupied with constructing and expanding the public school system or because it was not in the interest of public school leaders to talk about it. Whatever the reasons for its obscurity, choice is now being examined as a key factor in educational policy.[5]

CHOICE AS AN ESCAPE

One reason choice is getting more attention is that many who have traditionally chosen private schools for their children are finding it increasingly hard to pay for them. Another is that many parents who would not have thought of choosing a private school in the past are for the first time considering it.[6]

Sophisticated theories are hardly needed to explain why people who are dissatisfied with something try to "Exit" or choose an alternative. "Exit" is a natural reaction to dissatisfaction. The increasing discussions of choice in education reflect increasing disaffection with the public schools.[7] Choice provides an "end run" around the intractable problems of public school systems today. Instead of trying to make educational governance more responsive to the voice of parents, students, and citizens or to get school bureaucracies to share power or change the direction of militant teacher unionism, choice simply allows dissatisfied parents to pick a school better suited to their children's needs and their family's values.

Public school officials who complain about families abandoning public schools should ponder the degree to which they have contributed to the defection. School bureaucracies not only do not seem to notice poor quality education but they are also often particularly deaf to the voice of those parents who are dissatisfied. These may well be the very parents who could contribute the most if listened to. They are also the most likely to leave if they feel there is no hope of response. School officials are often their own worst enemies when it comes to maintaining support for the public schools.

CHOICE AS AFFIRMATION

As pointed out earlier, it would be a mistake to look at choice only as escape from unsatisfactory circumstances. Choice can be pro as well as anti. The parents who survey school systems in a number of communities before deciding where to live and raise their children are not necessarily withdrawing from a negative. They are choosing something they think will be of positive benefit to their children. Parents who become converts to the Montessori system, or who seek a special school to develop their child's artistic talent, are affirming values in their choices.

The alternative school movement shows how students' choice of school can put them into different learning relationships. The very act of selecting gives them a stake in the school they choose. Their choice represents an affirmation of their own values. Student behavior is often significantly transformed as a result, from rebellious or apathetic to cooperative and enthusiastic.[8] Anyone observing this phenomenon will see that the process is one of affirmation, not just escape or negation.

CHOICE AND MOTIVATION

Lack of motivation in students is a characteristic of the *relationship* between students and teachers or between students and schools, not a characteristic of the student alone. Choice can play an important role in those relationships.[9] The interaction between choice and motivation is not simple, however. It is not wise to assume that any kind of compulsion kills motivation or, conversely, that incentive is always plentiful when children are allowed to choose where to attend school and what to do when they get there. Successful education can take place under at least the outward appearance of compulsion; and harm can come to learners, particularly young ones, when the single message of the school is, "Do your own thing."

An approach that engenders and channels volition is better than education either by the rod or by the shrug. Without a will to learn, very little learning takes place, and to will is to have preferences, to choose. Whatever degree of control the educational bureaucracy thinks it has and however refined its management techniques, in most classrooms students have the final choice: they can "tune out" from the lesson—and thousands do just that.[10] Student choice is, therefore, an enormously powerful element in educational partnerships.

When a child is young, many choices are made for him, by parents or by school authorities. The question of who will make choices on behalf of a child is a major issue of educational and child welfare policy (see chapter 14), but there is a difference between making choices for children and simply "processing" them. Much of what is happening to children in public school systems does not represent a choice by anyone—the child, a parent, or a professional. Too many children are simply carried along as if on a conveyor belt.

Where choices are made by someone acting on a child's behalf, common sense and caring would assume that attention will be given to that child's specific needs, desires, and values and that the child will be consulted on certain matters. Unfortunately, common sense and caring were shown the door years ago in many school systems. A substantial part of the decisions affecting students are made without regard to individuals' values. It is revealing that the new federal requirements for providing an individual educational program (IEP) for each handicapped child, for instance, have created such an uproar. That the IEP system is often administered with the same bureaucratic legalisms and ineptitude that afflict much of public education no doubt adds to the difficulties, but taking each student's needs, resources, and prior learning experience carefully into account before determining a student's program places an unaccustomed burden on schools with no experience of person-centered education.[11]

The point is not that every educational decision must be made either by or on behalf of individual children. As we shall see in the discussion of loyalty, healthy, effective, and legitimate education can take place when individual choice is subordinated to group process. The need in educational policy is not to enthrone choice as the sole determinant, but to give it its legitimate place and to unleash the power it represents in terms of student motivation and parental trust. Schools could not function if a full-blown individual educational program had to be devised for every student in the manner now being attempted for handicapped children. Yet some of the spirit of individual choice called for in that program and some of the concern for the values, resources, and aspirations of students and their parents would improve educational programs for all children.

CHOICE AND ACCOUNTABILITY

Voice and choice can be interpreted as alternative methods of holding institutions accountable for their performance. Voice provides a kind of *political* accountability through which those who are dissatisfied attempt to change the institution. Choice, on the other hand, provides a kind of *market* accountability, through which dissatisfaction is registered by taking the business elsewhere.

We have pointed out that both types of accountability operate in

American education to some degree. There is a political process in which parents can complain or act politically to try to improve schools; and there is a choice system, used by millions of parents as their way of getting what they want.

The frustrations of the political alternative are well known to anyone who has tried it. How about accountability through choice? How well does it operate at present? While many parents exercise the option of choosing a different school when they are dissatisfied, many others do not, even when their children are failing in school and when political remedies have either not worked or have not been tried. It is instructive to consider why parents do not turn to choice, and it is not always because of lack of money. Usually, one or more of the following reasons can be identified:

1. The parents are not aware that there is a problem.
2. They do not think it is their responsibility to evaluate either their child's or the school's performance.
3. They know that the child is not learning satisfactorily but assume the problem is with the child.
4. They are aware that the problem may be with the school but feel they have no other option.

Each of these conditions bears investigation in considering how well choice currently functions as an accountability system.

UNTRUTH IN LABELING

Several recent lawsuits have drawn public attention to the fact that parents are sometimes not informed by a school of a child's educational progress or lack of it. In the *Peter Doe* case in California and the *Donohue* case in New York parents accused schools of neglecting to tell them that their children were failing to master basic school skills.[12] They said they learned the truth only when their teenagers tried to get jobs after having graduated from high school. These suits were unsuccessful; the courts were unwilling to establish a general legal right for children to be taught successfully. Both courts, however, recognized that school officials had not properly informed the parents of their children's lack of educational achievement.

The phenomenon of parents not knowing how Jane and Johnny

are doing in school is more widespread than a few scattered lawsuits suggest. Many schools, public and private, find it easier to keep the "customers" happy by giving their children passing grades than by dealing with the problem of failure.[13] The alternative is to make sure each student succeeds, but this requires techniques unknown to many schools. Grade inflation is only one indication of the failure of schools to teach. Another is the large number of high school graduates who obviously have not mastered a high school—or sometimes even an elementary school—curriculum. Failures among college freshman who have received A's and B's in high school are all too common.[14]

Parents may be faulted for not checking behind their children's grades for evidence of satisfactory learning. But if they do not check, and if the indications from the school are that all is well, their failure to choose an alternative education situation is not surprising.

WHOSE RESPONSIBILITY?

Many parents do not consider it their responsibility to verify school information about their children's educational progress or, if failure is indicated, to locate schools where success will be more likely. "Shocking," say those who insist that vigilance in education is a prime parental responsibility. Others, on the contrary, may ask why parents should be expected to second-guess the educational experts hired to evaluate their children's progress.

Embedded in the question, Whose responsibility? are important issues of political philosophy that have puzzled wise men for centuries. Most Americans, however, would probably agree to a simple solution: the responsibility falls both on parents and on school officials. It is reasonable for parents to rely on school experts to evaluate their children's progress in school, but parents should retain the residual responsibility to ascertain that the evaluations (and the school officials giving them) are themselves reliable.

In view of this common-sense judgment, why is it that so many parents in fact do not check on the reliability of school evaluations, especially when there is glaring evidence of poor educational results? An easy conclusion is that many parents are irresponsible. A more useful answer for educational policy is that the nature of the educational system teaches parents this kind of irresponsibility about their children's education. When the state sends children to schools that are failing—saying, in effect, as millions of parents are told, "There is nothing you can do about it"—the lesson comes through: "The education of your children is not your responsibility."[15]

Many parents, luckily, refuse to learn this lesson. They insist that their children be effectively evaluated and effectively taught; such parents, when there are problems, may either try to solve them in their children's present school or send their children to a different school. Too many parents, however, assume that the state is providing adequate education and that it is not for them to question what is being done; they are told that school officials are "doing their best" ("under difficult circumstances," no doubt), and they are given the impression that checking up on the schools is not welcome.[16]

While educators wring their hands and, as has become fashionable, complain that many parents show no interest in the education of their children,[17] they might better ask themselves about the role the system itself plays in encouraging this irresponsible attitude.

Anyone who doubts that school systems teach parents to be irresponsible should interview a school official. Ask who has the primary responsibility for determining how well a child is doing and for making sure he is in a learning situation where he can succeed, and see if the official can comfortably reply, "the parent." If he gives this answer, he knows he may face another question: "Then why can't parents choose another teacher or school for a child who is doing poorly?"

THE CHILD'S FAULT

If parents do learn that a child is failing, a common reaction is to blame the child rather than the school, and no thought is given to changing schools or programs.

Parents as well as teachers can have low expectations of children. Mothers and fathers who did not do well in school themselves, especially those who are poor or who generally feel like losers, are likely to accept the school's "winners and losers" game as the natural order of things—with their children, of course, expected to be the losers.[18] But poor parents are not the only ones who underestimate the abilities of their children. It can happen in successful middle-class families, sometimes through misdirected efforts to compensate for a child's learning problems, sometimes through rejection because the child's abilities or ambitions run counter to parental wishes.

Even parents who begin with high expectations for their children often make a downward adjustment as a result of school experience. With its great authority, the school can convince parents through grades or counseling reports that a child is slow, incapable, socially maladjusted, or mentally defective. It may be discovered years later that the child only had a hearing or visual problem, or perhaps a problem of learning style, and could have succeeded in a different school or program.

NO OPTIONS

Even parents who have high expectations for their children, know they are not learning as well as they could, and believe the school is at fault may feel they have no option to choose a different school. This is particularly true with the poor, for whom the constitutional right of choice means little.

"I should tell you something," says the mother of a fifth grader at P.S. 75 in the Bronx, the school with New York's lowest reading scores one year; "there ain't no learning going on in that school, and I can't afford to send him anywhere else."[19]

Many poor and minority parents have this experience. They know their children are not learning, but, for them, unsuccessful public schools are the only option. And if those schools operate on a "winners and losers" philosophy, poor parents are forced to play the game knowing their children will probably lose.

Human beings learn to adjust. When there is no choice, they come to accept reality as it is, even lowering their expectations for their own children, accepting incorrect information from the school, or, finally, absorbing the message that it is not their responsibility to care.[20] These are the lessons in education without choice, lessons learned by millions of American parents trapped in a system monopolized by professionalized bureaucracy.

As a method of accountability, therefore, choice does not function effectively for a substantial number of parents in our present system. The law guarantees a right of choice, but for all practical purposes and for some of the most important aspects of their children's education (such as the failure of the school to educate the child), there is no meaningful choice.

CHOICE IN THE FUTURE OF EDUCATION

Choice, as an inherent aspect of a democratic society, is going to become an increasingly important element in educational policy, whether in the form of demands for alternative schools and programs or through pressure for more radical plans, such as vouchers and tuition tax credits (see Chapter 14). The specific trends may wax and wane, but it is unlikely that the educational Humpty Dumpty of bland, homogeneous, "common" schooling will ever be put back together again. That Humpty Dumpty has fallen off the bureaucratic wall.

Educational policy is already shifting in interesting ways to take more account of choice. Alternative schools are becoming more prevalent. New approaches are being developed. A new Massachusetts law permits any twenty parents to get together and call for a course of their choice not being offered by the school authorities.[21] In Rhode Island parents can demand that the language of their choice be taught to their children.[22] Almost everywhere parents can choose to have their children exempted from sex education classes or salutes to the flag, and they have more rights every year to choose the programs for their handicapped children.

While not all provisions for choice may be wise, the advent of greater choice is in general a healthy sign. Choice is a sign of life, of people wanting to take initiative and assume responsibility. Docile acquiescence in whatever the state bureaucracy offers is a sign of the slow death of a people's independence. The goal for educational policy must be to take advantage of these signs of vitality and weave them, together with opportunities for more voice, into a new set of educational policies, practices, and institutions, in a context of loyalty.[23]

11 LOYALTY

Without a vision that is shared, without concerns and aspirations that are truly mutual, relationships are at best arrangements of convenience, and at worst the joint confinement of unwilling partners.

Jewish Theological Seminary, *High Holy Day Message*

Voice and choice are essential tools for the growth of individualism and the attainment of freedom. They are also fundamental concepts for understanding partnership in education. They are not, however, sufficient in themselves to explain human behavior or serve as the basis for educational policy. Nor are they sufficient even for the full realization of individualism and freedom.

The "I" that speaks or chooses never acts alone. A person's will is always shaped by his relationships with others. The individual un-attached—unloved and unloving, accountable to none but self and self's desires—produces not freedom but anarchy and anomie, conditions that breed mental illness, totalitarianism, or both.[1] Freedom, including voice and choice in education, must have a social context.

Many of the books, articles, and speeches that have guided American education to its present crisis have taken "education for freedom" as their theme. The goal has sounded glorious; the reality has been dismal. While the educational bureaucracy has stifled voice and choice, education's liberation movements, advocating such strategies as community control or laissez-faire classrooms, have likewise misunderstood the nature of education in a free society. Establishmentarians and liberationists have both neglected or downplayed a major ingredient of freedom and a major element in successful education: loyalty.[2]

Hirschman introduces the concept of loyalty to explain behavior not explained by voice and choice. He cites the example of a purchaser who continues to buy a product despite his dissatisfaction, or the efforts of a member of an organization who tenaciously expresses his views to effect change when he could easily express his values by resigning. The motivation in such instances is not immediate gratification, but loyalty.

Particularly important for educational policy is Hirschman's argument that loyalty helps explain "the conditions favoring coexistence of exit and voice."[3] Since I have argued that both voice and choice are necessary for education, an important function of educational policy is to provide a framework wherein both can operate appropriately. Yet, in a certain sense, they are rivals. When someone chooses to exit from an institution, he is no longer likely to use his voice to reform it. The more opportunity there is for exit, the less likely a person is to use voice to change things. Voice and choice are, therefore, divergent, and stable institutions cannot be built on the combination of these two modes of decision making alone.

Loyalty introduces a new element. Voice and choice, while opposite in one sense (in the one case, fighting rather than switching; in the other, switching rather than fighting), in another sense are the same—they both provide the means for individuals to express their personal will: "What do *I* want?" and "How can *I* get it?" Loyalty, on the other hand, relates the individual's will to the will of a group: "What do *we* want?" With loyalty, the dynamics of voice and choice change.

Some human affairs, as Hirschman points out, such as buying products in the marketplace, entail so little loyalty that choice—individual selection—is the only element involved in the decision. In other matters, such as membership in a particularly close-knit family, loyalty is so important that individual exit is unthinkable. In such cases, voice is the only option for those who want change. Most human situations, however, are more complex, and the mix of voice, choice, and loyalty is more intricate. An individual is rarely completely alone, asking "What do I want?" He or she is part of a variety of human groups which inspire varying degrees of loyalty. "What do I want?" and "What do we want?" are in constant interplay, and there may be many overlapping, and even conflicting, "we's." In these circumstances, voice, choice, and loyalty become the source of a rich array of human options.

"As a rule, loyalty holds exit at bay and activates voice," according to Hirschman.[4] A dissatisfied member, because of loyalty, might prefer to stay and fight rather than exit. Hirschman applies this concept to the case of parents "who plan to shift their children from public to private schools" but fear that this might "contribute to the further deterioration of public education in their community."[5] The loyalty involved might be personal loyalty to a group of friends and associates whom the parents would not want to "betray" by leaving the public schools, or it might be loyalty to the principles and values of public education. Most likely it would be a combination of the two. If the decision is to stay with the public schools, dissatisfaction would be channeled into voice, since choice has been ruled out. Conversely, if the parents decide to leave, they would have little motivation to use voice.

While exit tends to preempt voice, the threat of exit can enhance it; as Hirschman says, "the chances for voice to function effectively as a recuperation mechanism are appreciably strengthened if voice is backed up by the *threat of exit*, whether it is made openly or whether the possibility of exit is merely well understood to be an element in the situation by all concerned."[6] Perhaps this is why middle-class parents are more likely than poor parents to get responses to their school grievances. The more affluent parents can back up their demands with the implicit or explicit threat of moving to another school district or putting their children in a private school. In such cases voice and choice reinforce one another, rather than acting as rivals.

LOYALTY IN EDUCATION

Loyalty is of the greatest importance in education. It makes the difference between a school that is effective and humane, and one that is unproductive and uncaring. Loyalty sets the boundaries between healthy discipline, on the one hand, and repression or permissiveness, on the other. It gauges whether educational policies and practices are the legitimate expression of community will or illegitimate oppression of one group by another. It can make the difference between racial integration and "forced busing."

The power of loyalty can be seen clearly in many private schools. The "old school tie" is more than a cliché. The tie that binds alumni, students, and teachers often provides the motivation and matrix that make a school work.

Public schools in smaller towns often engender some of the same loyalty—to "our" school—and not always only because of the football team.[7] Urban public schools typically lack loyalty. A sense of membership is difficult to develop among heterogeneous and transient populations divided by class and ethnicity. Neither students nor teachers have much loyalty to P.S. 333, which has poor morale, low achievement, and never an activity to bring the community together. Individuals in such schools are sometimes loyal to one another or to a particular class or clique, but there is seldom loyalty to the school as a whole and even less to the school system.

Grafitti and vandalism, poor attendance, and bad student behavior are symptoms of the lack of loyalty. Exceptions stand out because they differ so sharply from the norm, and in these cases the exception can usually be traced to administrators, teachers, parents, and students who have developed a sense of loyalty to each other: they have formed a successful human group.

Despite its centrality to education, loyalty has been neglected in recent educational policy. There are at least three factors that help to explain this serious omission:

1. Loyalty is "irrational."
2. Loyalty is multiple and diverse.
3. Loyalty is often viewed as the enemy of individualism and freedom.

Each of these reasons must be explored in order to deal intelligently with loyalty as a significant element in effective educational policy.

IRRATIONAL LOYALTY

Loyalty evokes "a mystical bond instead of a rational contract"; it therefore does not fit easily into rationalized public policy systems.[8]

Educational planners are uncomfortable with loyalty; it upsets things when people do not behave according to rational roles and categories. The teacher who stays after school to help an uncooperative, hateful child; the parents who insist that Rosita and Kim Sung maintain their cultural heritages, while at the same time demanding "equal opportunity" for career preparation; the students who value peer group approval above personal achievement; or the principal who defends an incompetent teacher—are all acting "irrationally," but naturally. Human behavior is often not rational, but it is not thereby necessarily "bad."[9]

In *Small Is Beautiful*, E.F. Schumacher asks how the demands of freedom and discipline in education can be reconciled. Educational theorists and school officials struggle mightily with this issue, looking for rational schemes to explain and structure the dialectic between freedom and discipline. They all too often fail; yet countless parents and teachers bring off the reconciliation even though they are unable to write down their method in scientific terms. They do it by bringing into the situation a force that belongs to a higher level, where rational opposites are transcended; they introduce what Schumacher unashamedly calls "the power of love." He maintains that problems arising in human relationships cannot be solved by reasoning; if they could be, "there would be no more human relationships but only mechanical reactions; life would be a living death."[10]

The irrationality of loyalty—the mystical bond among people who care for one another beyond self-interest—is essential to successful education. Educational bureaucracy tends to program caring, love, and loyalty out of schools. School officials may not be individually loveless people, but they have allowed cold systems to take the place of warm loyalty in the pursuit of learning.

MULTIPLE LOYALTIES

The more complex a society, the more loyalties a person can have. A modern American can be simultaneously loyal to children, parents, employer, union, church, bowling team, political party, ethnic group, town, city, state, region, and nation, not to mention ideals and principles. Some loyalties, of course, conflict so strongly that individuals suffer mental breakdowns. Most people, however, manage to synthesize or at least juggle, their multiple loyalties successfully. The resulting pattern of human relationships can be intricate indeed.

A pluralistic society is by definition one with divided loyalties. They are a reality to be addressed in educational policy, and the challenge to individuals and social institutions is to learn how to take competing loyalties productively into account.[11]

Loyalty also comes in different types. All societies that have evolved beyond tribalism must cope with one type of loyalty based on personal, family, and ethnic ties and another grounded in commitment to the social abstractions—legal, religious, and political[12] — that hold the larger society together. Complications enough arise from divided personal and small-group loyalties; adding loyalty to abstract values such as "equality," "Islam," "a government of laws not of men," or the "Southern way of life" broadens the range of complexity and potential conflict. The small group "we" often clashes with the larger "We." A school official can be torn between wanting to help a nephew get a job and his loyalty to the merit system; a mother can oppose tracking students according to ability but fight mightily to get her son into the top track.[13] In such conflict-producing situations, people sometimes make a clear choice between two loyalties; at other times they compromise—or simply learn to live with inconsistency.

Both types of loyalty are legitimate and necessary in modern societies. Without loyalty to the small group—family, church, neighborhood—people lose their bearings and forfeit a context of meaning in which to define themselves, nurture values, and instruct their children. Without loyalty to the larger group, with its systems and ideologies, modern society cannot function. Government, industry, transportation, and communications require citizens to accept and support a set of legal, scientific, and universalistic values that are different from, and sometimes opposed to, small-group values and loyalties.

Romantics can get a hearing and sell books these days by advocating a rollback of modernity. Their appeals touch chords of nostalgia. The rollback is not going to happen, in part because people have already accepted modernity and its rewards; new values have taken shape. There is no choice but to live with both.[14]

Educational policy must be particularly sensitive to both small- and large-group loyalty. Each type must be developed so as to do the least violence to the other, and both must be given their place in individual development and in social organization. Schools sit at the crossroads. They are expected, on the one hand, to extend the process of family- and community-based education and, on the other, to prepare children for life in a complex modern society. This is true of private as well as public schools. Only in rare cases—for example, in Amish communities—is education designed to protect children from the modern world. Most families send children to school both to fulfill parental values and to broaden horizons—to confirm traditions and point the way to new values.

LOYALTY IN A FREE SOCIETY

Loyalty suffers in educational policy not only because it is irrational, diverse, and complicated but also because of a suspicion that it may violate individualism and freedom.[15]

We have seen too many cases where loyalty has been the enemy of freedom. Indeed, loyalty can stifle freedom if it is not balanced by choice and voice; in totalitarian societies, loyalty means the denial of individualism.[16] Nevertheless, there is no such thing as freedom without community, and there is no community without loyalty.[17] In a society or an educational system that is based on individualism, therefore, the important issue is not whether there should be loyalty but what kind of loyalty there will be; loyalty to whom and to what? and how related to the choice and voice of its participants?

Coerced loyalty—if it is loyalty at all—violates individualism, but loyalty freely given is a way to exercise freedom. One's voice is seldom heard, or one's choice achieved, except by joining with others. Whether this be three neighbors joining together to get their sidewalk fixed, or a church group, labor union, political party, or the society as a whole, it is the group process, with its attendant loyalties, that makes individualism possible.

Conformist behavior in American public and private life does not signify an absence of individualism or freedom. People conform, even intensely individualistic people, because of the benefits they derive from conforming. One such benefit is sanity, since people typically can tolerate only so much voice and choice. Another is acceptance, a sense of belonging. To "do what is expected" is not necessarily an indication of fear or coercion; fulfilling the expectations of others (be they ancestors, family, friends, or fellow citizens) can come from merely wanting to maintain social relationships. Conformity is part of the price of membership in human society, and most of us pay it unconsciously and gladly most of the time. The manner in which we eat, work, mate, and avoid antisocial behavior springs in large measure from a sense of belonging to a group or society that has rules and values.

Our behavior in matters of education is no exception. Parents send children to the local public school or to a private school not so much as a result of careful calculation of the relative costs and benefits of different kinds of schools but because of group expectations and values. Children conform to the norms of a classroom or their peer groups for much the same reason. Any decision to leave a group can be traumatic not only because it forces adjustment to a new context in which to implement one's goals but also because those who exit break powerful psychological bonds.[18]

Loyalty, to be legitimate in a free society, however, must be reciprocal. Students and parents are asked to be loyal to a school, but the school, in turn, must be loyal to them, or else there is no mutuality. There must also be mutual respect, which links loyalty to the true meaning of equality in our culture. Everyone is entitled to be respected as a person, to have his voice heard and to make his own choices. When there is equal respect, loyalty can enhance individualism. Jesse Jackson has his students shout *together* in massive group rallies, "I *am* somebody," and the whole environment seems to shout back, "You *are* somebody." The exercise expresses mutual loyalty as well as the strengthening of self-worth.

So likewise with schools, which, Jackson says, can work if people join hands. "If they don't join hands, the kids fall between the cracks. If the spirit declines, the will declines. A school is like a home. It needs unity and devotion, and a sense of sanctuary."[19] Unless a school is loyal to all its constituents, caring about their progress and development, it cannot expect loyalty in a society that values freedom and equality.

Ask any teenager in a ghetto school why so many youngsters fail to learn or why so many end up in jail, unemployed, or dead. Somewhere in the answer you will hear, "They don't respect us." Loyalty means respect.

A school without loyalty is not a school. Loyalty can come in many ways—through the leadership of a charismatic principal, through democratic participation of students, staff, and parents, through the common values of those who have sponsored or chosen the school, or through the extension of family, religious, or community values—but unless there is loyalty and a sense of community, a "school" is not a school. In American education today, there are many such "schools." They absorb the time and resources of students, teachers, and citizens, but they do not, and cannot, educate.

The values needed in schools today are not just codes of behavior, enforced by security guards and suspensions, but the ethics of mutual caring and respect and community commitment that *all* shall learn.

THE INTEGRATION OF VOICE, CHOICE, AND LOYALTY

With long-established institutions, such as public schools, or with decisions made long ago, such as religions embraced by one's ancestors, the activating force of voice and choice is often no longer alive, and loyalty lags. One of the functions of policy for institutions in a free society is the constant renewal of loyalty by reactivating voice and choice and reintegrating them into new patterns of loyalty.[20]

Loyalty at its strongest not only is integrated with voice and choice but is derived from them. Choice can produce loyalty directly by fulfilling values already embraced. Voice produces loyalty through a political process in which people's views and values are combined and modified to produce an agreed-upon result. In this case the loyalty is not only to the result but to the process that produced it and also to the people with whom it was hammered out.

The problem in education today is that there is too little loyalty of either kind—that produced by choice or by voice. Too often our educational institutions display no sense of community and no commonality of interest. The self-generated values of government, bureaucracy, and professionalization have become dominant and have militated against loyalty between students, parents, teachers, and citizens.[21]

The restoration of loyalty will require careful integration of voice and choice. Too much voicing of divergent views may weaken loyalty; but not enough voicing may make loyalty impossible, since people may feel that they and their views are not respected. Too much opportunity for choice may mean that people will not bother to use voice at all to improve things; but not enough choice may weaken voice by removing what Hirschman calls the "threat of exit."

Too much loyalty may mean that people will use neither voice nor choice to remedy defects; but not enough loyalty may make the whole enterprise fall apart.

To complicate things further, Hirschman points out that the particular combination of voice, choice, and loyalty that works today might not work tomorrow, and a combination that works in one community might not work in another—or if it works under one leader, it might not work under another. These complications might well make us wish for a simpler policy framework that would provide more exact and constant answers. On the contrary, one of the virtues of a framework based on partnership through voice, choice, and loyalty is that it helps us keep in mind the key elements—the real values of individuals and groups—even while conditions and personalities change, as they always will in human affairs. The model is suggestive rather than prescriptive. It will not provide simple answers but it will lead policy and action in the right directions.

The job of fitting voice, choice, and loyalty into a sound policy for educational partnerships must be accomplished through public policy determined by citizens, legislators, school board members, community leaders, and educators ready to face the present problems honestly, ready to dare to think new thoughts. It will be fatal to rely only on the officials now in charge of our educational establishment for leadership. Social managers in power are notoriously self-protective—and for understandable reasons. As Hirschman points out, organizational managers often wish "members to refrain from both exit and voice," and they therefore "will be looking for devices converting, as it were, conscious into unconscious loyalist behavior," that is, the kind of behavior that is "meant to *repress* voice" as well as choice. "While feedback through exit or voice is in the long-run interest of organizational managers, their short-run interest is to entrench themselves and to enhance their freedom to act as they wish, unmolested as far as possible by either desertions or complaints of members. Hence, management can be relied on to think of a variety of institutional devices aiming at anything but the combination of exit and voice which may be ideal from the point of view of society."[22]

We have delegated to professional bureaucrats not only the operation of schools but the formation of policy as well. As a result, we are getting "unconscious loyalist behavior," which leads to apathy and decay. The leadership needed to revive voice, choice, and loyalty in education must not be intimidated by professional educators who signal that only those with special expertise can deal with educational policy. Even in a rapidly changing world, the prime building blocks for the new policy framework are available to everyone in America's overarching and still agreed upon ideology, which includes respect for the individual, for families and small groups, and for the universal values needed to live in the modern world. The American philosophy encompasses the belief that a society is composed of its parts and, at the same time, that the whole serves to protect the parts—*e pluribus unum.* The "I" and the "we" of voice, choice, and loyalty need to be put together in creative ways, and it is civic and political leadership of the highest order that must find the right combinations for the coming decades.

As we look in Part 3 at some of the major policy problems facing education, let us examine whether a better framework for leadership is provided by shifting the policy focus in education from bureaucratic "service delivery" to partnership through voice, choice, and loyalty.

III APPLICATIONS

12 EQUALITY REVISITED

At worst, we end up with intensified injustice: inequality with a federal
blessing.

Jonathan Kozol, *Prisoners of Silence*

Equality has been the dominant public policy issue in American education for the past quarter-century. The Supreme Court's 1954
desegregation decision touched off an era of debate and discussion
that still echoes through the halls of Congress, state legislatures, the
courts, and educational journals and popular media.

Yet we remain a long way from resolving the problem. For a society supposedly based on equality, there is an astonishing degree of
inequality in American education. Some Americans receive an
education equal to the best in the world; other Americans, however,
get an education that can only be called abysmal. We announce an
ideal that "all men are created equal" and proclaim an educational
system to implement it, but many students end their educational
careers more "unequal" than when they began.[1]

Educational equality has proved a complex and difficult issue,
but there is no way American society can dodge it. The inequalities
are too real; their social consequences will continue to press upon us
as long as they persist.

This chapter, however, is not another recital of the shameful story

107

of American educational inequality. Rather, it is an attempt to look at some of the current debates on educational inequality and suggest that the problems at their heart can be dealt with more effectively by understanding education in terms of partnerships based on voice, choice, and loyalty than in terms of the prevailing policy concepts based on professional service delivery.

"REVISIONISTS" VERSUS "APOLOGISTS"

Much of the recent debate about equality and education has turned on the assertion by a number of writers and scholars "that schooling serves the well-to-do better than the poor and, by and large, helps to reproduce rather than alter the class structure" of American society.[2] Such a dictum debunks the traditional American myth of equal educational opportunity and is therefore seen as a revisionist point of view.[3]

The revisionists have made a considerable contribution to the understanding of both the history and the current condition of American education. Their work has shown that from the earliest days public schools served the interests of some groups more than others. Although there is not agreement on every point, revisionist scholars share a consensus about the nonequalizing results of American education which raises the ire of public school defenders, who resent what they see as an unfair "attack on the schools."[4]

Typical of these debates is the heated exchange between revisionist historian Michael Katz and Diane Ravitch, whom Katz has dubbed one of the "apologists" of the public schools. Ravitch, with the backing of the National Academy of Education and the Ford Foundation, came forth in 1978 with *The Revisionists Revised: A Critique of the Radical Attack on the Schools.* She has been widely acclaimed and her book reviewed as a devastating attack on the revisionists. She questions their analysis and their motives and argues that the schools have, with a few "lapses from the standard," served the cause of equal opportunity.[5] She cites as evidence the increased number of poor and minority children going to college and the general expansion of the middle class over the past hundred years. She accuses the revisionists of ideological bias in failing to see the accomplishments of the American public school system.

Michael Katz, in turn, has attacked Ravitch's book, pointing out how she failed in any serious way to challenge the revisionists' basic analysis of social and educational inequality and distorted the arguments of the revisionists for her own ideological ends. He also protests the prestigious backing of her work, which he fears will dampen critical analysis in the future.[6]

These and other attacks and counterattacks among revisionists and apologists might be dismissed as tempests in scholarly teapots if they did not have an important backwash effect on educational policy and practice. For, while few parents, citizens, or school officials have followed either the arguments or the evidence in detail, the fuss has left many people with the unfortunate impression that there is respectable scientific support for the pernicious idea that schools cannot be expected to make much difference for poor children.

Such a message is ironic. It appears to the public as a finding of authoritative social scientists concerned with changing the educational system, but it is the defenders of the present system who use it to block change. If poor children cannot learn, they argue, why criticize schools for not teaching them; and if schools do not make much difference, why should the public be up in arms about their quality? Although revisionists intended to make a case against the inequities of American schools, their arguments are used instead to maintain the status quo.

The irony is compounded when it is realized that, before the debate began, few ordinary parents and citizens expected schools to abolish social class or eliminate the advantages of the rich. People generally hoped that the schools would do a good job of educating children and that this would have its own effect in promoting equality. In their own down-to-earth way, they have known all along that schools do make a difference. They have also known that, by and large, poor children go to worse schools than rich children and that many children (especially poor and minority children) go to schools where they fail to gain even a rudimentary education. This glaring, common-sense fact about educational inequality is often lost in the debates about equal educational opportunity, as the critics point to the general inequities of American society and the defenders point to the many accomplishments of the public schools.

Part of the problem is the tendency in present social policy to divert attention away from the schools themselves and from the inequities inherent in present educational relationships (see Chapter 16); but part of the problem is that, even when the schools are looked at directly, the present emphasis on education as a service focuses attention on the "inputs" and "outputs" of the service-delivery system rather than on the relationships among the participants and the ways in which they promote inequality.[7]

SERVICE INPUTS AND OUTPUTS

Two major concepts have dominated recent thinking about equal educational opportunity: equality of inputs and equality of outputs. These two concepts have been exhaustively discussed by theorists and translated into innumerable legislative and educational programs. Neither concept has been fruitful in reducing inequality. They have missed the mark because they have been applied to the fundamentally faulty concept of education as a service. They have, in fact, reinforced the focus on services instead of relationships.

Equal Inputs—The Limits of Equal Services

Under the prevailing framework for educational policy, in which schools are presumed to deliver educational services to children, equity in education should be a simple matter: if the services delivered are equal, then the education is equal.

The equal input concept was a major aspect of the famous Coleman report, entitled *Equality of Educational Opportunity,* which measured a number of objective ingredients that make up the educational service-delivery system. Surveying such things as physical facilities, laboratories, and the amount of staff training, the Coleman researchers found little difference in these "input" factors among schools serving different racial groups. The conclusion reached by many—and reinforced in subsequent years by media reports of the work of Moynihan, Jencks, and others—was that since the "inputs" of educational service were roughly equal, the education must therefore be equal. Conversely, if the "output" (learning) is unequal, which it certainly is, the reason must lie outside the school, that is, in the home, or the social milieu of the student, or, even more deterministically, in the genetic inferiority of the low achievers.

This "services" approach to equality is unable to deal with the contradiction presented by two schools, with similar student bodies and each with the same input of science laboratories and teachers with masters degrees, etc., that produce different results. Yet it is clear that students in some schools learn much more than their peers of the same social class in another school with the same inputs of the type usually measured. One school might be a successful learning environment, while the other might be destroying children's minds and fostering hostility and alienation.[8]

While one cannot condone giving worse or fewer services to some than to others, equal service inputs are no guarantee of equality and provide little guidance to the real problems of educational inequality in our schools.

Equal Outputs—The Limits of Compensatory Education

Since equalizing inputs proved so unsatisfactory, some theorists and practitioners turned to the idea of equalizing outputs. They argued that equal inputs are not enough; equality in education requires that efforts be made to equalize educational achievement.

The demand for more equal achievement might have had a beneficial effect if the focus could have been kept on real outputs, that is, learning. Under the dominant service-delivery concept, however, "equal outputs" is quickly translated into "more than equal inputs." This is predictable: if you want more outputs from the educational service machine, you increase the inputs. Thus more counselors and special reading teachers were hired for schools with low achievers; more equipment was bought, and special remedial curriculums were added. Billions of dollars have been spent in these "compensatory" programs designed to produce more equal educational outputs.

Unfortunately, the "more than equal inputs" encountered the same problem as the "equal inputs": they were applied to fundamentally flawed institutions. With all the extra staff and equipment, schools without productive learning relationships between teachers, students and parents, were, and are, doomed to failure. The organizational charts may be perfect, the staff-student ratios improved, the teachers fully certified, and the equipment multiplied; but still little or no learning takes place in thousands of American schools.

It has all been very discouraging. Many legislators, administrators, and school board members have devoted great effort to getting compensatory laws and programs enacted, and many school officials and teachers have worked hard to implement them, but the results are disappointing. Although some successes have been reported, the Congress and most fair-minded people who reviewed the programs have had to conclude that by and large they have failed to make any substantial dent in the massive school failure of poor and minority children.[9] In some cases they even worsened the situation, disrupting the regular curriculums, which at least had some structure and continuity.

EQUAL EDUCATIONAL RELATIONSHIPS

No system of education built on a service-delivery concept will achieve its goals because it cannot deal with human idiosyncracies. Real people always complicate life for bureaucrats and planners. Charts, job descriptions, role definitions, written lesson plans, and the like can be shields from reality. Service systems can provide beautiful, abstract equality for all children and at the same time ignore the flagrant inequality rampant in the real world.

I have suggested that instead of thinking of education as a service, we should conceive of it in terms of partnerships among teachers and students, school and families, and school systems and communities. Education in these terms can never be exactly "equal," since each relationship is based on the individual characteristics of the people involved. Real equity, as distinct from abstract equity, must deal with the uncertainties of human relationships and the lack of exact measures by which to determine whether one educational relationship is comparable to another. This will take us beyond equal inputs and compensatory services. Relationships involve people, their expectations and decisions, their voices, choices, and loyalties.

Within this framework people can see the striking inequalities in learning relationships built into our present school systems. They can also see that children and their parents have unequal opportunities to remedy ineffective educational relationships.

How can these inequalities be attacked and overcome? Two types of reform have addressed these fundamental questions in recent years: community control, to give people more voice in the educa-ton of their children, and educational vouchers, to give people more choice. The search for equality in education must lead us to examine these two quite different approaches to more productive and equitable educational relationships and to explore why neither of them has yet produced significant change in American education. Thereafter, in connection with our examination of families and communities, we will look again at the relationship between social equity and educational equity to see whether a concept of educational partnerships provide a more productive route to equal educational opportunity.

13 COMMUNITY CONTROL

Nowhere is the discrepancy between ideology and practice more obvious than in the hierarchy of a centralized bureaucracy.

Erik Erikson, *Childhood and Society*

Seldom has a movement been so much talked about and yet so little understood as the movement for community control of the public schools. Confusion surrounds the phrase "community control," in part because the terms of the debate have been influenced by members of the educational establishment who have alternately feared the movement because they misunderstood it and misunderstood it because they feared it. Some of the confusion, however, also arises because community control includes at least three quite different strands, which educators, the media, and even their advocates often fail to distinguish.

1. *Minority Group Power.* Community control for many black, Hispanic, and other minority groups is rebellion against white or majority group control over the education of their children. It emphasizes group identity and group political action. With or without antiwhite rhetoric, it derives its main momentum from resentment over the poor education provided to minority children. Its chief educational goals are improved student achievement and heightened pride and self-esteem.

2. *Political Democracy.* For liberal reformers, community control is aimed at forcing the educational bureaucracies, especially in big cities, to be more accountable and responsive to the public. It focuses on the need for better mechanisms to achieve representative democracy in education and for more effective supervision to make school personnel carry out the public will. As a means of increasing political accountability, this sort of community control often advocates decentralization of the decision-making authority in large systems.

3. *Debureaucratization.* A third strand is an attack on bureaucracy. Instead of emphasizing the need for greater political or bureaucratic accountability, it would make educators more directly accountable to parents and children in schools and classrooms. Its stress is on community, and it would redefine many "control" questions in terms of positive and productive relationships between students, parents, teachers, and citizens.

These three strands of community control obviously overlap; some people see all three as desirable and mutually supportive. Each, nevertheless, has different policy and political implications, and they are so different in some respects that they represent competing causes. All three demand greater participant voice, but voice operating in distinct ways and with different aims. Furthermore, each of the three types of community control has both radical and moderate spokespersons, so that differences in style and political tactics have interacted with differences in substantive agendas to increase confusion. Added to this are the ambiguities growing out of the relation of all three strands to the concept of decentralization, which might mean only an internal shuffling of bureaucratic responsibilities but could become more radical when linked with ethnic rebellion, new forms of political accountability, or changes in bureaucratic values and structure.[1]

The misunderstandings about the different strands in the community control movement have greatly impaired the quality of the public policy debate. What to one person looks like the "conservative" idea of giving city people the same right to locally elected school boards traditionally used in small town America (and in some cities in the nineteenth century) looks to another person like turning schools over to the wildest of radicals, posing a "threat to the American purposes."[2] What to one observer could look like a progressive effort to generate citizen responsibility could look to another like encouragement of a reactionary, tyrannical "cult of localism."[3] What some see as a necessary escape from destructive, pathological educational bureaucracy, others interpret as the dismantling of the political and administrative system needed to govern large and complex school systems.

Confusion has led to stalemate. Despite all the sound and fury, very little has changed. Even in New York City, where the upheaval over community control reached its peak, school and classroom practice by the end of the 1970s was remarkably similar to what it had been two decades earlier, before the commotion began.

This can comfort those who have opposed community control, except in one respect: along with the survival of the old structure, the problems have survived as well. Minority and poor children in massive numbers still fail to get the most minimally acceptable education. Urban school systems continue to lose public credibility and support. The force of urban school bureaucracies still deadens the initiative and motivation of teachers and students alike.

We cannot tell whether community control could be an educational success, because thus far it has been a political failure. Real community control has never been tried—in any of its various forms—beyond a few pilot programs; it remains an unexplored educational strategy.[4]

For a movement that has aroused such intense emotional and political reaction, there has been surprisingly little effort to sort out what it has all meant and where we should go from here. Some people have concluded that there is no place to go at all; they have reconciled themselves to a future in which urban public schools will forever remain ineffective, unaccountable, and bureaucratic. Others, unwilling to accept such a future, are beginning to conclude that some alternative to public school systems is needed—at least for cities, or at least for poor and minority children.

Before reaching conclusions about whether there is hope for urban public schools and about possible alternatives, it is important to look more closely at the three main types of community control— minority group power, political democracy, and debureaucratization—and relate them to the policy framework suggested in this book.

BLACK SEPARATISM VERSUS LIBERAL UNIVERSALISM

Leonard Fein, one of the most thoughtful commentators on the community control debate, directs virtually all of his thought and perceptive analysis to the first type of community control—the demand for minority group control over the education of minority children. In his 1971 book-length essay *The Ecology of Public Schools: An Inquiry into Community Control*, Fein argues that the proposals for decentralization and community control in the 1960s escalated into a cataclysmic battle because they raised the most profound and threatening ideological issues for American society—a clash between the universalistic values of democratic liberalism on which our public education system has been built and the "profoundly subversive" values of black separatism.[5] This clash creates an anguished dilemma for educational policy, according to Fein.

Fein sees the positive values in a school system based on "secularism, rationality, and universalism."[6] The ideology of this system holds out the promise of fairness to all; equal treatment regardless of family background, religion, or race; protection of minority voices against the tyranny of majorities; professionalism based on merit; a rationally ordered service-delivery system accountable to the public through representative government. For blacks it offers the goal of a society in which color would become irrelevant and racism would no longer exist. These are glorious goals, liberal not in the narrow partisan sense, but in terms of the mainstream ideology of American society as a whole.

Yet Fein knows that something is profoundly wrong with the way these ideals are translated into reality in the education of minority children: a centralized bureaucracy expected to protect the right of individual voices against the tyranny of majorities is a cruel joke.[7] Whose voice is being protected? Certainly not that of black parents. To deny minorities the elementary rights of self-government in the name of integration compounds the mockery; presenting centralized urban school systems as the protector of integration only lends weight to Stokely Carmichael's quip that "integration is a subterfuge for the maintenance of white supremacy."[8] Rhetoric about the ideals of an effective, rational, and professional service-delivery system makes the contradictions even worse for parents whose children do not gain the most basic learning tools and come out of school headed toward a life of incompetence and alienation.

Furthermore, Fein not only sees the contradictions in applying liberal, universalist ideology to the problems of urban and minority education but also understands the strength and pride that can be gained from group identity, the initiative that can come from assuming responsibility for one's own affairs, and the legitimacy schools could gain if they were more accountable to those they are supposed to serve. More fundamentally, he recognizes "that the mass, undifferentiated, atomized society—that is, the secular society—is psychologically disabling, socially chaotic, and politically unstable."[9] He sees community control as in some sense a corrective to these disabilities as they affect education.

Fein's analysis leaves him deeply disturbed. The values of both liberal democracy and community control seem valid; yet he sees them in direct conflict with each other. He sees the community control movement as "a profound rejection of the core of liberal ideology," "a departure from the American past and the American belief." He argues that the emergence of community consciousness among blacks "flagrantly violates the traditional liberal ethic of universalism. It parochializes society instead of secularizing it; it evokes a mystical bond instead of a rational contract." It is, therefore, "profoundly subversive."[10]

The solution to this dilemma, according to Fein, is to grant community control of schools to blacks as an "exception" so that the prevailing liberal ideology of the public school system can remain intact. Some might say "Right on" to this suggestion, but this solution, despite the brilliance of much of Fein's analysis, is ideologically monstrous, politically impractical, and, most of all, unnecessary. In offering such an unsatisfactory solution to an avoidable problem, Fein makes two fundamental mistakes common in the community control debate. First, he sees the issues of control only in political terms. Second, he sees the demand for community as an unusual bid for separatist, racial power. By putting these two assumptions together, he presents community control as the demand of a particular ethnic group for overt political control over a government agency—clearly an illegitimate demand within the American political tradition.[11]

Community control as it emerged in black neighborhoods came to be framed in this way because real grievances of the type set forth by

Fein exist and cry out for ideological debate and resolution. In the 1960s people were willing to take ideological positions and fight about them: a Stokely Carmichael declaring the legitimacy of Black Power and an Albert Shanker defending his power with liberal universalism. Furthermore, the antagonists fought politically as well as intellectually; minority leaders rallied their troops with cries of "black is beautiful," and teacher unions with slogans about job security and due process. And, of course, the racial implications escalated all the other issues to a high pitch of emotion and anxiety.[12]

Given the news potential of the debate, the media added to the polarization. They highlighted the most extreme voices rather than the most reasonable. Angry outbursts between black militants and defenders of the system made good copy; they entertained and titillated audiences; they sold newspapers.

But the shouts failed to deal with the real issues: tens of thousands of children not being educated, parents wanting some voice in the education of their children, and citizens getting fed up with paying more and more for worse and worse education.[13] These issues were more real to many people than either black separatism or liberal universalism. Nor are they inherently revolutionary or subversive issues, but concerns that one might reasonably expect to be handled within the American political system.

Why, then, did these issues get lost? In part it was because the system was in the hands of officials who saw it to be in their own interest, with the help of a few charismatic radicals and the press, to channel the debate into unnecessary wars over black separatism. As Fein himself admits, the great mass of black Americans did not buy what Carmichael was selling; they hold the same democratic ideals treasured by most other Americans, maybe more so, since their survival depends on them. By and large, black Americans want what America has said it is supposed to deliver, including a decent education for their children and some accountability from their government. What, then, was the threat when blacks raised voices against prevailing educational policy and practice in the 1960s?

The threat was that America, at least its large urban educational systems, was not prepared to deliver on these simple, nonrevolutionary expectations most Americans take for granted. These systems *could not* deliver on these expectations. Its critics claim that they were purposely designed not to deliver to black or poor children.

Whether intentional or not, these systems have proved ineffective and unworkable in meeting the challenge of urban education.

The primary threat of the early community control movement, then, was not to traditional American ideals but to ineffective and unresponsive educational bureaucracies. That threat came not from militant black separatists, of whom there were relatively few, but from frustrated, angry parents and their allies who concluded that the time had come to make fundamental changes in urban public school systems. The protesters may not have been clear or united about what they wanted, but the threat of change was clear enough to unite the educational establishment against them. The main crisis was not primarily an ideological struggle between black separatism and liberal universalism but a political struggle over who would control urban public schools.

PROFESSIONAL VERSUS POLITICAL CONTROL OF PUBLIC EDUCATION

What Diane Ravitch calls the "Great School War" of Ocean Hill–Brownsville in Brooklyn was actually only a battle in a much larger political struggle—the struggle of the citizens and parents across the country to regain control over their public schools.[14] Ocean Hill–Brownsville was a battle the community control forces lost, but the larger struggle over political democracy remains unresolved.

Ideological issues of the type Leonard Fein ably analyzes were indeed involved in Brooklyn in 1968 and have been involved elsewhere, but they must be seen in the context of broader issues of why urban public education is so abysmally ineffective and how people can begin to relate to their schools as responsible parents and citizens rather than as docile and apathetic "clients" or angry and militant antagonists.

To put the ideological issues in proper perspective it must be realized that, while black separatism is a threat to liberal principles, liberal, universalist orthodoxy has never been fully enthroned in American public education. American education throughout most of its history has been characterized by a balance between universalistic principles and all sorts of parochial, particularistic, class, ethnic, and community interests. American public schools were not born as bureaucratic institutions; they began to approach the more extreme forms of bureaucracy only in this century. In nineteenth-century cities, balances of various sorts were typically struck between professional and lay control and between universalistic and community values at the school and classroom level. Even as the balance began to shift toward the professional and bureaucratic side, the rhetoric and myth of lay control and community accountability were preserved.

It was professional educators, not black militants, who first began to challenge the traditional balance of lay and professional control. Myron Lieberman, in *Education as a Profession* and *The Future of Public Education,* bluntly argued that all professional issues in education should be decided by the professional staff, and he defined virtually all educational decisions except the most general goals as professional.[15] Such thinking came to characterize an increasing number of school administrators and teachers in the 1950s and 1960s. Professional leaders stood forth boldly with the confidence gained from additional credentials and an increased awareness of growing political and organizational power. Educators could not understand how lay people, who had no expertise, should exercise power which should, by all right and reason, belong to professionals. The belief was honest, and it was professed, at least on the conscious level, for the sake of improved education. But it was a belief bound to create a political struggle even if there had been no civil rights movement. The demand for professional control of education is a far greater threat to traditional American ideology than any attack black militants ever mounted. School staffs had gained increasing de facto control over public schools in a process covering many years, but once they threw down the gauntlet as an overt challenge to lay control, it was certain to be picked up.

Unfortunately for the professional control forces, the bid for legitimation of their power came just at the time serious doubts were being raised about the competence of professional leadership. Lingering questions about why Johnny can't read and why Russia's Sputnik beat America into space made the late 1950s and 1960s a bad time to assert professional hegemony. Had the schools been performing to everyone's satisfaction, people might not have noticed this new ideology of professional control, and those who did might not have objected to it. But with serious questions raised about the wisdom and effectiveness of public school educators, the assertion of professional control seemed doubly threatening to traditional American assumptions about democratic government. Public institutions are supposed to be controlled by the public, and institutions as close to people, their values, and their children as schools particularly could not be seen as the exclusive domain of teachers, principals, professors, union leaders, and faceless bureaucrats, who often did not even live in the community.[16]

It was into this context that the civil rights movement injected its own challenge. The first item on the agenda—desegregation—made it unavoidably clear that public schools had been used not just for professional ends but for political purposes, namely to enforce a caste system of second-class citizenship on black Americans, most obviously in the South but elsewhere as well. The myth of professional, nonpolitical education was exposed as a screen for white political control, which operated to the disadvantage of blacks. It was truly ironic, therefore, when desegregation efforts were condemned as a use of the schools for political purposes.

The next item on the agenda—the plight of tens of thousands of black and minority children who were not getting an education regardless of segregation or desegregation—pressed the question of political power further. Various members of the educational establishment, virtually all of them white—superintendents, commissioners, professors, and teacher leaders—were genuinely trying to find out what was wrong and do something about it, but when black leaders saw that little that was effective was being done, they began to ask, "Why are these white professionals deciding about *our* children's education?"

This question, it is true, sometimes took the form of the demand for group-conscious minority power found so threatening by Leonard Fein. But it also echoed a totally American question being asked in rough, unsophisticated terms by citizens and parents of all races and colors: "Who are these bureaucrats who have taken over our schools, and why are we letting them do it?"

Blacks were indeed among the most vocal challengers of the legitimacy of professional control of education, but they were not alone in declaring that the schools were not performing satisfactorily, and, in a traditionally American way, demanding a voice in deciding what to do about it. Blacks had a special edge to their complaints because professional control usually meant white control and because, when dissatisfied with the quality of public schools, they had fewer alternatives, such as moving to another community or choosing a private school. Americans had long ago realized that democracy involves interest group politics as well as the independent political action of separate individuals. Blacks had, and still have, an identifiable group interest in education—their children are subjected to widespread discrimination and ineffective education. A case could be made that it was only as their legitimate demands for accountability from school authorities were met with bureaucratic and professional protectionism that the community control movement took on a more militant flavor. Black parents were in effect told that, even though their children were getting a miserable education, they could have no voice in doing anything about it. This is a message no group in America should accept. It was not, then, that "black separatism" rose up suddenly as a sort of alien and subversive threat to liberal ideals, as Fein suggests. Rather, the denial of basic American democratic ideals created fertile ground for the growth of black political action and ideology.

Even the remedies proposed, namely, smaller political subdivisions of large city school systems, was within the American tradition. If some of the subdivisions would be predominantly black, that would make them no different from the thousands of other local school districts that are dominated by one group or another—Anglo-Saxon Protestants, Italian Catholics, Norwegian Americans, or whomever. Why should predominantly black districts suddenly be "un-American"?

Ironically, since local control of education has particularly strong roots in American culture, it was "Americanism" that was thrown up in opposition to these demands for community control of schools. Authoritarian cultures more easily conceive of education as a state function and, therefore, an activity that the rulers can decide to provide however and by whomever they choose. In the United States, however, public education is traditionally seen as a communal enterprise organized to help families carry out what were initially seen as family responsibilities. As the country became more urbanized and heterogeneous with the influx of immigrants, the dominant elite began to see public schools as a way for "us" to educate "them." But as the immigrant groups, both old and new, began to come of age and assert their rights to first-class citizenship, their demand for a voice in the education of their children was inevitable. To expect less would be to deny the most basic democratic ideals of American society.

THE ATTACK ON BUREAUCRACY

It would be a mistake, however, to see the community control struggle only in terms of battles for racial or political control of public schools. Something more is involved—something, though less dramatic than either the racial or the political confrontation, that may in the long run be more revolutionary than either of them. This is the effort to debureaucratize, to "desystematize," the system over which the struggle for control is being fought. This third type of community control is the effort to develop closer and more productive relationships between students, teachers, parents, and communities—in short, to create partnerships for learning rather than mechanisms for delivering services. This strand of the community control movement puts more emphasis on community and less on control, although the methods of political control have an effect on the possibility of developing productive educational relationships.

The debureaucratizing strand is more revolutionary than the other two in that it would change the basic structure of urban public education, rather than just who controls it. Furthermore, if the bureaucratic structure of education is changed, the issues of control and ethnic identity would take on a different focus.

It is instructive in the 1980s to reread the famous Bundy report of 1967, which kicked off the furious battle over community control not only in New York City but also across the nation. So quickly did the fight center on political control that one tends to forget how much of the early discussions dealt with the need to change the *relationships* of the participants in the educational process. The very title of the report, *Reconnection for Learning: A Community School System for New York City*,[17] signaled the orientation of its authors.

The starting point for the Bundy panel, appointed by New York Mayor John Lindsay to help carry out a New York state legislative mandate to decentralize the school system, was a school system "caught in a spiral of decline," with "vast numbers, if not the majority of the pupils, . . . not learning adequately." The panel concluded that the first step toward renewing the system was to provide a means of "reconnecting the parties at interest so they [could] work in concert." It stressed the need to reverse the "fear, suspicion, recrimination, and tension; by strengthening the ability of all participants to turn their talents and energies toward making things happen, instead of devoting their lives to holding one another in check. In short, the best that the proposals could accomplish would be to set in motion a gradually growing process of mutual confidence."[18]

The panel was "convinced that responsibility for what the student achieves is shared jointly by parents, the community at large, and the school system, to say nothing of other agencies that influence the urban environment." It cited the (New York City) Public Education Association's plea for "the fullest possible participation of community groups working with the local school board and the district superintendent and his staff in a cooperative effort to improve education." It quoted Dr. Kenneth B. Clark's remarks that when a school's "job is well done, the parents are partners in the enterprise. Each parent shares responsibility with the school for the achievement of his child." The Bundy panel called for a "dynamic" school partnership with parents, and said: "We see this sharing of responsibility as a part of a fundamental redirection of the process of education, designed to make education more relevant to the student, to bring it closer to his feelings and concerns, and to connect all the members of the school community with one another."[19]

McGeorge Bundy and his colleagues were not isolated voices urging new relationships for learning in the late 1960s. The Coalition for Community Control, a citizen's group formed to foster the Bundy proposals, issued a pamphlet, *Community Control Is Community Responsibility*, that spoke of "the enormous educational power that can be generated both inside and outside the schools when a community begins to support its schools and support education and learning in the home."[20] Mayor Lindsay spoke of the goal of school decentralization as that of improving the quality of education in the city through "reconnecting the parties concerned with public education in a constructive, creative effort."[21]

The Public Education Association welcomed the decentralization effort as "today's most important educational experiment" and emphasized the importance of changing human relationships in the educational enterprise:

The process of building a new structure of self-government is a process of self-renewal. It is a human process, and herein lies its important difference from the educational "innovations" of the past 15 years. All of the new machinery, new curricula, and new buildings of recent years, have been put into our education without dealing with the human equation. They have missed the mark because our most important problems are human problems: problems of the spirit, of the will, of integrity and self-respect; problems of human relationships and communication. . . .

The process of human renewal, however, must extend beyond the community boards themselves if this new experiment is to mean anything. Already there are signs of increased citizen and parent activity at the level of each school. The involvement of the paraprofessional will significantly change the human equation in our schools. School volunteers will increasingly be seen as an essential element of the educational process and not just as an extra benefit as they are too often seen today. The involvement of businessmen is another significant addition to the human equation.

Once our youngsters begin to sense that education is not just a matter of being turned over to an often alien institution for processing, but is rather a human process in which many types of adults and even older students are committed to helping them grow up to be competent and whole adults, then the process of education will once again be back on its feet.[22]

The concern for new relationships was not limited to New York City. Every large city in the country suffered from the problems of massive educational failure, parent and student alienation, and unresponsive educational bureaucracy. Many of the liberal and radical ideologies called for rejection of the impersonal and uncaring relationships that characterized big city education. The movement for decentralization in Detroit, Boston, Washington, D.C., Oakland, California, and elsewhere resounded with many of the same conditions and goals cited in New York.

With all the talk of reconnection, partnership, and changed human relationships, how did the community control issue so quickly come to be so completely and bitterly dominated by the question of who should control? How did the aspect of community drop out of the equation and the debate?

Part of the answer, as already mentioned, is the manner in which the media highlighted the most controversial issues and personalities. But a larger part of the answer is that most of the protagonists, as well as the scholars and media commentators covering the issue, were locked into the service-delivery concept of education and had political tunnel vision of a kind that asks first about the power structure. If the focus of educational policy is on a governmental service-delivery system, the issue of who is going to be in control is necessarily preeminent. Even the Bundy report, with its talk of partnership and parental responsibility, confused its idea of community partnership with that of holding professional staffs politically accountable for delivering school services.

The concept of education as partnership changes the focus of community control. In the first place, it conceives of education not primarily as a governmental-political process. While a public school is a governmental agency operating within a political and bureaucratic system, the *teaching-learning* process operates by quite different values—not by representative government, political accountability, or bureaucratic control, but by direct accountability among teachers and students, among students and their families, and among families and schools. Unless these direct, mostly face-to-face, psychologically intensive relationships are developed, little learning is likely to take place.[23] Once they have been established, most transactions take place within this nonbureaucratic, nongovernmental context.

The issue of control in this nonbureaucratic mode of educational transaction is very different from the question of who should control the "delivery system." The crux of the matter is not who controls, but how the various participants can interact most productively, how the voices of the various partners can appropriately be heard so that human loyalties and educational partnerships can flourish. The question of the political control of government-run schools is not obliterated by a partnership model of education, but when partnership for learning is the policy, government management of schools is put in a different light.

The notion of community also takes on a different cast. As long as education is treated as a service delivered to atomized individuals, each one an abstractly "equal" unit, the emergence of community consciousness among these "clients" and "targets" is seen as a threatening development. But if education is understood in terms of partnerships, a sense of common purpose is encouraged among students, families, and teachers. A concern for community, therefore, is not a violation of professional-client relationships, but a necessary adjunct of the educational process.

The partnership model does not assert the right of any group to separate political jurisdiction outside the democratic system; it does assert, however, that there be opportunity for people as they really are, with all their idiosyncrasies and ethnic and religious identities, to establish mutually beneficial relationships. This concept was once traditional in American education, and it can still be found in small towns and rural areas.

THE LIMITS OF COMMUNITY CONTROL

Although the three strands of community control discussed in this chapter are different and can come into conflict in their extreme forms, each represents a necessary emphasis for education in a democratic society. Ethnic group educational politics (the first strand) is legitimate in a democratic society as long as it does not seek to delegate governmental functions directly to racial subgroups. As Leonard Fein points out, ethnic politics in America has usually served as a launching pad for lower-status groups to gain the self-confidence to enter into the social, economic, and political mainstream rather than as a step toward separatist political structures. Political accountability (the second strand) is dictated by basic democratic values; as long as schooling is provided by government, people must have a voice in its management. Finally, partnership between parents, teachers, students, and citizens (the third strand) is necessary if schooling is to be effective and legitimate.

Serious questions arise, however, about whether any of these kinds of community control of education is possible in America today, especially in urban settings.

How can there be community control when there is no sense of community? A fair question. The pluralism of American society not only has intensified over the last century but is now becoming legitimated as a permanent feature of the society rather than just a transitional phase along the way to a homogenized American culture. Few political jurisdictions are functioning communities.

A sense of community can be developed on a small scale, in individual schools, classrooms, or minischools, where face-to-face relationships can bridge cultural, religious and value differences. But many decisions are and will continue to be made at higher levels, within broader political jurisdictions. Indeed, the protection of minority rights has traditionally required the intervention of government at higher levels to overrule the parochialism and discrimination of local majorities. Do we have sufficient common values on a broad base to govern education as a community enterprise at all levels where decisions must be made? As John Dewey pointed out, "The machine age in developing the Great Society has invaded and partially disintegrated the small communities of former times without generating a Great Community."[24]

Community control requires "community," and American society may no longer be capable of it in education. If not, then the necessary underpinning for the legitimacy of public education may no longer exist.

There is another problem: the political power of the professionalized bureaucracy to which we have delegated education may by now be so strong that it can overpower all efforts at community control of whatever kind. One of the most thoughtful and persuasive proponents of this view is economist Jacob Michaelsen, who himself served as a member and president of his local school board in Santa Cruz, California, and ultimately reached the conclusion that community control of public schools is no longer possible. Building on E.G. West's "economic theory of democracy," he sees our present educational structure as inevitably producing an alliance between teachers and principals in which "control over their jobs most often takes precedence over the needs of individual children and their families" and in which there are "the essential conditions for insulating school management from citizens generally; namely, the assurance of a budget independent of satisfied consumers." Michaelsen concludes, therefore, "that the bureaucratization of the schools may, indeed, be an irreversible process" and that "community control will not be able to overcome the structure of incentives inherent in the bureaucratic form of school organization under representative government."[25]

Even the partnership type of community control is a threat to many professional educators. It can weaken their exclusive power to define children's educational needs and define how much public funding is needed to meet them. Furthermore, teachers who see themselves as the experts and sole purveyors of education have a hard time accepting parents and students as empowered partners in the learning process.

As for parents themselves, many of them are only too happy to accept a passive role. If the professional authorities say "leave it to us," it is natural for many parents to relinquish their responsibility for the education of their children. Those who do raise their voices, furthermore, are often easily co-opted, simply by having their individual demands met while no change is made in the basic system of bureaucratic-professional control.

Doubts about the possibility of effective community and parent voice in public education must be taken seriously. There is too much evidence of their validity to brush them aside. Only in individual classrooms and schools where a teacher or principal is committed to a strong parental role or when controversial issues such as busing or sex education attract wide public attention is there likely to be much opportunity for parent and community voice, and then often to no avail, or to too much avail, as when a militant majority on such issues forces its will on a vanquished minority.

As a result of these doubts about the possibility, or even desirability, of solving our educational problems through the political process, increasing numbers of thoughtful people are reaching the conclusion that we must give up on voice and find an alternative. Whether we must accept the judgment that voice is no longer a viable route to educational partnerships is a matter of epochal importance that this generation of Americans must face. For there is, for the first time in a hundred years, an alternative to the concept of politically governed schools which is being taken seriously, namely, education by choice, or educational vouchers, to which we now turn.

14 FAMILY CONTROL

The case for family choice rests on the belief that there is no social consensus over what are the proper goals and means of education.

Stephen Sugarman, *Where*

If community control provides no easy path to learning partnerships, educational vouchers are an alternative that would sidestep the complexities of representative government, the need to find consensus amid pluralism, and the frustrations of dealing with entrenched professionalized bureaucracies. Vouchers, however, raise their own set of problems, as we shall see at the end of this chapter.

THE CONCEPT OF VOUCHERS

In contrast to the concept of community control, with its diverse meanings, the concept of educational vouchers is simplicity itself: take the $1,500 to $3,000 now being spent annually on each child in public schools and put it into the hands of parents (or students themselves if they are old enough) in the form of a voucher, so that they can choose and pay for their own schools in the marketplace.

Voucher proposals come in various forms and with differing social philosophies and consequences, but the basic concept remains the

133

same: choice, rather than voice, would be the primary way in which families would express their educational values and establish their relationships with schools.

The contrast with community control is clear: if parents are dissatisfied with a school, why suffer through long and fruitless PTA meetings? why endure indifferent, arrogant school officials? why bother to elect a decent school board that would have little chance of reforming the schools anyway? why fight with powerful teachers' unions over the life and future of your children? why appeal to commissioners of education or the courts? why organize a Black Power or back-to-basics movement to get your voice heard and values respected? Simply move your child to another school that you like better!

Under a voucher system, instead of schools being accountable to families and citizens collectively through a political process, they would be accountable to each family individually, through the market process. In this scheme, parents acting as customers, displeased with a chosen school, need only pick another provider.

BACKGROUND OF THE VOUCHER IDEA

The concept of educational vouchers goes back at least as far as Adam Smith. Smith is said to have got the idea from his own educational experiences at Oxford, where he studied virtually unsupervised and concluded that the professors were so comfortably endowed that they had no incentive to satisfy anyone other than their colleagues. The faculty at Oxford had an eighteenth-century equivalent of what present-day economist Jacob Michaelsen complains of in American public schools, namely, "the assurance of a budget independent of satisfied consumers."[1] In *The Wealth of Nations* Smith used the universities as an example of the evils of protected monopoly: "The endowments of schools and colleges have . . . not only corrupted the diligence of public teachers but have rendered it almost impossible to have any good private ones."[2]

Thomas Paine and John Stuart Mill also advocated educational vouchers. Although Paine emphasized the rights of the family and Mill the rights of the child, both saw educational choice as the necessary ally of liberty, and saw government-controlled education as its natural enemy.[3]

In more recent times advocacy of educational vouchers has come from two strikingly different quarters. On the one hand, laissez-faire economists, led by Milton Friedman of the University of Chicago, have argued in the tradition of Adam Smith that education in the marketplace would be more efficient, varied, and suited to parents' preferences than the education provided by government bureaucracy. These economists maintain that much of the ineffectiveness and insensitivity of present public schools comes from their monopolistic character. They argue that not only efficiency but also equality of educational opportunity would be better served by providing each child with access to the educational marketplace through government-financed vouchers. In advocating his voucher plan in 1955, Friedman suggested that the "role of government could be limited to assuring that the schools meet certain minimum, common content in their program."[4]

The other source of voucher advocacy is on the political left. Egalitarians and some radicals concerned about poverty and inequality in American society have argued for educational vouchers as the most direct and effective way to redress the educational disadvantages of the poor, who suffer the most from our present educational system and have the least power, economically or politically, to do anything about it. Christopher Jencks has been the most widely publicized exponent of this view. Jencks, however, has proposed a voucher plan with significantly more restrictions than Friedman's plan; without restrictions, he and others fear vouchers would increase social and racial segregation and educational inequality.[5]

A TRIAL FOR "LIBERAL" VOUCHERS

Although Friedman's ideas have a longer history, it was Jencks's "liberal" plan that got the first foot in the federal government door, through a project promoted by the federal Office of Economic Opportunity in 1969. The OEO was hardly a hotbed of free market ideology; its political and intellectual roots were more in the New Deal than in laissez-faire economics. Nevertheless, OEO had been set up as a separate government agency, reporting directly to the president, because of skepticism about the old-line social service bureaucracies. This skepticism was particularly strong as applied to the public education establishment. Millions of federal dollars had been poured, with little visible effect, into city schools. There was a proliferation of new programs, added staff, and professionally designed "innovations" but very little change in the basic relationships between students and their schools and little or no improvement in academic achievement. The OEO concluded that some way had to be found "to provide families with economic and political leverage on the system," and the voucher idea seemed at least worth trying.[6]

Aware that an unregulated voucher system would be subject to criticism as a promoter of segregation, class stratification, and "hucksterism" preying especially on the poor, OEO gave a grant to Jencks to formulate a proposal that would provide the advantages of choice while minimizing these undesirable consequences. Jencks's plan, called a "regulated, compensatory" voucher system, prohibited schools from charging more than the amount of the voucher; required them to accept all applicants (or choose among them by lot); provided an increased voucher amount (a "compensatory voucher") for poor children to encourage schools to take them (and to provide the extra resources presumed needed for their education); and required outside school evaluations and information to help parents make informed choices.

Not surprisingly, Jencks's plan was "greeted with alarm by conservatives as another example of needless and meddlesome bureaucratic interference."[7] It also met with hostility from many professional educators who saw in the plan a direct threat to their power and an indirect affront to their status as providers of education.[8] The uneasy professionals were joined in opposition by many liberals who, while not wedded to existing educational arrangements, were concerned about the possible negative consequences of vouchers on the future of public education.[9] The opponents were not comforted by the OEO's assurances that the plan was only an experiment, since it was the kind of experiment whose success could have dire consequences for the public school system.

In short, the Jencks plan got little political backing. With much effort, between 1970 and 1972 OEO found only six school districts willing even to consider the proposal, and after initial studies financed by the OEO, all but one of them dropped the idea. The reasons for the cold reception were varied and complex. According to a Rand Corporation study, they included "previous political upheaval involving the schools, the opposition of local teacher organizations, the indifference or suspicion of parent groups, and widespread opposition to making private and parochial schools eligible for public funds."[10]

The one district that did not drop out after the initial study was Alum Rock, a medium-sized school district of 15,000 students, near San Francisco, California. The history of what happened to the voucher idea in Alum Rock is instructive.

THE ALUM ROCK EXPERIMENT

In developing a program with the Alum Rock school district, the federal officials intended to create a "basic structural change where parent choice rather than bureaucratic decisions determined the allocation of educational resources."[11] In other words, like the conservative voucher proponents, they saw *market* mechanisms (choice) rather than political and administrative mechanisms (voice) as the way to empower parents and improve education. Such basic structural change did not, however, occur in Alum Rock.

OEO's approach to initiating voucher experiments was to negotiate with school systems, which in turn meant negotiating with the various local public school interest groups, including the school boards, parent groups, and teacher organizations. In five of the six systems in which this approach was tried, the negotiations, as indicated, broke down before any experiment was tried. The same thing almost happened in Alum Rock. A study panel of teachers, parents, and community members was ready to reject the proposal until it was agreed to delay the decision pending state legislative action permitting vouchers. An alert and aggressive school superintendent, Dr. William Jefferds, eager to get additional federal funds and seeing an opportunity to test his own ideas on decentralized school administration, used the delay as an occasion to get an OEO staff training grant to pave the way for a larger allocation of federal money. OEO, fearful of losing its last remaining chance to try an experiment using vouchers, put its foot in the narrow crack of the door that Dr. Jefferds held open, even though the district had not made any real commitment to a voucher plan. When the California legislature failed in the fall of 1971 to allow private schools to participate in voucher projects, Dr. Jefferds used his favorable bargaining position to press OEO further, and he secured agreement to proceed with an "internal voucher" experiment limited to the public school system, with private schools to be added if and when the law permitted.

Negotiations between OEO and the Alum Rock school system went on for three years. The resulting plan set up a system that not only limited choice to public schools but maintained school sizes regardless of parental dissatisfaction; enforced seniority and excessing rules so that no teachers would lose their jobs because of the shrinking of unpopular programs; refused to provide information to the parents on the comparative student achievements in the various schools and programs; and, after an original flirtation with budget decentralization, recentralized fiscal decisions when funds became scarce. In short, few of the important features of a voucher plan remained.

Although the Alum Rock project failed to provide a true experiment in free-market education, it did provide some experience with parental choice. Fifteen percent of the parents chose programs outside their neighborhood schools—a figure viewed by some as showing little interest in choice but by others as showing a great deal of interest, given parents' natural preference for neighborhood schools and the limited choices provided by the project. If there had been true market conditions, the shift of 15 percent and the potential of more shifts if people became dissatisfied would have introduced a considerable competitive element into the school system.

Meanwhile, though not in the original Jencks plan, the project also provided a new slant on "teacher power." Teachers were not only given leeway to design the separate minischools from which parents could choose; they were also given control over the $250 compensatory voucher for each "poor" child who chose their program. As Denis Doyle observed, "A teacher who attracted fifteen to twenty compensatory voucher children found herself presiding over an educational gold mine"—to the point where many of the teachers "could not spend the money as rapidly as it poured in." Summing up the experience, Doyle quipped: "What had begun as the last OEO 'power to the people' program ended as a 'teacher power' program."[12]

David Selden, past president of the American Federation of Teachers, liked what he saw in Alum Rock. His initial categorical opposition to vouchers was changed by two visits to the project. Selden became convinced that, "under the right circumstances, vouchers might open the door to a new form of learning that could go far toward humanizing the American elementary school." The "right circumstances," as described by Selden, included programs "run by teachers, with heavy parental involvement," but with the teachers deciding "how the compensatory voucher money will be spent. They can spend the funds on materials or personnel, virtually without restriction. This emphasis on teacher control is the main reason teachers generally favor the plan."[13]

School-level teacher control of educational decisions, as opposed to centralized bureaucratic control of personnel, financial, and administrative policy, has a number of attractive aspects in terms of partnership, especially if combined with real parental choice. The small size and intimate relationships in the Alum Rock minischools made them conducive to partnership relations, but as federal and local funds became scarcer after the third year of the program, both teacher autonomy and school-level decision making in Alum Rock were curtailed.[14]

Alum Rock was a case in which the "organizational structure of the school system successfully resisted attempts to be changed from a monopoly to a market system." The public monopoly agreed to provide more choices for its customers, which itself may have been beneficial, but as the Rand Corporation Study pointed out, "The beliefs in consumer sovereignty underlying a voucher system were not congruent with the beliefs underlying a public monopoly."[15]

A BRIEF OUTING FOR "CONSERVATIVE" VOUCHERS

If OEO in general, and Jencks's vouchers in particular, enjoyed only a tenuous political hold in 1970 and 1971, they were doomed after the Nixon landslide in 1972. The new president's instructions to his new OEO director were forthright: disband the whole federal poverty agency. The Alum Rock voucher experiment was also to be abandoned and a "proper" Friedman-type voucher project tested elsewhere. New Hampshire was considered a suitably rock-ribbed, individualist climate for a more laissez-faire experiment, and funds were provided for voucher feasibility studies in eight New Hampshire districts and in East Hartford, Connecticut. Before much study could take place, however, oversight of vouchers in Washington was shifted from the collapsing OEO to the newly formed National Institute of Education, where the prime focus was research, not social change, and where all activist inclinations, of the right or the left, were inhibited by the agency's troubled relations with Congress. Meanwhile, the people in all eight New Hampshire districts decided they did not want even this "free enterprise" relationship with the federal government, and the school principals in East Hartford decided that vouchers were too threatening to be tested. The whole idea "spelled intolerable diminution of their (the principals') role."[16] None of the communities had much concept of what vouchers were about, and little effort was made by federal officials to increase their understanding or to overcome opposition.

By 1976 the federal initiative in experimentation with vouchers had collapsed. At this point the lessons with regard to vouchers could be read in a number of diverse ways:

1. Vouchers are a bad idea; they have been tried, and either they do not work or nobody wants them.
2. Vouchers are a new idea; it will take more time and effort before people understand them.
3. Vouchers are a controversial idea; they can be expected to generate political opposition, which can only be overcome with more political finesse than was used by OEO.
4. Vouchers are threatening to public school systems and will never be accepted by public school constituencies.

VOUCHERS RESURRECTED: COONS AND SUGARMAN

Briefly, in the mid-1970s, it appeared that the idea of vouchers had passed from the scene. One effort to introduce them in Michigan was beaten back by strong public education and teacher union opposition. Although Friedman's ideas still made sense to those who accepted his general outlook on American society, mainstream educational policy makers were searching for answers elsewhere.

The voucher issue was reopened in 1978 by John E. Coons and Stephen Sugarman in *Education by Choice: The Case for Family Control.*[17] This book is important for a number of reasons. First, the authors have liberal credentials: Coons was active in the civil rights movement, and he and Sugarman together played a leading part in the movement for greater equity in public education funding—a movement that produced the famous *Serrano* decision in California and a series of court cases and political actions to change state aid formulas in most of the states of the union.[18] Sociologist James Coleman, in his foreword to *Education by Choice,* calls the book a "product of a quest by Coons and Sugarman for equity in education" and urges its readers to see it as a proposal that "holds promise for far more than equity in the educational and social benefits it can bring." Here was something that could not so easily be brushed aside by school officials, as could Friedman's ideas, as an effort to rebuild nineteenth-century capitalism on the school grounds. Nor did it have the trappings of 1960s antipoverty planning.

Even more significant were the authors' proposals for action—action very different from that used by the OEO in negotiating with Alum Rock and other public school systems. Soon after the book was published, Coons and a number of associates launched a petition drive to get the issue on the California ballot as a popular referendum. They failed to obtain the approximately half-million signatures needed to get on the 1980 ballot, but they have vowed to continue, the success of Proposition 13 in 1978 and Proposition 4 in 1979 being seen as examples of how substantial changes in government policy can be obtained despite the organized opposition of public school interest groups.

Debates over educational vouchers are heated—understandably so, since important values are involved. This is all the more reason why the issue should be approached with more than rhetoric and slogans. Many arguments for vouchers are solid, and many of the objections are insubstantial. Yet there are serious drawbacks. The two following sections consider, first, the provoucher arguments and, second, the problems.

ARGUMENTS FOR FAMILY CHOICE: VOUCHERS

Competition

One of the most inviting aspects of vouchers is the single-jump escape they provide for most of the problems of educational bureaucracy, professionalization, and government accountability. These problems derive from trying to run education as a government enterprise, for which collective decisions must be made on behalf of the public as a whole. Even if government run schools should remain one of the choices under a voucher system, much of the curse would be removed since parents (or older students) would have to take the blame for buying into the public system, which could be bypassed if it failed to do a satisfactory job.

Choice would necessarily mean that the public schools would have to compete with private and parochial institutions. No longer would government schools have "the assurance of budget independent of satisfied customers." They would be on their mettle to provide education that satisfied both the cultural and the academic expectations of parents. With such an arrangement, schools as unproductive and unsatisfactory as many of our present public schools would be likely to find themselves out of business.

Another virtue of a competitive system would be that parents would not have to remove their children from a school to make public educators notice them; the mere fact that they *could* move their children might keep school officials alert to the parents' educational goals and to the community will.

Choice and Student Motivation

While much is said about the potentially healthy effect of competition on the motivation of teachers and administrators, less is said about the effects of choice on the motivation of students and parents.

Teachers rue the lack of student motivation, particularly among lower-class and minority students and lazy, indifferent, or surly middle-class students. But, as pointed out in Chapter 10, lack of motivation is seldom a characteristic of students; it is almost always a characteristic of the *relationship* between students and teachers, or between students and schools. If we want to deal with motivation, we must deal with the kind and quality of these relationships.

Choice is likely to have a positive effect on student-teacher relationships. Of course, most of the choices in voucher proposals for elementary and secondary schools would be made by parents, and what parents choose for their children is not always greeted with delight. This would not necessarily negate the positive effects of choice, however. Compulsion does not always lead to resistance; it depends on application and context. While children may not make the decision, the fact that someone close to them has done so can still have a powerful effect. Furthermore, modern parents are learning their own limits when it comes to compelling Andrew or Maria to "like" school. For better or worse, parents today are forced to listen to and learn from the opinions voiced by their children.[19] Even elementary students know it if a playmate attends a more interesting school than their own, and most would not hesitate to tell Mom and Dad about "this great school" their friend goes to if a policy of choice existed. Children also know when parents distrust a school. Their attitudes are affected by adult values. Children can develop their own independent and positive relationship to a school, but this is much less likely when parents are hostile to the institution.

Accommodating Pluralism

A voucher system would provide a way to accommodate the pluralistic values in American society. As said earlier, education is never value free. That being the case, whose values will prevail? In a common system for all children, decisions about values are made either by the professional bureaucracy or through an imperfect and often acrimonious political process. When clashes of value are too great, the political process cannot accommodate them, and compromise has a limited capacity to please. It can produce a result that leaves everyone dissatisfied or a "muddled middle" that so confuses a school's values that children are left with no clear guidance. At the same time, the adoption of one group's values over another's may lead to alienation and psychological withdrawal by those whose values are disregarded.[20]

Some countries, such as the Netherlands and Belgium, have dealt with sharp divergences in religious and cultural values by providing government-subsidized school choice.[21] American society, it can be argued, is at least as pluralistic, not only religiously and culturally but also in terms of competing philosophies (consider "open" versus "traditional" schooling, for example). Rather than attempting to reconcile these differences through the political process, vouchers would permit people to pursue their own values in schools conforming to their value preferences.

Choice by vouchers not only would permit people to escape the divisiveness of cultural clashes in the political arena but also would strengthen particularistic institutions that assert their own values and provide a community for cultural expression. Many social analysts are concerned that such private institutions have been weakened in recent years by the onslaught of all-encompassing government, which robs them of their functions.[22]

Vouchers would be a financial boon to church-run schools. Parochial school systems now short of funds might instantly be restored to fiscal health; indeed, if the voucher payment approximated the current expenditure per pupil in public schools, many church schools would have far greater resources than ever before and probably a considerably expanded clientele.[23] This would unquestionably provide a boost to religious education and also to the religious institutions themselves. A parochial school, even one strapped for funds, is often the mainstay of a congregation, providing social and intergenerational relationships that reinforce religious commitments. Many denominations that have traditionally avoided parochial day schools might open them.

Voluntary associations would also be strengthened, for the same reason. Individuals who have banded together for any cause will usually have their bonds strengthened if their children are educated together under the banner of the group. We might find vegetarians, antiabortionists, environmentalists, Libertarians, or Socialist Workers opening schools in order to increase their group cohesion and intergenerational continuity.

Strengthening the Family

Dealing with the pluralism of values through choice rather than the political process would strengthen and empower American families. Most parents do not have the time or resources to participate actively in the political process. In a small, relatively homogeneous town, parents may be expected to participate sufficiently in the school system to iron out problems and reach common agreements. But in modern urban or suburban America, with its transiency and cultural diversity, the chances of most parents giving voice to their values and having their voices heard is greatly diminished, even if the professionalized school systems were open to parental influence, which many are not.

Many parents do not want to participate directly in the management of their children's education; but to make a choice of schools is not to accept full management responsibility, and doing so could give them a much greater sense of involvement and responsibility.

Education by choice is also likely to strengthen a child's sense of the family bond. Children who are aware that their parents have carefully chosen their school are in a different psychological climate from children who are sent to a school by the state. Children who attend a school chosen by their parents know where to turn in case of difficulty, and those to whom they turn have the power to act. The parents' responses might not be to the children's liking, but happy or not, the complaints have a chance to register, and voicing and listening to grievances strengthen a family.

"The Best Interest of the Child"

Parental choice may strengthen the family, but will it help the child? What if the parents make choices that are not in the child's best interests? This has been a major justification for shifting power to government.

The strongest argument made by Coons and Sugarman for education by choice is that parents are more likely than anyone else to make choices in their children's best interests. They are well aware that there is a "vast ocean" of educators and child development experts prepared to tell parents what is best for their children, but the experts are in such disagreement that they constitute a veritable Babel of expertise. Experts on children offer no "collective perception on what is best for the child."[24] Given the conflicting and uncertain expert knowledge, the real question, the authors say, is, Who shall decide? Coons and Sugarman argue that authority should rest in the hands of the agent most likely to allow the child voice in the decision and the agent most apt to know and care about the child, in case the child's wishes need to be overridden.[25] They argue that parents fulfill these conditions better than any other agents of society.

Coons and Sugarman do not claim that parents are perfect, only that they are more likely to be caring and interested in their children than are strangers in the educational bureaus or experts from the universities. They see parents as better educational guardians than "the professional cadre of a school or a district," not because teachers or school officials do not care about children but because their institutional roles put them in a position where they are less likely to know a child, to listen carefully to his or her concerns, or to have the healthy self-interest derived from having to "bear the responsibility for mistakes made in judging the interests of the child."[26]

It bears saying, too, that many public school officials have little experience or expertise in choosing schools for children. Students are usually assigned to public schools by geographic zone and grade level. They often know little about individual records of performance or psychological traits, two important factors in making good decisions for a child. Even incompetent parents usually know a great deal about their children; and more parents than are given credit by experts care very deeply about those they bring into the world.

More Direct Partnership

Choice opens a more direct route to partnerships between teachers and parents and between families and schools. Partnership is a state of mind more than a description of functions; it need not always involve active participation. Some parents may choose a school where they have nothing to do with curriculum because of their level of trust in the school. Others may choose a school that encourages or requires participation. In either case, the mere act of choice creates a degree of partnership because it creates a bond that is likely to be felt by all parties—the teacher, the parents, and the child.[27]

Choice as a Right

Quite apart from the practical considerations of how a system of choice might correct the inefficiencies and antieducational aspects of present public school systems, a philosophical argument can be made for the right of parents to choose where their children go to school.

Peter Berger and Richard Neuhaus suggest that "the right to make a world for one's children is a fundamental human right."[28] They see the violation of this basic right as one of the greatest crimes of totalitarian societies and one of the most worrisome tendencies of democratic societies, in which the monolithic bureaucratic structures of modern government creep toward totalitarian models.

As I said earlier, the right to choose for one's children is not obvious. Since the beginning of human history, many societies have considered child rearing a community enterprise as well as a responsibility of natural parents. Nevertheless, the individualistic value structure of modern democratic societies seems to imply a right of parents to have substantial control over the educational destiny of their children.

In one sense this argument is superfluous, since the constitutional right of parental choice in education is already established. The question, however, is whether this legal right has much meaning for thousands of parents who feel trapped in unsatisfactory public schools. The question of a right to choice in education therefore becomes primarily a question of discrimination.

Choice and Social Discrimination

If parents have a legal right to choose their children's school, then a serious problem of social discrimination exists in present public educational policies if wealthy parents can exercise this right but poor parents, for all practical purposes, cannot.The right to select a school is not like the right to buy a Cadillac. Owning a Cadillac is not a human right, and no one suggests that everyone ought to have one. Education differs from products to be purchased in being both a social necessity and a legal obligation imposed on individuals. The current system discriminates by compelling poor parents to send their children to schools that they may feel are antithetical to their values and detrimental to their children's interests.[29]

If all parents were compelled to send their children to schools about which they had no choice, such a policy might be considered nondiscriminatory (albeit unconstitutional). If only those who have no other options are so compelled, the issue become one of discrimination.

The shadow of discrimination against the poor in the present educational system is lengthened by federal taxing policy, which subsidizes those who already have the money to send their children to exclusive suburban public schools. Thomas Vitullo-Martin's research has shown that

> if a family is in the 50% federal tax bracket, the net increase in its total tax obligation of a $3,000 rise in property taxes is only $1,500. . . . The local government raises its revenue by $3,000, but the federal government simul-

taneously decreases its revenue by $1,175. . . . The aggregate effect of the tax deduction system on a high-income community is that the federal and state governments pay a higher percentage of the community's tax obligations—up to 70% of local taxes in some New York suburbs compared with less than 15% of city taxes. . . . The net effect of federal intervention in education is to subsidize the wealthiest families in the wealthiest districts far more than the central cities and their residents.

Since, as Vitullo-Martin points out, "the most exclusive schools in America are suburban public schools," the present laws compel the poor to enroll their children in mediocre public schools and, at the same time, subsidize the choice of exclusive public schools for the rich.[30] This makes a mockery of Horace Mann's ideal of a common school system.

Concern about the discriminatory way in which choice now operates has led some educators, most notably Theodore Sizer and Phillip Whitten, to recommend vouchers for poor families, rather than for all families.[31] A variation on this idea has been more recently suggested by Barbara Lerner, who proposes giving vouchers to those children who are failing in the public schools. Her idea is that this would give such children an alternative chance to succeed and provide a useful spur of competition for the public schools, without encouraging a mass exodus of those sutdents who are doing well in them.[32]

ARGUMENTS AGAINST FAMILY CHOICE

Opponents of vouchers draw grotesque pictures of what would happen under a choice system. They predict the collapse of all education or the seizure of young minds by religious or subversive elements. Some of the objections, which we will examine first, have little validity. Some, however, which we will examine at the end of this section, must be taken seriously.

Administrative Chaos

A choice system, some people claim, would be a nightmare to administer because of the diversity of programs and the uncertainty of enrollment in any particular school or program. The short answer to this is to ask any honest public school administrator how simple it is to administer the "one best system." A great deal of the administration of the public system could be eliminated in a choice system. Individual schools would have to be administered, but much of the unproductive educational administration above the school level would no longer be needed.

The introduction of vouchers and greater choice would, to be sure, entail administrative problems, as does any process dealing with thousands of people. A voucher plan, however, could not possibly match the administrative superstructure now plaguing American public education.[33]

Hucksterism

Critics say that education put on the "open market" would engender slick advertising to woo parents into shoddy private schools.[34] They cite the notorious scandals of fly-by-night vocational schools as visions of the educational future. Some hucksterism would arise, but choice of elementary and secondary schooling would be monitored by parents, and a network of information on desirable schools would be likely to emerge. Many, if not most, parents would probably elect neighborhood schools, and choice of a distant institution would usually not occur without some evidence of its superiority. Furthermore, unlike a refrigerator or some other consumer item, the continuous process of education provides opportunity to change a choice if it does not work out.

These safeguards against educational frauds would exist even without the governmental assistance in evaluating schools which many voucher plans propose. Were the government freed of the responsibility of operating one system for all students, it might be more apt to enforce some kind of educational "truth in labeling" and mandate honest reporting so that parents could learn what is happening to their children, as they often cannot in the monopolistic public system in which the professional experts decide what parents are to be told.[35]

Lack of Market Behavior

Somewhat parallel to the concern about hucksterism is the fear that business monopolies would take over American education if vouchers were introduced. A scenario can be sketched showing family choice education trodden down by monolithic franchise schools and educational supermarkets serving schooling à la McDonalds. Critics maintain that the presumed increase of choice and the enhanced pluralism would disappear under the weight of bland, commercial uniformity.

This seems unlikely. Franchise schools could appear, but it is hard to imagine any greater "bland uniformity" than what we have in public schooling today. Furthermore, if education is as difficult to administer successfully on a massive bureaucratic basis as it appears to be, it is unlikely that it will attract many business monopolists. They would want to think twice before undertaking to contend with massive numbers of schoolteachers, children, and their parents.

Choice and the Political Process

Fears that a system of choice would lead to administrative chaos, hucksterism, and commercial exploitation are among the more trivial criticisms of voucher plans. There are more fundamental problems, however, the first of which is political. Simply put, do people want education to be assigned to the marketplace? Do they want to be governed primarily by choice instead of voice?

This question may initially seem simple-minded. If offered, would not everyone want a choice? And if some do not, why not extend choice to those who do? The issue, however, is not that simple. It might seem that everyone would want as much choice as possible, but in terms of human psychology and social instincts, that is not always true. In trying to explain the bizarre behavior of the members of the People's Temple who surrendered their wills and their lives to James Jones in Jonestown, Guyana, one psychiatrist speculated that "our society is so free and permissive and people have so many options to choose from that they cannot make their own decisions effectively. They want others to make the decisions and they will follow."[36]

A will to totalitarian control is obviously antithetical to democratic society, but people nevertheless find it socially and psychologically practical and even necessary to limit choices. Although some might prefer to drive on the left side of the road and some on the right, virtually all want only one rule, even if it reduces their freedom of choice. Decisions about the education of children are obviously more important than left- or right-hand driving, but the very importance of educational decisions can make people hesitant to shoulder them. A social instinct may well inhibit many parents from wanting to make educational choices by themselves and may also make them fearful of unlimited choice for parents in general.[37]

Consider the case of a small nineteenth-century town of a hundred families debating whether to set up a public school. If 60 percent of the families wanted a public school, the town might still deem it unwise to proceed until a larger proportion of families join in. If 90 percent of the families agreed to send their children to the public school, however, and a building were built and teachers hired, there would develop a kind of "we're all in this together" feeling that would make it at once hard to drop out and easy for a majority to oppose public subsidies for parental choice.

Many Americans have a "we're all in this together" attitude toward the public schools. They may prefer a different school for their own child but still be against opening choice as a general policy, for fear that the time-honored system might fall apart. The people who voted against the voucher proposals in New Hampshire and Michigan may have done so out of a deep conservatism, a desire not to change the social or educational equation in their community. Pragmatically, a choice system may be too radical a change to be politically viable. Inertia is a human condition. Change fosters fears, even when it promises benefits. Many Americans find it hard to conceive of life without a public educational system.

THE SOCIAL GOOD

Underlying people's reluctance to accept a shift to a voucher system may be a more substantial objection than inertia, an objection relating to the general social good.

What are the social purposes of education? How do these purposes relate to the best interest of the child? Coons and Sugarman base their provoucher argument on a sharp distinction between childrens' interests and society's interests. While they see both as the legitimate concern of education, they evaluate them independently. They first consider educational policy as if "our society's sole objective in education is the best interest of the individual child," and they conclude that family choice is the best policy. Then they consider, as a separate matter, that "the welfare of children is not the only concern of the schools. . . . Educational policies are often designed to benefit either organized groups or the total society and may or may not be consistent with the welfare of the individual child." In this social context, they see the prime purposes of education as "the maintenance of a consensus supporting order and liberty" and "the achievement of racial integration." Both, they argue, would be better served by family choice than by the present system.[38]

Coons and Sugarman are aware of fears that choice would pose "a threat to the consensus that underlies an ordered liberty" and the concern that "any encouragement of individuals by government to cluster according to their own values is a step in the wrong direction, a dangerous extension of cultural pluralism that threatens to fuel intolerance and to undermine social cooperation." Yet they discount these fears. Family choice, as Coons and Sugarman see it, would reduce alienation, lead to greater trust, and "cement a stronger political bond among our diverse peoples" than the present system of compulsory conformity through the "herding or propagandizing of children." They project a system of schools of choice as more successful than our present public schools in supporting "that civic agreement, partly explicit (in the guarantees of the Constitution), and partly implicit (in the individual will to protect the rights of others), that maintains the structure of ordered liberty.[39]

With regard to the social goal of racial integration, Coons and Sugarman argue that "incorporation of elements of choice in systems of integration eventually should achieve more than the current efforts of courts and legislatures. Successful white efforts at racial exclusivity through choice should be relatively few, and all-black schools should be largely self-selected. Most important, the integration attained would be stable and fraternal, hence more likely to beget further integration.[40] This assertion has infuriated civil rights veterans familiar with both the "free choice" evasions long used to preserve segregated public schools and the "segregation academies" that have sprung up to avoid court-ordered desegregation. The rosy predictions of Coons and Sugarman would probably not come true in many situations. They almost certainly underestimate the degree to which people would either directly or indirectly choose racially constituted schools. Their position, nevertheless, deserves consideration in view of Coons's experience in desegregating public schools and the lack of progress through other means. His position is based on two main considerations:

1. Desegregation by legal compulsion has reached its peak and is likely to achieve little further progress, both because of the growing conservatism of the courts and because present conditions provide little political impetus for further forced mixing.
2. Voluntary choice would not only promote more integration, but more educationally beneficial integration, because of what Nancy St. John calls "the psychological power of self-determination."

Coons and Sugarman see choice as a system under which black families would be able to make for themselves the trade-off between a neighborhood school and integration and to make their own decisions about the relative benefits of this choice for their children. "If integration is to suceed," they conclude, "it may be wise to modify our strategies in ways which take greater account of the needs of individuals."[41]

These arguments for the merits of meeting society's needs through greater respect for the individual needs of children are powerful. Coons and Sugarman stumble over a fundamental problem, however. The interests of children and the interests of society are not as easily separated as they imply—at least not in a democratic society, which can have no interests other than the combined individual and collective interests of its people.[42] To some extent liberty requires the ability to see individual interests as distinct from collective interests. At the same time, an underlying premise of a democratic society is that if the social interest is "for the good of all," the interests of individual members are best served by adding their support to the common good even though that can mean subordinating their own preferences. There is a contradiction in presuming that in a democratic society something that would be good for children would lead to a bad society and, vice versa, that something could be good for society that would be bad for children.

The separation of the interests of the child from the interests of society leads Coons and Sugarman into a trap. They see the available options solely as either "private choice" or "public compulsion" the latter evoking images of a government that would "deliberately use a child as the instrument of social policy inconsistent with his well-being."[43] When anything that is not "private choice" is treated as "public compulsion," private choice certainly seems preferable. But what if a particular institution is seen as a "public choice"—a community enterprise, something a community affirms as a group? Any kind of group decision or action involves the subordination of some degree of individual will. Does that automatically mean "compulsion"? It can instead be seen as the price paid for mutual endeavor and, what is more important, for a sense of community.

The greatest weakness of Coons and Sugarman's argument for choice over voice is their underestimate of a sense of community as a preeminent goal of public education in America. The discussion of the "consensus supporting order and liberty" in their book misses the point in describing the present strategies of public education as aimed at the assimilation of ethnic and other groups into the larger society and indoctrination of the assimilated population into "some unitary conception regarding the proper ends of human striving."[44] Such goals are easily discredited, but these are not prime social purposes of public education. Far more basic is the creation of a sense of community wherein pluralism and divergent values can be maintained.

The idea of a common school did not come from a society that had already developed its cohesion and common purpose, though that may have been the case in Puritan New England or towns settled by single ethnic or national groups. As a national institution that spread rapidly in the nineteenth century, public education was not so much a way to reflect community as to build it. Whereas contemporary educational revisionists may see the common school movement primarily as the effort of a dominant Protestant elite to socialize disparate immigrants and rural Americans into a disciplined industrial work force, this can hardly be a full explanation of the motives of the thousands of citizens who worked for the development of public schools, raised money for them, and sent their children to them. The need for social cohesion is not something felt only by greedy industrialists, and there was clearly more behind the development of the public school system than the creation of a Protestant, capitalist melting pot.

One may legitimately ask how social cohesion can result from trying to forge a common school out of so many disparate values. Does not such an effort lead to animosity rather than cohesion? It certainly can if the divergence is so great that the center cannot hold.

Where the center can hold, however, common public education is one of the means by which *unum* can be built out of *pluribus*.

Stephen Sugarman has said that "if both the goals and means of education are uncertain," the answer "is to turn away from the issue of 'what is best' and to ask instead who should be given the power to decide what education is best for children."[45] His answer is to give the power to individual families. He fails to see that the process of deciding on the common good, even when it is fraught with conflict, is a primary way to develop community in a diverse, democratic society.

Freeman Butts observes that public education has had a *public* and *political* purpose from the beginning. A primary purpose of public schooling "was to prepare the young for their new role as self-governing citizens rather than as *subjects* bound to an alien sovereign or as *private persons* loyal primarily to their families, their kinfolk, their churches, their localities or neighborhoods, or their ethnic traditions."[46] How many people fully shared this republican purpose is unknown; but at least some of this purpose was, and still is, an important part of the public school ideal of many Americans.

What Coons, Sugarman, and other voucher advocates propose, therefore, is quite radical. They would redefine education as primarily a *private* affair. In their scheme, the primary question would no longer be what serves the public but what each family sees as serving its individual interests—the "wants of a single family rather than the needs of society." The charge that vouchers would be "selfish and antisocial" is not just name-calling;[47] it alludes to a deeply serious issue.

Schools of choice would perform a different function from that of public schools. They would serve as extensions of the home or of particular religious, ethnic, or ideological groups, whereas public schools serve as an experience in the public world. Some private schools function partially as public institutions in this sense—schools such as Exeter and Andover, which enroll students from many backgrounds and geographic areas, provide both academic and extracurricular experiences designed to help lead the student beyond his home background. But the main justification for family control is to permit the other kind of choice, not provided by public school; namely, of a school designed to reinforce family values.

Shifting from publicly provided education to private choice

would enhance the role of families as institutions but would reduce their political role. As Sugarman says, we would be "turning away" from the political process, presumably because of the great difficulty of trying to arrive at political consensus. Families would become politically atomized, each encouraged to look out for its own children. Without a political role in education, parents would probably become more politically impotent than they are at present. Granted that ideals such as equity and respect for students' values are far from being realized in our present system. Nevertheless, should education come to be seen primarily as a private matter, whence would come the motivation for equity and justice for all children? What would prevent dominant majorities from setting the value of the voucher at a level that would benefit the middle classes and the rich but leave the poor unable to buy adequate education—and do so legitimately, since education would be a matter of looking out for one's own. The result, in all probability, would be a system in which class and ideological segregation became an even greater problem than racial segregation. The issue would not be what we Americans, we New Yorkers, or we Peorians want for our children, but what we Smiths, we Baptists, or we Socialist Workers want for our children. This sentiment is appropriate for family, church, and ethnic group affairs, but if only these values were brought into the public arena, one of the prime purposes of public education, and one of the prime values of American society, would be jeopardized.

Even greater divisiveness than at present could result. The state would have to decide which private schools would be eligible for the public subsidy through vouchers. Unnecessary but severe church-state controversy could flare. State authorities, and perhaps state legislatures, would have to decide when a legitimate black studies school became an illegitimate black power school, or when a legitimate conservative school became an illegitimate Nazi training camp. The situation could become politically intolerable, ironically violating one of the most cherished of American values, a value that many voucher advocates especially want to preserve: the protection of private affairs from the heavy hand of government.

Family choice, inviting as it is, raises the most profound questions about the purposes of education in our society, and perhaps about the purposes of the society itself. We will have to look deeper than the single remedy of choice to find valid educational policy for the decades ahead.

15 A PARALYSIS OF POLICY

If a man will begin with certainties he shall end in doubts; but if he will be
content to begin with doubts, he shall end in certainties.

Francis Bacon, *Advancement of Learning*

Neither community control nor vouchers have as yet effected a cure
for America's education malaise. Despite many reform efforts, public schools remain professionalized, government-run bureaucracies,
failing disastrously in the cities and headed for increasing trouble in
suburbs and rural areas as costs mount, effectiveness declines, values
diverge, and public support falters. Most reforms have been little
more than efforts to improve, without changing, the faulty service-
delivery model of schooling; and most have been dismal failures.
Furthermore, the two reform movements that have at least addressed
fundamental issues in a way that might restore partnership to a
central role in education, lead in opposite directions, with community control calling for greater participation and accountability in
public schools and vouchers leading toward escape from public
schools through private choice. The result is a paralysis of policy.
The United States today has no clear consensus on public educational
policy, and people do not know which way to turn.

A NECESSARY CONTRADICTION:
VOICE AND CHOICE

A resolution of this policy dilemma requires a closer look at the differing orientations of community control and family control—that is, of voice and choice.

Community control holds that the main problem with present public educational systems is that professionalized government bureaucracies have become unresponsive to their clients and that, to correct this situation, parents, students, and citizens must be given more voice in educational institutions and policies. From this approach have flowed such proposals as decentralization, school site management, parent advisory councils, and various other plans to whittle down or sidestep bureaucracy so that students, parents, and teachers can develop a more productive relationship in public schools. The voice approach accepts education as a public enterprise but holds that the present governmental system is no longer "of the people, by the people, and for the people" but rather is, at best, "of the bureaucracy, by the professionals, and for the people" and, at worst, "of the bureaucracy, by the bureaucracy, and for the bureaucracy." Community control holds that public education must become a partnership "of the people, by the people, and for the people" before it will be effective and legitimate.

The other concept, family control, suggests that education will be made more effective and legitimate not by giving people more voice but by giving them more choice over the schools to which they send their children. Advocates of this approach claim that it would make schools more effective through competition and more legitimate by avoiding the value conflicts that are inherent in making collective educational policy for people with diverse values.

Two fundamentally different concepts of education underlie the approaches of voice and choice. "Voice" sees education as something that "we the people" provide for "our" children for the good of a community as a whole and, therefore, as something that must validly express the will, or voice, of the people. "Choice" projects education as the responsibility of individual families; it would provide a way for parents to express their will individually rather than collectively. "Voice" sees education primarily as a public good, presumed to benefit families as well; "choice" sees education primarily as a private good, presumed to benefit society as well.

The educational systems produced by pure voice or choice approaches would be radically different. "Voice" at its extreme could give rise to a system of compulsory attendance for all children in government schools but democratically run, with all having a voice in their governance. "Choice" at its extreme could mean either the abolition of public schools altogether, leaving parents with the full responsibility of providing for their children's education, or an unregulated voucher system, in which the government's role would be to pay the bills for parents, who would have the greatest possible freedom in selecting schools for their children.

With voice and choice embodied in separate, conflicting proposals, the advocates of each position are at loggerheads, fighting for control over educational policy. This battle has already begun. After a hundred years of dominance, the voice approach is under fire. Many people are abandoning efforts to reform public schools through the political process and are instead seeking ways to escape from them.[1] Although this debate is useful in raising important issues of educational policy, a fight to the finish would be counterproductive. The principles of voice and choice, though pulling in opposite directions, should not be separated; nor should one be allowed to conquer the other. Neither alone is sufficient to provide a sound basis for educational policy in a free society. Education is necessarily both public and private—a general responsibility of society and a private responsibility of families and individuals. It is both a matter of public policy, which all have voice in shaping, and of private commitment, reflecting individual values and initiative. The challenge is to achieve the proper balance between the public and private aspects of education.

Education in the United States is already both public and private in a variety of ways besides the constitutionally guaranteed right of parents to select between public and private schools. It is public in that the state regulates certain aspects of private education and in the ethos of public service and citizenship that permeates virtually all private as well as public schools.[2] American education is private in that substantial portions of the total educational process, even for those attending public schools, are still controlled by parents, churches, private business, neighborhoods, gangs, and voluntary associations—private, ultimately, in their influence upon and response elicited from individual students. Despite compulsory attendance laws, there is no compulsory learning, and if there were, we might not like it. At least in our kind of society, ultimate control over learning rests in private hands and always must as long as we want to remain free.

From the earliest days of American society, education has been both a public concern and a private responsibility—more in some parts of the country than in others and more at some times than at others, but never only a private responsibility of parents or a public responsibility of government. Much of the community concern for education in the early years was expressed through religious and voluntary associations rather than government. That did not imply an absence of public emphasis on learning, however. Leaders such as Jefferson and Washington stressed the importance of education to the new Republic, and they saw it as a responsibility of the society as a whole. Government educational policy has been a continuing part of our history from the 1647 Massachusetts "Auld Deluder" statute, which required every community to provide schooling, to the provisions for public schools in the federal land ordinances of the 1780s, and into the nineteenth century, when governmental initiative began to prevail over other public expressions.

The combination of public and private concern for education is not unique to American society. In virtually all societies, the education of the young is a function of the community as a whole as well as of families and parents. True, the community element is not exercised through government in every society, but the processes by which any culture develops, spreads, and perpetuates itself in succeeding generations extend far beyond the family. Language, tradition, mores, ceremonies, the example of elders, work patterns, technology, and economic relationships all educate children. It is literally not possible in any society to leave education to the family alone.

The issue, then, is not whether education should be public or private, dominated by voice or by choice, but how the public and private elements can be effectively combined.

To summarize, one difficulty in the United States in the past hundred years has been the increasing governmentalization, bureaucratization, and professionalization of education and the decreasing sense of personal responsibility for education on the part of students, parents, citizens, and individual teachers. Rather than being seen and felt as a partnership of mutual and coordinate responsibilities, education has increasingly come to be seen as the government's responsibility, with students, parents, and communities cast in the role of passive recipients of the state's services and teachers cast in the role of docile functionaries of a state bureaucracy.

Voice and choice each have contributions to make in rectifying this disempowerment of the necessary partners in education. Both derive from and give expression to people's values and aspirations. They should not be seen as contradictory principles but as coordinate principles, each having its appropriate role and both essential to counteract the disempowering effects of professionalized government bureaucracy. Yet neither the current prevailing policy framework nor the two contradictory reform efforts of community control and family control have been able to bring them together.

The missing element in the policy discussions thus far is the third element of the proposed new policy framework—loyalty. We have looked at the mechanisms through which individuals, families, and communities might relate to schools—voice and choice—but we have not looked at how individuals, families, and communities relate to each other. In the debates over community control there has been too much emphasis on control and not enough on community and, in the discussions about family choice, too much emphasis on choice and not enough on family.

One source of the difficulty in finding consensus on educational policy is the confusion in American society about issues of loyalty, about how families and communities relate to individuals and government. Problems about loyalty have been inherent in the American experiment from the beginning—in the necessary tensions between conflicting loyalties to self, family, friends, church, ethnic group, employer, and government. We have coasted for many decades on formulas for relating these elements that, regardless of how well they may have worked in the past, must now be reexamined in order to develop an educational policy that will deal effectively with the issues of the decades ahead.

The beginnings of this reexamination are now under way with new policy thinking about the family. But family policy, while beginning to break from the service-delivery mentality of the past, is becoming trapped in its own type of economic and social science determinism that places students and parents in the position of help-less victims. In the chapters that follow we will examine how this determinism has developed, how it can be escaped, and how the relationship between families, individuals, and communities of various types must be taken into account in restructuring educa-tional policy in terms of partnerships based on voice, choice, and loyalty.

16 FAMILIES AS VICTIMS

> The family is emerging as a key symbol in an ongoing assault on institutions and professions . . . a continuation of Romantic mutinies against a modern professionalized service society.
>
> Joseph Featherstone, "Family Matters"

Among the most important social policy developments of the last two decades has been the renewal of interest in the family as a social institution—the willingness to rely on the family rather than ignore or supersede it because of its presumed weaknesses. Curiously, this important shift in social thinking has had little effect on educational policy or practice. Even though education is one of the most prominent factors in family life and family life is a major factor in education, most of the recent studies on the family have little to recommend on educational policy.

This chapter examines how recent family policy studies, like recent thinking about equality, steer us away from sound thinking about education and how a different approach is needed to arrive at effective educational policy.

THE SHIFT IN POLICY REGARDING FAMILIES

In 1903 Charlotte Perkins Gilman wrote in her study *The Home: Its Work and Influence:*

163

There is no more brilliant hope on earth today than this new thought about the child . . . the recognition of "the child," children as a class, children as citizens with rights to be guaranteed only by the state; instead of our previous attitude toward them of absolute personal ownership [by their parents]—the unchecked tyranny, or as unchecked indulgence, of the private home. . . . Civilization and Christianity teach us to care for "the child," motherhood stops at "my child."[1]

Social policy theorists such as Gilman had concluded that the American family, beset by urbanization and modernization, was disintegrating and could no longer be trusted to care for itself or its children. Ellen Richards, a leader in the professionalization of social work, argued that the school was "fast taking the place of the home, not because it wishes to do so, but because the home does not fulfill its function. . . . If the State is to have good citizens . . . we must begin to teach the children in our schools, and begin at once, that which we see they are no longer learning in the home."[2]

Not all American social policy has been as aggressively social service oriented as that of Gilman and Richards, but a good deal of it, from the turn of the century onward, has tended to look on the family as a source of weakness rather than strength and has turned to social agencies—mostly governmental, bureaucratic, and professional —to make up for failings in the family.

An important shift away from this antifamily posture is in progress. Christopher Lasch, in *Haven in a Heartless World: The Family Besieged*, quotes Gilman and Richards with disapproval. Lasch echoes many other scholars and authors of liberal, conservative, and radical persuasions in rejecting the view of the family as an institution that produces "misfits, emotional cripples, juvenile delinquents, and potential criminals" and that, therefore, needs to be displaced by professional and governmental child-rearing agencies.[3]

The recent trend away from this sort of social service imperialism has obvious implications for educational policy, especially since the newer thinkers see the schools as being among the most "imperialist" of social agencies, guilty of "disfranchising,"[4] "monopolizing,"[5] "invading,"[6] and "denigrating"[7] the family. Their views on the harm done to children by ineffective schools and insensitive educators is often eloquent and biting.

It is odd, then, that the major family policy studies in recent years have had so little to recommend about to educational policy. To understand this, we have to review some of the history of how "the family" has come to be included on the current social policy agenda.

THE MOYNIHAN REPORT

A shift in social policy toward a more positive view of the family had an unhappy beginning in the 1960s. Daniel Patrick Moynihan, then assistant U.S. secretary of labor, wrote an internal memorandum about the "crumbling" Negro family.[8] The Negro family, he said, was strangled by a "tangle of pathology," which produced all sorts of social ills, including unemployment, crime, illegitimacy, and poor school achievement. He decided that government intervention was needed "to strengthen the Negro family so as to enable it to raise and support its members as do other families."[9]

This famous Moynihan report, written in March 1965, was not initially released to the public. Moynihan's intended impact was inside the government "at the highest levels," and in this intent he was successful.[10] On June 4, 1965, at Howard University, President Johnson delivered a notable speech, "To Fulfill These Rights," in which he highlighted "the breakdown of the Negro family structure" as perhaps the "most important" national social problem, "its influence radiating to every part of life." He called the family "the cornerstone of our society" and put forth the call to "work to strengthen the family."[11] Moynihan helped to write the speech, which was clearly based on his earlier memorandum.

As the measures needed to "fulfill these rights," the president (and Moynihan) recommended the same remedies now being put forth, fifteen years later, by various panels and commissions on the family; namely, more jobs, better income, improved housing, and welfare "designed to hold families together." After initial positive responses to the president's speech, however, the Moynihan report itself, when released during the summer of 1965, became the target of the most scathing political attack, not from conservatives who feared that it might expand the welfare state, but from blacks and liberals.[12]

The main criticism was that Moynihan had singled out the Negro family for his eloquent description of "pathology," "collapse," "disorganization" and the resultant crime, ignorance, illegitimacy, unemployment, and other undesirable social consequences. The report (officially titled *The Negro Family: The Case for National Action*) became public just as the riots in the Watts section of Los Angeles were reawakening consciousness of race issues throughout the country, and very soon it was branded "racist"—a label that has plagued the report and its author ever since.

Were not many white families also "pathological"? And were there not many black families as stable and responsible as many white families? Why, then, single out black families? The report itself said that "a considerable number of Negro families have managed to break out of the tangle of pathology and to establish themselves as stable, effective units,"[13] but that did not save it from attack. Nor did it save the movement toward a more profamily social policy from several years of distraction as the battle raged over the charge of racism in the Moynihan report.

If the racial aspects of the Moynihan controversy could have been brushed aside by agreeing that the problem was surely not just a problem for black families, perhaps social policy could have focused a little sooner on the importance of the family as such, but, once the issue had been made one of race, the debate shifted to thrusts and counterthrusts about the black family. The ensuing squabble distracted attention from important issues about the role families play in social life, and, in particular, how they interact with schools.[14]

Unfortunately, the debates over the Moynihan report came just as educational policy was also being influenced by the Coleman report, which was widely interpreted (by Moynihan among others) to show that family background was the prime factor in school failure.[15] The impression left from the combination of the Coleman report, with its emphasis on home factors, and the Moynihan report, with its talk about "the tangle of pathology" of Negro families and their effect "on the school performance of Negro youth growing up with little knowledge of their fathers," was that the problems of school failure by poor black children was one of well-nigh insuperable social pathologies—conditions far beyond the reach of educational policy or school practice. This mindset was deeply entrenched by the time the new family studies began to appear in the mid-1970s.

NEW APPROACHES TO THE FAMILY

By the mid-1970s new thinking about the family began to show up in various studies and commission reports. Mary Jo Bane came out in 1976 with *Here to Stay,* a strong assertion that the family was alive and strong in America, not "crumbling" and not fading away under either the weight of its problems or the onslaught of "social service imperialism." Bane presented data undermining a number of the "myths" on which intrusive social services were based:

> The extended family is not, in fact, declining; it never existed. Family disruption has not increased but has only changed character. The proportion of children living with at least one parent has gone up, not down. The increased proportion of children living in single parent families results to a great extent from mothers keeping their children instead of farming them out. Mothers have changed the location and character of their work, but there is no evidence that this harms children. Nor is there any evidence that contemporary families have fewer neighbors and friends to call on for help and companionship now than in the past.[16]

While this description may understate the problems families face in modern society, the basic policy conclusion Bane draws from her analysis is increasingly accepted as correct: until social "programs are designed to incorporate the very real and very strong values that underlie family life in America, and until they are perceived as doing so, they are doomed to failure."[17]

Most of the more recent family studies have adopted this point of view of emphasizing family strengths instead of family weaknesses. The Carnegie Council on Children reminds us that "98 percent of American children grow up in families now and are likely to do so in the future."[18] Richard deLone, the council's associate director, argues that efforts by social agencies to "stand in for family functions are poor substitutes for families" in many cases.[19]

These changed perspectives by themselves could have led to major rethinking of educational policy, but they were joined by an outlook even more pregnant with implications for changes in school policy: the idea that some of the family's loss of functions and responsibility in modern society is due to overzealous "helping professionals" and social service bureaucracies. Christopher Lasch is particularly eloquent on this point:

> With the rise of the helping professions in the first three decades of the twentieth century, society in the guise of a nurturing mother invaded the family, the stronghold of those private rights, and took over many of its functions. The diffusion of the new ideology of social welfare had the effect of a self-fulfilling prophecy. By persuading the housewife, and finally even her husband as well, to rely on outside technology and the advice of outside experts,

the apparatus of mass tuition—the successor to the church in a secularized society—undermined the family's capacity to provide for itself and thereby justified the continuing expansion of health, education, and welfare services.[20]

"The history of modern society, from one point of view," says Lasch, "is the assertion of social control over activities once left to individuals or their families"—a process that has had a "shattering impact . . . —the impact of the so-called helping professions—on the family."[21]

Richard deLone's *Small Futures,* a study done for the Carnegie Council on Children, devotes a whole chapter to "Help That Can Hurt." He discusses how dependence is encouraged by welfare, how the child-care system places children "at the mercy of the state," and how the present educational system results in "the reproduction of social inequality." Elsewhere in the book he describes the creation of the public school system in the nineteenth century as a case in which "public policy seized upon the child as the place to resolve the tensions of liberal capitalism," and he sees the Progressive reform at the turn of the century as helping to "transform education from a process of interaction between teacher and learner into a problem of instructional management."[22]

Kenneth Keniston, chairman of the Carnegie Council, likewise describes the acceptance of public schooling in the nineteenth century as an "inroad on traditional family functions," which "began to replace family education rather than assist it," and complains of the social institutions that put down parents and "sap their self-esteem and power."[23]

As Joseph Featherstone has pointed out, many modern critics see "government, bureaucracy, and the professions as the enemy, and the family as the victim of intrusive power of the centralized state."[24] This theme of the "family as victim" is clearly a reaction against the "family as villain" message seen in the Moynihan and Coleman reports and the accompanying "don't-blame-us" attitude of educators.

This new focus on the strength of families and the disempowering effects of the "helping professions" could well have led to strong recommendations for changes in school policy. But it did not. Astonishingly, despite all their astute analysis of the debilitating effects of modern social service bureaucracies, many of the leading thinkers in this area and two of the main national policy panels—the Carnegie Council on Children and the National Academy of Sciences panel on family policy—avoid any serious discussion of educational policy and any significant proposals for education reform.

The Carnegie Council's *All Our Children* announces that it "deliberately omitted a discussion of the importance of public education in the lives of children."[25] *Small Futures,* the special report by Richard deLone, which the council originally announced would go into the problems of education more fully, declines to "enter these mazes" of the "governance, accountability, staffing, programming, funding, and coordination" of social service systems like schools.[26] It makes almost no recommendations on school policy. The National Academy's *Toward a National Policy for Children and Families* frankly says that it gives "only passing attention" to issues such as "inadequate education," which it admits "deserve serious attention in view of their impact on families and children."[27]

How has it come about that these powerful thinkers and prestigious panels on family policy have almost nothing to say about educational policy? There are two problems, and they are related. In the first place, the main conclusion of these studies is that the preeminent problems facing families and children are economic and the basic remedies needed are increased employment and a redistribution of income, rather than changes in social institutions like schools. Second, the social determinism that sees families as the helpless pawns of an unjust economic system has an effect similar to that of the service-delivery mentality in keeping parents and students in a passive role with respect to social policy—a role that makes effective educational change impossible.

Lasch, despite his biting irony about the "helping professions," ends up emphasizing the "heartlessness" of our economic and social system as the major source of problems and the major area for social policy reform. The Carnegie Council on Children and the National Academy of Sciences, armed with impressive data and analysis, reach the same conclusion: it is the economic and social structures of society, rather than institutions like schools, that must be changed. Kenneth Keniston epitomizes this focus on economic reform to the exclusion of educational reform when he says that liberal reforms "have failed in their lofty goals. . . . the inequalities that spurred reform in the first place . . . simply cannot be altered by education."

> For well over a century, we Americans have believed that a crucial way to make our society more just was by improving our children. We propose instead that the best way to ensure more ample futures for our children is to start with the difficult task of building a more just society.[28]

There is in this thinking clear evidence of the continued baleful influence of the Coleman-Moynihan thesis. The Carnegie Council's assumption that "family income, parental education, race," etc., are the factors that "appear to determine most of the differences among children in school performance" certainly contributes to its disposition not to look closely into why schools do not work for so many children and what might be done about it.[29] But these reports also reveal a deeply entrenched social and economic determinism of their own that virtually blocks any possibility of seeing educational change as a route to equality or social improvement.

In describing the injustices of our economic and social system, deLone says that unemployment "correlates strongly with mental illness, family breakup, and child abuse" and that unemployed parents can "communicate feelings of futility and worthlessness to their children."[30] Lasch says that "the growing child experiences poverty through the intermediary of his parents, and the quality of that mediation unavoidably influences his psychic development."[31] He points out that middle-class as well as ghetto youth suffer from a "personality structure" that has failed "to internalize parental authority" and has been adversely affected by "the general deterioration of the social environment."[32] He says we must recognize "the ways in which poverty and racism reverberate in every area of life, embedding themselves in cultural patterns and personality and thus perpetuating themselves from one generation to the next."[33]

Lasch, deLone, and the others would deny that they "blame the victim."[34] They intend, instead, to blame the social system for an unfair distribution of income. Nevertheless, whether fault is conceived to lie in the "depravity" of the poor, as presumed by many nineteenth-century social theorists, or in the "pathologies" of the poor, as assumed by twentieth-century liberal reformers, or in the "stacked deck" of social and economic injustice, as assumed by the more recent critics, the result, from an educational point of view, is much the same: families that produce children who are not expected to succeed in school.

Children afflicted with "mental illness," "feelings of futility and worthlessness," and "personality structures" that have failed to "internalize parental authority" and children whose "psychic development" has been affected by "poverty and racism" are clearly not going to be seen as promising students. The school, therefore, is not a focus for reform. Even if families are not blamed for these pathologies, they become the source of school failure.[35] The deterministic trap is reentered, except that now the problem is further removed from the realm of educational policy, since the culprits in school failure are remote, impersonal social and economic forces.

Recent social policy analysis on the family, therefore, like the policy thinking about inequality to which it is closely related, introduces a kind of double determinism: schools cannot do anything to improve education because the problem is with the families, and families cannot do anything to improve education because their fate is determined by the social and economic system.

So much care is taken not to blame the victim that individuals and families are in danger of being stripped of all responsibility. And, while policy planners may genuinely want families empowered and may hope that this can be achieved in some future just society, their arguments tend to disempower families in the here and now by treating them as helpless victims in the grip of social and economic influences.

Richard deLone is not unaware of what he himself calls "the error of determinism." He says we must not see the child as a "passive creature," the product of genes and environment, with little active, autonomous participation in his or her own development."[36] Rather, the "individual actor, the child, must be considered" if we are to escape from determinism. But then deLone does a curious thing. When we look at this thesis to discover how the child can be an "autonomous" participant, we find more determinism. According to deLone, the "crucial new variable" that the child as "an important actor" introduces is "his or her own theory of social reality," providing "a kind of diagram of the social universe, including his or her location in it, as well as a kind of map of his or her likely future." This map serves as a "feedback loop in a self-steering process" that "in turn helps guide the child's own development."[37] Where does this "map," or "feedback loop," come from? From "the experiences characteristic of different social class and racial situations, plus the history of the group to which an individual belongs," and this provides the child "with information that is given beyond the child's control."[38]

In demonstrating his theory, deLone recounts an interview with Joseph, a black second grader living with his mother, who is a lunchroom worker. "If Joseph could read the statistics he would know that his chances for a professional job are slim; indeed the army is a fairly high career aspiration, given the history of his race and the odds facing the child of a single parent whose own earnings are limited."[39]

So much for escaping from determinism. This approach to policy leads to what Featherstone has noted as "the prevailing defeatist intellectual fashion in education"—an attitude that leaves policy planners "resigned to the limits of what schools can do compared with the changes in the realms of jobs, housing, and health care."[40]

There is a correlation between the disempowering nature of deterministic social policy and the disempowering tendencies of the service-delivery approach to social services. In both, people are treated as passive receivers, either of social forces or of social services. These pawn-people are not seen as possible initiators of action or generators of value. They could not become, in such a policy framework, empowered partners in the educational process.

Recent family policy studies offer powerful arguments for social and economic justice for families. The Carnegie Council on Children and the National Academy of Sciences speak for many concerned Americans when they say that too many people are poor and helpless, their lives blighted, their children poorly educated, and their lack of opportunity a threat to the entire society.

Nevertheless, to be reminded that society is unjust gives little guidance about another basic problem: what to do about schools. These reports have virtually nothing to say about how schools should be run, what should be taught, how teaching can be improved, how schools should be paid for, who should control educational decisions, or, most urgently, why education for poor children is so rotten and what can be done about it. Not only is educational policy neglected, but the deterministic orientation of these reports seriously undermines effective educational policy making. These reports come perilously close to saying, "Poor children do poorly in school; therefore, to improve education for the poor, we must first abolish poverty." This kind of deterministic thinking must be laid aside before any sense can be made out of educational policy or family policy or the relationship between the two. How can it be overcome?

EDUCATIONAL EQUALITY VERSUS SOCIAL AND ECONOMIC EQUALITY

One can indeed argue that as long as social and economic inequality exist, there will never be· educational equality. Millionaires will always be able to provide a better education for their children than poor people. Even if all schools were "equal," the rich could still hire tutors, provide their children with the benefits of travel, and give them an abundance of enriching early childhood and home experiences.

At the same time, educational equality can and must be separated from social equality to arrive at sound educational policy. The ability to read and think, and access to the literature, science, art, and history of one's own culture and that of others, provide a kind of equality quite apart from whether they lead to economic or social advancement for the individual or change the class or economic structure of society as a whole. And in many cases they clearly do lead to improved economic and social status.

Just as a good education is no substitute for an adequate income, so a decent income is no substitute for an education.[41] Families and children need both. One way to escape from the determinist and defeatist attitude toward education in recent family policy is to recognize the distinction between educational equality and economic equality. To achieve educational quality and equality we must look at educational issues and understand what will and will not contribute to productive learning relationships for children. This in no way detracts from the need for social and economic justice or from the relationship between economics and education; it only prevents these concerns from distracting attention from the need for changes in education.

THE LIMITS OF SOCIAL SCIENCE

Another step in overcoming the double determinism that renders both schools and families helpless is to separate social science from social policy. They are not the same. Social science can only analyze what is; social policy is an effort to determine what ought to be. In deciding what ought to be, it is well to be guided by what is, but the "is" can never supply the "ought." Some of the problems of recent policy analysis come from this ancient confusion between empirical and normative thought, and nowhere is the confusion more dangerous than in education. To develop social policy, present reality must be matched against human values, aspirations, and initiatives, which social science cannot determine.

Particularly prominent in the analysis used by the Carnegie Council and the National Academy of Sciences, and particularly dangerous for education, is the preeminent tool of social science—probability. Probability can only tell us what happens "in most cases"—for "most families," for "most children from poor families"—or what "the odds" are of escaping conditions that make it "probable that an individual's experience will be bounded by the historical requirements of a class."[42]

Educational policy can take account of statistical probabilities, but its values cannot be based on them. In education, of all places, policy must be based on indeterminacy, not determinism; on futures, not pasts; on people's potential, not their "probable" limitations.

The reality described in recent family analyses is entirely plausible as a *statistical probability:* this is what happens on the average. But, as deLone admits, "there is major difference between what is probable and what is strictly determined."[43] Statistical probability is the wrong basis for educational policy. Joseph, the lunchroom worker's son, did not need to "read the statistics" to know "the odds" against him in our society; yet we would not want either Joseph or his teachers to guide their learning or teaching on the basis of these "odds."

Keniston, like deLone, recognizes the difference between the probable and the strictly determined. The "most vital endowments" that can be given to children, he says, "are those of the body, mind, and spirit," and he acknowledges that birth into a poor family "by no means irrevocably dooms a child to social judgments of infirmity, stupidity, or demoralization—there are millions of witnesses to the contrary." At the same time, the basis of his policy orientation is that poverty "makes all three of these outcomes [infirmity, stupidity, or demoralization] *more likely*" (emphasis added) and that redistribution of income must, therefore, be the priority in social policy.[44]

Educational policy, and family policy as it relates to education, must proceed in exactly the opposite direction, basing their strategies and programs not on the "more likely" outcomes of poverty but on the possibility of exceptions, like the "millions of witnesses" who do gain an education and who are provided with "endowments of body, mind, and spirit" by their families despite their poverty. Educational policy must be based on positive assumptions of what schools and families can do.

The trap of determinism can be avoided, in other words, simply by rejecting it. Determinism is an artifact of the mind, a habit of thought that is particularly well nourished by the methods of social science. It is legitimate for certain intellectual purposes but lethal for education. Determinism has no place in teaching children or in establishing school policy.

Specifically, social determinism overlooks three types of empowerment involved in the educational process: the power of education itself, the power of individuals, and the power of families.

THE POWER OF EDUCATION

The deterministic outlook sees education as part of the "cultural apparatus" that "reproduces in its members" the existing class structure.[45] Social science describes here what education "is" for "most" children in our society. But this perspective gives no indication of what education can and ought to be; therefore, it cannot be the basis for educational policy. Education, when properly carried out, has a power of its own—the power to free the mind, regardless of the shackles of class or race. Learning how to use their minds intelligently, informed by the accumulated wisdom of human culture, may not guarantee people jobs as bank presidents or equalize their incomes; it can, however, empower them to think effectively for themselves, a power that lies at the base of individual freedom and initiative.

Education can enable people to develop a "theory of social reality" different from that "given" by their social class experience. Education opens new worlds for people, introduces them to ideas and human experience not part of their daily lives and family backgrounds. Richard deLone is simply incorrect in saying that education "cannot alter the developmental situation from 'within the child'—that is—cannot alter significantly and systematically the process by which an individual constructs a social theory of reality and participates in his or her own development."[46] He has, in fact, described one of the main purposes of education in a free society. The fact that many (most?) schools *do not educate* in this sense provides an agenda for educational change, not an excuse for defeatist educational policy guided by scientific determinism. To base educational policy on the probabilities of social science is but another way to institutionalize low expectations.

THE POWER OF INDIVIDUALS

The determinist tends to disregard individual exceptions since his science proves that "most" poor children cannot expect to succeed. Why not? Because they are poor. Determinism always ends where it begins. *Most* poor children may end their school days uneducated ‚at the present time, but nothing in social science says that any particular individual must remain ignorant, or even that most must remain ignorant forever. Individual human beings have remarkable resilience and initiative. Despite the most adverse environments and experiences, the human mind and spirit can accomplish remarkable things. It happens too often to be discounted as unrealistic that the child who is a hopeless failure in one setting becomes a productive student and citizen in another.

The proper framework for education is to look at people as individuals able to learn instead of abstractions defined by the probabilities of poverty and ignorance. The "venerable cultural myth that each individual is a master of his fate" may seem a dangerous "misconception" from the point of view of social science, as deLone claims,[47] but it is exactly the perspective required for educational policy that does not disempower students and render them passive and inert recipients of unsuccessful "service delivery."

One of the characteristics of students measured in the Coleman study was their "feelings of control of their environment." The data showed that "at least in parts of the country, Negro pupils are more likely than white pupils to be exposed to fellow students who have feelings of powerlessness over their environment."[48] Educational policy based on probabilities accepts feelings of powerlessness as a fact for poor and minority children. But effective educational policy must appeal to that potential in every individual to assume control over his own fate. As Erik Erikson has pointed out, "The process of American identity formation seems to support an individual's ego identity as long as he can preserve a certain element of deliberate tentativeness of autonomous choice. The individual must be able to convince himself that the next step is up to him."[49]

THE POWER OF FAMILIES

Finally, determinism leaves out the power of families as generators of value and initiative. In the deterministic view, families, like schools, are mechanisms for the transmission of the existing social system. Families are one of the vehicles through which children form their "inner maps of the social world," which are seen as such powerful "determinants of their aspirations . . . self-images, . . . and their real futures."[50]

Families do have a powerful influence in setting values, which are sometimes negative and sometimes positive. There are too many cases to ignore in which the single mother, poor and disadvantaged, is a powerful positive influence on her children, giving them the self-confidence and motivation to learn and become successful adults. Positive values are clearly more difficult to impart when poverty and social decay weigh upon a family, but they must not be seen as impossible, or even improbable, in educational policy.

Even social science's probabilities cannot document that "most" poor families are incapable of providing positive reinforcement for their children. We do not know what most families would do if decent and effective education were available to all children and families were given the opportunity to play responsible roles in supporting it. These conditions do not now exist. The "delivery" of educational services has not only provided grossly unequal educational experiences for different children but has also deemphasized responsible roles for parents. The way in which families are seen in the deterministic outlook for policy dominated by social science may be very different from the way they would actually behave under educational policies based on different principles. The following chapter explores the role of families seen not as helpless victims of social and economic forces but as partners in the educational process—partners whose productive involvement depends on the proper balance of voice, choice, and loyalty.

17 FAMILIES AS PARTNERS

In real life, parents are not helpless, voiceless victims.

Sara Lawrence Lightfoot, *Worlds Apart*

Public educational policy has been paralyzed, as the survey of chapters 13–15 revealed, with two important routes to fundamental change—community control (voice) and family control (choice)—leading in opposite directions. I suggested that resolution of this dilemma required a reexamination of the role of families and communities and how they relate to each other (loyalty). In chapter 16 I discussed recent rethinking in regard to the family but found it unhelpful for educational policy because of its deterministic perspective. If families are to play an active role in education, they cannot be seen either as the helpless pawns of blind economic and social forces or as abstractions in ideological or scientific theories, no matter how progressive or well intended. The view of the family that is useful for educational policy runs counter to this "helpless victim" image and sees the family as an important institution, with values and resources both unappreciated and underutilized in current policy.

THE FAMILY AS EDUCATOR

Educational research has begun to focus on the importance of the family as educator.[1] It is now being recognized that much of what a child needs to know, both before and during the school years, is learned in the family. Schools have their own special contribution to make, but they share with the family the teaching and learning of basic language, cognitive framework, self-concept, and social skills.

The role of the family as a transmitter of values to children is also receiving more attention. Whether the values transmitted are seen as too authoritarian or permissive or as the conduits of ignorance or undesirable social mores, families nevertheless have a powerful influence on the values of their children, and in our kind of society they have a right to have such influence within very broad limits. Furthermore, this role is increasingly recognized as important for educational success and social development. Children without a value base derived from the family are more vulnerable to anomie and mental illness, even if at some point they rebel against their upbringing.

The implications of these new views are that a sound educational policy requires seeing the family as a resourceful, primary partner in the educational process. Frank Riessman was one of the pioneers in urging that educational policy be based on the strength rather than the cultural deprivation of students and their families.[2] Others, such as Sara Lawrence Lightfoot, Hope Leichter, Donald Erickson, Lawrence Cremin, and Benjamin Bloom, have made similar arguments.[3] If families have weaknesses and problems, and many certainly do, be they poor, middle class, or rich, there is no real choice in most cases except to build on their strengths so that they can participate as partners in achieving the educational goals virtually all families share with the rest of society.

VICTIMS, VILLAINS, OR PARTNERS

An immediate advantage of the partnership concept for education is the assistance it provides in escaping the dilemma of whom to blame for educational failure. The service-delivery concept of education makes families either victims or villains. When learning does not take place, the client can blame the provider, and the provider can blame the client. In modern education the provider has had the upper hand, and both the power and motive to blame the family— sometimes with "benign" intent ("We'll educate you regardless of your culturally backward family") and sometimes with malign intent ("We cannot educate you because of your culturally backward family"). As parents have become more frustrated and politically active, they have tried to turn the tables and blame the educators for not providing their children with an education.

Arguing about whom to blame is an unproductive enterprise. Both perspectives have validity; families are weakened and disempowered by current social conditions and by social service bureaucracies. At the same time, families are not by nature perfect, and in many cases they do not provide the healthy socialization, nurturing, ego development, early learning experiences, and support for learning that help make schooling successful.

A stalemate caused by mutual recrimination for failure is unnecessary. The partnership concept provides a more productive framework. It can recognize the problems facing families without rendering them powerless.

RESISTANCE TO FAMILIES AS PARTNERS

Shifting to a partnership policy in education will not be easy. Most schools and school systems, like many other institutions, still operate on the premise of the irrelevance or weakness of the family. Most, perhaps unwittingly, are still agents of what Mary Jo Bane calls "social service imperialism". The family's role is seen as little more than that of producing children and feeding, housing, and clothing them so that they can go to school. Educational policy has been *school* policy; families might be the concern of social workers or priests, but not of educators. Many habits of both mind and practice must change before educational policy can fully incorporate an understanding of the family as an important participant in education.

Sara Lawrence Lightfoot describes how present social policy has "created a conceptual dichotomy of the child's existence into socialization and education, the one shaped by the family and the other by the school." Such a separation not only "permits researchers to neglect the process of socialization within the schools and education within families" but causes them to neglect the "relatedness" of schools and families. She points out how this puts policy at odds with reality. Her observations and interviews with hundreds of parents and teachers confirm that in the real world "the issue of family-school relationships" is a "dominant theme in the lives and experiences of parents, teachers and children" and a major factor affecting educational effectiveness and legitimacy.[4]

Both educators and parents, however, have a tendency to preserve the dichotomy between home and school, harmful though it may be. It is more comfortable to live with a policy that permits mutual recrimination than to assume mutual responsibility. As long as education is seen as a service to be delivered, educators can concentrate on perfecting the delivery mechanism, regardless of its results, and parents can focus on how educators are failing to deliver the desired product.

Even for those who want to strengthen the ties between home and school, the relationships have become more complex and difficult than they were when parents had more control over child raising and school was less important. For parents to send their child to the local schoolmarm for a few hours a day in the winter months to learn the three R's was very different from today's parents dispatching their child six hours a day, nine months a year, to an institution over which they have little control and which purports to provide not only an academic education but guidance on how to deal with drugs, sex, driving, and sometimes even death. In addition to the official curriculum, the school's social and peer culture provide powerful influences that many parents find foreign, if not repugnant, to the values they wish to pass on to their children.

One way educators have responded to the difficulties of educational relationships in modern society is by retreating into their separate world of professional service delivery—to *serve* families but not to *collaborate* with them. For their part, parents often try to avoid the problem either by withdrawing from the hassles of trying to relate to the school or by withdrawing their children from the public schools altogether. It should be clear by now that we have paid a heavy price in social alienation and educational failure for these disengagements between family and school.

The partnership concept does not avoid the tensions and value differences between schools and families, since they are inevitable in human relationships, but it does provide a better framework for dealing with them. It makes withdrawal more difficult, but it also acknowledges that education is an uneasy partnership.

AN UNEASY PARTNERSHIP

Tensions and potential conflicts are inherent in educational partnerships because schools and families play different roles. The first step in forging successful school-family partnerships is to recognize that families and schools are different social institutions with different value systems and different types of loyalties.

In her book on the family, *Here to Stay*, Mary Jo Bane addresses the tensions between family values and the values of public institutions such as schools. "Equal treatment," for instance,

> implies an ethic wherein all men and women do unto others as others do unto them; strangers and brothers are treated similarly; and people are judged by what they do rather than what they are. Family loyalty follows quite different principles, treating people on the basis of special relationships, compatibility, and affection. Family members make no pretense of treating each other equally or of treating strangers the same as themselves.[5]

Others have noted these differences in home and school values as well. J.W. Getzels refers to the "discontinuities in value codes and language codes" between families and schools.[6] David Tyack has described the "growing dissonance" between school systems and various groups of families as the country became urbanized and more culturally pluralistic.[7] To some extent the whole "revisionist" school of educational history can be seen as describing the conflict between the values of school systems and the values of students and families.

Sara Lawrence Lightfoot, in *Worlds Apart*, sees discontinuities and conflicts as "endemic to the very nature of the family and the school as institutions, and they are experienced by all children as they traverse the path from home to school." In describing the sociological perspective, she summarizes the perceived differences between the two worlds as follows:

> In families, the interactions are *functionally diffuse* in the sense that the participants are intimately and deeply connected and their rights and duties are

all-encompassing and taken for granted. In schools, the interactions are *functionally specific* because the relationships are more circumscribed and defined by the technical competence and individual status of the participants. . . . There are contrasts between the *primary relationships* of parents and children and the *secondary relationships* of teacher and children. . . . Children in the family are treated as special persons, but pupils in school are necessarily treated as members of categories.[8]

She speaks of the "struggles . . . waged daily as parents and teachers argue (often silently and resentfully) about who should be in control of the child's life in school," with the result that teachers often end up seeing the "parent-mass as a threatening force" against which they join together "in fear (and disdain) . . . for institutional support to protect their interests."[9]

To the extent that the public educational ideology of rationality, abstract fairness, objectivity, and professionalism has become the secular religion of our society, family-type values can be seen as heresy. The psychological and political conflicts that develop at times take on the flavor of religious wars. The battles over textbooks in West Virginia, Indiana, or Long Island—or over sex education almost anywhere—show how emotional such confrontations can become.[10]

The pervasiveness of tensions underlying school-family relations can be seen in the fundamental dilemmas that have plagued educational policy makers for years: Should children conform to schools, or schools to children? Are schools assisting families in educating their children, or are families assisting schools? Do children belong to their families or to society as a whole? Who should make the final decision when a conflict arises between school and family on sex education, discipline, text books, or curriculum?

These questions arise from two quite different educational perspectives, which must be accepted and synthesized in effecting educational partnerships—the same two perspectives, indeed, that were discussed earlier as giving rise to the divergence between voice and choice and between the public and private aspects of education. One perspective sees proper socialization and education of its children primarily as a social function, necessary for society's survival. As this perspective was expressed by Horace Mann,

> the society of which we necessarily constitute a part, must be preserved; and in order to preserve it, we must not look merely to what one individual or family needs, but to what the whole community needs; not merely to what

one generation needs, but to the wants of a succession of generations. . . . They who refuse to train up children in the way they should go, are training up incendiaries and madmen to destroy property and life, and to invade and pollute the sanctuaries of society.[11]

The other perspective views the education of children primarily as the responsibility of parents, who have a "fundamental human right . . . to make a world for" their children.[12] In this view, the process of educating one's children, or at least of directly controlling those who educate them, is an important part of "making a world" for them. For the state to "usurp" this function deprives families of their basic rights and breaks the essential bonds that enable education to be effective and legitimate.

As pointed out earlier, each of these two contrasting, obviously oversimplified perspectives has some merit; yet neither alone can be accepted as showing the total picture. In our kind of society, children cannot be treated as the exclusive responsibility of either parents or the society as a whole. They are both the "nearest and dearest" possession of a family and the embodiment of society's future.

Since both the society and parents have a role in the education of children, they must act as partners despite the built-in tensions between them. The service-delivery or provider-client concept too easily permits the student to be seen as the responsibility either of, on the one hand, the parents (who can arrange for his education through public or private schools) or, on the other hand, of society as a whole (which undertakes to deliver whatever education it deems necessary for the social good). The partnership concept cannot discount either role. It recognizes the legitimacy of the two roles in the educational process. Accepting both roles necessarily entails accepting the potential for conflict between them, but it has the merit of forcing policy makers and practitioners to try to "design creative ways of living with both," as Bane urges.[13]

CREATIVE AND UNCREATIVE TENSIONS

Some of the discontinuities between family values and school values are productive; others are not. Distinctions and careful balancing is necessary for effective educational partnerships.

Too much dissonance, or discontinuity, between the values of the family and those of the school is likely to be unproductive. For example, Erik Erikson reports on the school experience of Dakota Indian children who, despite "intelligence . . . slightly above that of white children," nevertheless "withdraw from competitive activities" or, in some cases, refuse "to respond at all" in school. "To be asked to compete in class goes against the grain with the Dakota child, and he criticizes the competitive ones among his fellows," says one study, and "this difficulty, paired with the inability to speak English and fear of the white teacher, leads to frequent instances of embarrassed withdrawal or running away."[14] One does not have to go to the extreme of clashes between native American and white culture to find instances of students being virtually forced out of a productive learning relationship because of cultural discontinuities between student and school.[15]

Certain *types* of value clash are also likely to be unproductive. The bureaucratic values of the school cited in Part 1 and by Lightfoot, Bane, and others can be, and often are, carried to the point where effective learning partnerships are impossible. Teachers whose natural instincts properly lead them to want to reach their students on a human level constantly complain of being blocked by the bureaucratic ethos of their schools.

Differing school and home values can, however, be productive if properly blended. If schools were not different from homes, there would be no need for schools. Even bureaucratic values, usually missing at home, are important for inducting students into the more impersonal and abstract relationships of the public worlds of work, technology, law, and citizenship. Exposure to these values is one of the reasons parents send their children to school. They understand that school provides experiences in helping the child grow beyond the home. In school children encounter new values in a context more representative of public civility than the family can offer. In George Herbert Mead's terms, school is where children often receive their first intensive exposure to "generalized others."[16]

Such school-home differences need not lead to trauma. When teacher gives Johnny a *D* and mother comforts him with love, no fatal inconsistency is present; two different spheres of life may be operating, each quite properly in its own way. If one of the results of differences in values between home and school is "divided loyalties" —divided, for instance, between the more particularistic values of the home and the more universalistic values of the school—learning to live with such divided loyalties is a necessary part of modern living. Problems arise not from trying to live with both but from not learning how to live with both. The combined home-school experience is important for developing the skill to negotiate public and private worlds.

DEFICITS, STRENGTHS, AND DIFFERENCES

In relating schools to families, battles are often fought needlessly because quite different issues and circumstances are lumped together as if they all had to be decided by the same policy. Some people want schools to "assist" families in ways that other people call "usurpation" of family prerogatives. What to one is a useful element of civic education is to another an affront to deeply held religious or moral values. Some of these clashes are truly important and must be faced as differences in ideology or educational philosophy, but some are caused by the failure to distinguish between different kinds of problems in the relationships between families and schools. In particular, we must distinguish between situations of *deficit, strength,* and *cultural differences.* Failure to do so is one of the reasons we are in what James Conant has called "a rather mixed-up state of mind about the relation of the child, the parent, and the state."[17]

Consider the following situations:

In *Family A,* the father is absent, the mother an alcoholic; the eight children are seldom fed, clothed, or adequately cared for. The children live in one room with little opportunity to do homework. They have no sense that their mother has any expectations for them in school. They do poorly in school, and state officials think something should be done to make up for the *deficits* in the home life of the children.

Family B is poor, and the father is missing, but the mother has high educational aspirations for her children and keeps after them in regard to their homework. She speaks, however, with a heavy accent and is embarrassed to talk to the teachers about the trouble her children are having in school. The teachers feel there is nothing they can do, because the mother never comes to "open school night." The mother thinks the teachers do not respect her children because they are poor and look different from the other children. She does not know what to do about this. Although she does not explain it this way, she feels she has *strengths* that the school could use if she and the school could find a better relationship.

Family C has both father and mother and strong family values. The children have been good students in school and respectful both of their parents and of their teachers. Everything went smoothly in school until the oldest son entered high school. The school authorities have told the boy he is talented in math and science and should take the advanced classes and prepare for college. His parents, however, consider colleges dens of inquity; they want the boy to take a vocational course and use his math and science skills to learn an "honest trade," like auto mechanics. The boy is torn between two loyalties; he wants to follow the school's advice and go to college, but his parents forbid it, and he loves his parents. He is caught between real *cultural differences* between his family and his school.

Different categories of problems call for different policies. Family A has *real deficits*. We may dispute the kind of help needed, whether the children should be taken away from the mother or kept at home and given extra help. Some intervention, however, may be the only humane course. Family B has *real strengths*—the mother's aspirations for her children and her willingness to help if a productive relationship with the school could be established. The problem here is one of lost opportunity to use strengths, strengths that could help the school do its job. Family C, however, demonstrates *real differences*. What appear as strengths to the parents are seen as obstructions to education by the school authorities. Yet they cannot be described as deficits; there are differences between home and school purposes which the school must respect, try to overcome, or reconcile.

The educational policy landscape is full of real deficits, strengths, and differences. While sometimes what appears to one person as a strength will appear to another as a deficit and to yet another merely as a difference, there are many situations in which there could be agreement if school and home genuinely tried to work together. We do not have to choose once and for all in educational policy between policies based on deficit, strength, or the differences and apply one approach to every situation; the problem is to decide the approach appropriate to a given situation.

PARENTS AS PARTNERS

Parents clearly have a special role, and special rights, in the education of their children. Children are dependent for many years, during which someone must speak and choose for them. In tribal and traditional societies, where custom, ritual, and community consensus determine so much of human behavior, there is less need to decide who will perform this role on behalf of children. In modern society, however, where so many decisions must be made, both in daily living and in important life choices, someone must make these decisions for children, and for most areas of the child's life this responsibility is assigned to parents.

As modern societies become more complex and professionalized, the decision-making role of parents becomes even more complicated. The Carnegie Council on Children says that American parents have a "new job" in "choosing, meeting, talking with, and coordinating the experts, the technology, and the institutions that help bring up their children." The council refers to this as an "executive" function.[18] Richard deLone, in *Small Futures,* calls it the role of "managing partner."[19]

Whether parents are "executives" or "managing partners," they have great difficulty in playing this new role since, as the Carnegie Council points out, they have little authority over "those others with whom they share the task of raising their children."

> On the contrary, most parents deal with those others from a position of inferiority or helplessness. Teachers, doctors, social workers, or television producers possess more status than most parents. Armed with special credentials and a jargon most parents cannot understand, the experts are usually entrenched in their professions and have far more power in their institutions than do the parents who are their clients. . . .
>
> As a result, the parent today is usually a coordinator without voice or authority, a maestro trying to conduct an orchestra of players who have never met and who play from a multitude of different scores, each in a notation the conductor cannot read. If parents are frustrated, it is no wonder; for although they have the responsibility for their children's lives, they hardly ever have the voice, the authority, or the power to make others listen to them.[20]

DeLone emphasizes that "some parents are less able than others to play the role of managing partner effectively," because of "imbalances in power and status that may intimidate parents, making it difficult for them to penetrate the barriers of professional mystique and institutional obduracy that can turn meetings between professional service providers and poor clients into exercises in domination and frustration."[21] Anyone who has attended parent meetings will recognize this as a problem that, while it especially affects poor families, can apply to middle-class families as well.

For parents to fulfill their responsibilities in educational partnerships, they must be able to make their voices heard and their choices effective. If they feel something is wrong, they must be able to take appropriate action on behalf of their children, or the partnership is a sham. Likewise, even if nothing is "wrong," the voice and choice of the parent should be part of the educational equation. Jesse Jackson's technique in Operation Push of having parent and student sign a homework contract is a way of incorporating the commitment and loyalty of the parent in the learning partnership.[22]

STUDENTS AS PARTNERS

While parents speak and act for children in the years of youth's dependency, it is assumed that individuals can decide for themselves by the time they reach adulthood. The development of autonomy does not occur overnight on a child's eighteenth or twenty-first birthday; it develops continously as the child grows up. From an early age children begin increasingly to speak and choose for themselves on an ever-widening range of questions. Education can be interpreted as part of the process by which children find their own voice and learn to make their own choices.

A particularly important shift in perceptions of the family's role in education is recognition of its importance in the development of autonomy in children. Liberal thought for many years has treated the family as the source of narrow parochial values from which the child has to be "liberated" by the secular rationalism of modern education and culture. (This has been an important ideological justification for so-called social service imperialism in education.) While some of this perspective has validity for educational policy, autonomy is increasingly seen as linked with a strong family base. "The child's need to establish for himself a stable and self-respecting position in relation to the extended world is a commonplace of modern psychology." The family is viewed as a prime source of psychological strength and, therefore, as necessary for "acquiring fully autonomous morality."[23]

The argument for autonomy is not an argument for permissive child rearing or school policy. On the contrary, permissiveness, if it means letting children do whatever they want, is probably one of the worst ways to develop autonomy. Equally bad, however, is an educational policy that fails to provide for the continuous growth in a child's ability to speak, act, think, and choose independently.

The service-delivery model of education is a threat to this type of maturing autonomy. It discourages young people from assuming responsibility for their own learning. It promotes passive students, waiting for education to be delivered to them. Students, on the contrary, must be the preeminent partners in the learning process. If learning is the goal, the student is its prime producer. Children can be taught, but they cannot be "learned"; they themselves must learn. From the time infants begin to look around their cribs to make sense of their environment, their own mental processes are at work integrating experience and transforming it into meaning. Neither parent nor teacher can deliver learning to a child. Parents, teachers, peers, and anyone else involved in teaching bring stimuli, information, and context to which a child reacts and from which he or she selects. The activities of a school are but a specialized part of the environment in which children learn. These activities can be helpful, or unhelpful, in enabling the learner to integrate knowledge; but they are not learning. Only the learner can do the work of learning.

Even in traditional and "authoritarian" learning situations, successful learning has been a partnership. The hunter showing the neophtye how to use a bow or the blacksmith introducing the apprentice to his craft is involved in partnership with his student. A parent or a teacher may have varying degrees of authority over a child and may possess either substantive or procedural knowledge that the child does not possess, but unless the child joins in the learning process, no learning takes place.

The fact that the student must be in partnership with whoever is immediately teaching him is the most fundamental element in any educational policy, one that is easily forgotten in bureaucratized and professionalized educational service-delivery systems. Successful learning partnerships are intense with emotional interaction. The student and teacher need not love, or even like, each other, but their relationship is emotionally charged; their values and egos are constantly on the line. A learning partnership between teacher and student, once established, takes on a life of its own; it becomes a sizable reality to be recognized and respected by all others involved in the educational matrix.

In short, learning relationships involve powerful interactions between families and schools and complex loyalties among the key partners—students, parents, and teachers. Each of these prime participants in the educational process, however, also has loyalties that extend beyond family and school, to peers, neighborhood, church, ethnic group, political ideology, professional networks, and so on. Since in modern society loyalties are multiple and intricately related, the concept of partnership in education requires us to look at a context broader than the triangle of student, parents, and teacher.

18 NOT ALL IN THE FAMILY

The more one looks at the family the more it isn't there.

Hope Jensen Leichter, *Families and Communities as Educators*

We saw in the last chapter that learning partnerships involve powerful relationships between families and schools as well as complex interactions of voice, choice, and loyalty among the key partners—students, parents, and teachers. Any proposal for recasting American education that puts heavy emphasis on the family, however, must deal with some serious problems, none more perplexing than the elusiveness of the family itself.

Hope Jensen Leichter, an educator who has thought much about families and education, wrote in 1978 that the more she tried to focus on "the family" the more the concept tended to "disappear." One can start with individuals, she says, and see how various institutions affect their education or start with the school and see how it relates to individuals, families, and other institutions. But "the more one looks at the family, the more it isn't there."[1]

In terms of educational policy, what is one to make of a partner who "isn't there"? The disappearance of the family is precisely what many school officials cite as a major problem in today's education. Too often, from the school's point of view, either no stable family exists or the family seems to have willingly surrendered its child-

193

rearing responsibilities to the school. But a more useful perspective is to see that the socialization of children involves multiple influences in the nonacademic world. It is misleading to look for purely familial influences in isolation from the complex web of interacting loyalties of which the family is only a part. Assessments of the sources of a student's attitude toward school, authority, career, or other factors that affect learning must take account not only of the immediate family but also of friends, neighbors, church, the corner candy store, and a whole host of influences that make up the ethos of his community.

Even such intimate matters as how to feed and discipline children may be as much affected by the opinions of friends and neighbors as by family values. As a child grows up, outside influences increase and become more "public." Peer culture and television make it impossible for parents to keep their children in a completely private world of family. Few parents, in fact, want their children isolated from the larger world, even though influences outside parental control may produce acute anxieties.

With so much emphasis now being placed on the importance of the family in education, there is a danger of focusing on the immediate household to the exclusion of the full range of relationships that provide the value base for a child's socialization and education. Looked at in this broader context, an "intact" suburban family that has moved from place to place to follow a husband's career may have a more restricted human environment than a "broken home" in the ghetto, with a rich tapestry of neighbors, friends, fellow church members, and various "aunts" and "uncles."

The point here is not to romanticize ghetto family life or to ignore the real deficits that exist in many families of all classes. Rather, it is to suggest that an educational policy that promotes productive learning relationships for children must look at how the school relates not just to the immediate family but to the extended family, community, neighborhood, ethnic group, church, and other loyalties that provide the child with the world of meaning he or she brings to school.

An important educational difference between a ghetto child and his middle-class counterpart may not be so much that the former does not have a stable family as that his functional "family" has no relationship, or a negative relationship, with the school. It is this crucial perspective that tends to get lost if one focuses only on the immediate family and its deficits. As Leichter points out, "if one arbitrarily narrows the domain that one regards as education and the domain that one considers family, one creates blinders at every point." She urges "a more flexible paradigm" in order to see more clearly the family's role in education and its relationship to other forces and institutions.[2]

MEDIATING STRUCTURES AND EDUCATION

One way to broaden our view beyond the immediate family is through the concept of mediating structures. As described by Peter Berger and Richard Neuhaus in their monograph *To Empower People: The Role of Mediating Structures in Public Policy,* these "people-sized institutions" are seen as "value-generating and value-maintaining agencies in society," which stand "between the individual in his private life and the large institutions of public life."[3] Mediating structures include not only families, neighborhoods, churches, voluntary associations, and other traditional groups that play an important role in the lives of nearly all Americans but also nontraditional groups, such as communes and self-help organizations (for example, Alcoholics Anonymous), which are increasingly used by individuals to mediate between themselves and a "heartless" society.

Mediating structures have a powerful influence on education, both individually and in their interaction. Leichter analyzes how the family—still the prime mediating structure—"screens, interprets, criticizes, reinforces, compliments, counteracts, refracts, and transforms" school experiences, television, visits to museums or the zoo, or peer group experiences; in short, how it "mediates the educational experience of its members." She points out how the family has an especially strong influence because family membership goes on over time and the return to the family on a daily basis makes the family a critical locale for the discussion and interpretation of experiences that take place elsewhere."[4]

Despite its great importance however, the family "disappears" as a separate entity as a child grows and his value system comes to be influenced by a variety of other mediating structures interacting with each other. The multiple influences on a child make it difficult to separate the family as an isolated entity. As one study found, "parents simply do not have that much control over their children's development; too many other factors are influencing it."[5]

Next to the family, the mediating structure that has received the most attention from educators is the peer group. James Coleman has pointed out that just at the time when it becomes "more important that teenagers show a desire to learn, the developing adolescent culture shifts their interest further and further away from learning." Efforts to counter this influence often fail, not because parents or teachers are not available or do not care but because to take advantage of adult influences "the student must cut himself off from the activities of his friends, and in effect remove himself from the pursuits which would make him 'part of the crowd.'"[6]

Any parent or teacher of teenagers is familiar with the power of peer groups and knows that it is not just in extreme cases, such as the recent wave of conversions to religious cults, that teenagers find alternative mediating structures that are more influential than families or schools—and more influential *as educators.* Children *learn* a great deal from the "pursuits which make them 'part of the crowd.'"

Most of the emphasis on peer groups has been on their negative influence—their power to draw young people into drugs, promiscuous sex, or "hanging out" instead of studying. But educators and parents make a mistake if they focus only on the negative side. Even when the results are bad, the learning process is often impressive. The most exquisite application of effort, long practice, discipline, and constant correction from peers goes into learning how to make a good layup shot, master the latest dance step—or roll a reefer with proper aplomb. More benign examples of peer education include learning how to drive a car or behave in social situations. Some of the most powerful examples occur in peer tutoring of academic subjects, a technique greatly underutilized by educators.

Self-help groups based on peer influence were common in nineteenth-century America and helped educate many people who received little or no formal schooling. While he was still a slave, Frederick Douglass joined the East Baltimore Mental Improvement Society, and, despite his slave status, he was assigned "several times a prominent part in its debates." He later noted his educational debt "to the society of these young men."[7] The idea of self-help (which, by the way, usually means *mutual* help) is today gaining strength in society at large and among educators. The New York State Board of

Regents has announced an effort to encourage study circles, of the sort "popular in Sweden for many years, where more than one-third of the adult population is involved in this type of activity."[8]

Neighborhoods and networks of interconnecting families can also play an important part as mediating structures in education. Lawrence Cremin has pointed out that Bernard Bailyn, one of the most creative historians of education, overlooked this phenomenon in emphasizing the nuclear family in early New England education. Families may well have arrived from Europe and set up households as nuclear units of father, mother, and children, but within two or three generations most New England towns contained a significant network of family relationships linked to churches and other community institutions. These networks, as Cremin says, "go far in explaining the educative basis and power of the colonial New England community."[9]

Many modern neighborhoods have powerful networks of relationships among kin and friends that provide a context of meaning and values for those involved. Some of these do, and many more could, support effective educational partnerships both in school and in the community.

COMMUNITIES GREAT AND SMALL

Before settling on mediating structures as the only groups with important influences on education, it is necessary to realize that people also derive meaning and loyalty from membership in large groups, which go beyond family and other face-to-face relationships. The values derived from large-group loyalties can be as strong as those derived from the more intimate relationships of mediating structures. The person who overrides family ties in the name of religious beliefs, patriotism, or the "merit system" is pursuing values that operate on a different level from small-group loyalties. Large-group loyalties and values are often expressed in symbols and abstract systems of belief that can bind people together over wide boundaries of space and time.

The increased importance of large-group values and loyalties is one of the characteristics of modern society. As Robin Williams has pointed out, "the passage from 'traditional' to 'modern' society involves a movement toward more complex, highly differentiated and specialized social institutions and social roles," together with "a different sort of political order, one serviceable to a much expanded notion of the relevant community, as the shape of social life changes from the order of the village to the order of the nation."[10]

Josiah Royce and John Dewey saw decades ago that the idea of the "great community," based on abstract concepts that extend beyond family and local community, is essential to modern society, especially to modern democratic societies where government is "of laws, not of men."[11]

Almost invariably, however, large-group loyalties are mediated by small-group memberships. What international religion exists apart from its local congregations? Loyalty to Amalgamated Products takes on concrete human meaning through loyalty to the research division, or perhaps to the Amalgamated softball team. In the political sphere, as Alexis de Tocqueville pointed out, local assemblies of citizens constitute "the strength of free nations."[12]

Part of Berger and Neuhaus's argument for a mediating structures approach to public policy is that small-group mediation is necessary not only because of the organizational needs of large groups but also because of the psychological needs of individuals. People may form values in relation to abstract loyalties, but the values take on meaning and emotional weight in intimate human relationships, which create mutual obligations and supports on a direct person-to-person basis. John Schaar, in his book *Loyalty in America*, expresses a related view when he says that "ethical codes rest not merely on rational judgement. They stand ultimately upon emotional attachments."[13]

Modern social existence involves a multiplicity of overlapping loyalties—loyalties to different kinds of groups, both large and small, with powerful interplay between small- and large-group loyalties. This has profound significance for the way in which individuals relate to society and to school.

Before leaving this overview of the different kinds of group membership that may influence education, we must look at one further complexity: the relation of all this to American individualism.

INDIVIDUALS AND GROUPS

American society contains a paradox: it proclaims an ideology of individualism; yet we exist everywhere in groups. There is nothing unusual about our groupishness, which is normal; humans are social beings. In fact, Americans participate in networks of memberships and associations more numerous and complex than in many societies that make no pretense of being individualistic. What is paradoxical about American society is that, despite the clear social reality of our existence, most public policy treats us—we treat ourselves—as if we were only individuals, as if we were a group of 200 million separate, free, and equal units linked together only by the abstract relationships of law, contract, and universal principles.

The truth is that individuals cannot exist apart from human groups. We gain our identities and self-confidence as members of them. Groups permit us to raise our voices, make choices, develop loyalties, and learn who we are as individuals. Individualism, then, is not incompatible with group loyalties; it depends on them, even though at times they conflict with one another and with universalistic principles.

How do we deal with the paradox of projecting ourselves as individually free, yet needing to be in groups? One way is through choice: modern society provides such an array of groups that one can to a large extent choose one's affiliations, defying even such strong group-forming realities as race, religion, or ethnic background. Strong, well-defined groups that provide the greatest human support often supply the psychological strength needed to break away and seek different and more satisfying involvements. For better or worse, even family loyalties in America are to a significant degree a matter of choice.[14] This of necessity makes the groups weaker in some respects, but it does not lessen the *need* for group loyalties; it only increases the need for individuals to learn how to negotiate the interplay between their individualism and their group loyalties.

The role that choice plays in American culture in helping to reconcile individualism and group loyalties reemphasizes the importance of choice in education, since education is a prime area for this reconciliation. It is to a large extent through education that children learn how to function as strong, autonomous individuals within a multiplicity of group loyalties, large and small. Education cannot play this role, however, unless its ideology is rethought and the role of government, bureaucracy, and professionalization is redefined to allow for the voice, choice, and loyalty that enable people to be at the same time free individuals and loyal members of groups.

19 REDEFINING THE ROLE OF GOVERNMENT, BUREAUCRACY, AND PROFESSIONALISM

> We ought to describe schools in a language appropriate to a family rather than to a factory.
>
> Christopher Jencks et al., *Inequality*

Renewed interest in families, neighborhoods, and other "mediating structures" in modern society is significant for several reasons: (1) it reflects growing awareness of the importance of small "people-sized" groups both for the psychological health of individuals and for the welfare of society as a whole; (2) it represents a modification of the individualistic-universalistic ideology, which tends to see society only as a collection of individuals linked by abstract relationships and governmental institutions; and (3) it is related to a growing disenchantment with government bureaucracy on the part not only of "conservatives" but of citizens and scholars of all persuasions.

These shifting viewpoints, however, raise many questions, nowhere more pointedly than in public educational policy. In education the dilemmas, paradoxes, and contradictions of individualism, small- and large-group loyalties, government bureaucracy, and professionalism all come together to demand resolution.

Present educational policy is grounded in the oversimplified ideology of individualism now coming into question. Teachers and school administrators recognize the existence of families, ethnic groups, and

201

communities, but the official value system discounts them and calls for dealing with every child "regardless of race, religion, or family background." This ideology has great merit. It underlies appeals for justice and freedom and supports much of the important modernizing function of schooling. Its merits, in fact, should be strengthened and implemented more effectively. Yet the ideology must be modified. This is the most fundamental change required in educational policy today.

In its simplest form, the political assumption underlying public education—the assumption that supports governmentalized, bureaucratized, and professionalized education—is that "we the people," as individuals acting collectively through government, have delegated the function of educating our children to government school systems, which will deliver education to children on a free and equal basis. The revised conception must be based on the premise that neither "we the people" nor our children are merely a collection of individuals; we are collections of families and communities of all sizes and types, and education involves relationships between people *seen as members of these communities.* Failure to see education in this way will lead to continued ineffectiveness and illegitimacy of the educational process. What is needed is not, as Leonard Fein recommends, an "exception" to present individualistic ideology, so that the "community" of blacks and other minorities will be recognized, but acknowledgment that *all* children are parts of communities.[1]

Along with offering a more flexible paradigm for evaluating the role of the family in education, the mediating structures concept suggests an ideological framework for taking "people-sized" groups into account. The Berger-Neuhaus thesis suggests that American educational institutions and other social services have become enslaved to the megastructures of government, large bureaucracies, national textbook publishers, and labor collectives, to the detriment of the initiative and responsibility of students, parents, families, neighborhoods, and voluntary groups.[2] The dominance of megastructures makes it difficult to develop and maintain the relationships crucial for learning. We have seen that successful education requires a partnership, and the mediating structures thesis shows how one side of the partnership—the learner side—is deemphasized, weakened, and discounted in current policy. The learners themselves as people, their families, their associations, their worlds of meaning, are increasingly disregarded by the megastructural system. For many students, the school situation provides little opportunity for participation as a real partner; thus little learning occurs. In some cases there is even negative learning, that is, the learning of self-hatred, alienation, incompetence, and failure.

The mediating structures thesis also asserts that the megastructures that increasingly shape our lives threaten the basic values of society—such as the right of people to make a world for themselves and their children and to choose and express their own values. Drawing on the work of Durkheim, Weber, and more recent social observers, Berger and Neuhaus see a highly technologized, secularized, and rationalistic society as a source of increasing anomie, alienation, and dehumanization, leading to loss of identity and erosion of personal values. Ultimately, at the megastructural extreme, they see looming the threat of totalitarianism. When masses of people have no grounding in values of their own, no effective mediating structures to help support their private worlds, they turn to the state and national collective identity as the only reliable sources of meaning and human relationships. Berger and Neuhaus warn that these are the conditions in which "the political order must be secured by coercion rather than by consent. And when that happens, democracy disappears."[3]

To Empower People identifies a common base of values among Americans—whether liberal or conservative, Republican or Democrat, Catholic, Protestant, Jewish, Muslim, or atheist—who reject the path toward totalitarianism. Berger and Neuhaus do not suggest that modernity be abolished: hardly. They advocate instead new ways to empower people within modern society. Such empowerment involves, first of all, an awareness of the increasing influence of anonymous and distant government, faceless and unaccountable corporations, unresponsive bureaucracies, and the instruments of mass opinion manipulation, and then invention of ways to strengthen mediating structures to provide the necessary base for strong values and strong individuals.

A relationship exists between the Berger-Neuhaus explanation of educational ineffectiveness and their concern for the violation of basic American values. One reason for educational ineffectiveness is the incongruity between our cultural values and the values inherent in present educational bureaucracies. If America could be reconciled to full government control over the lives of its citizens and to a correspondingly efficient, professionalized bureaucracy to effect such control, we might be able to make such a system "work." Happily, we have not succeeded. Americans do not want such a society. We want a society that will respect a substantial degree of individualism and pluralism of values, life styles, and aspirations. We fear—and rightly fear—a bureaucracy that is too efficient serving a government bent on full social control.

In solving our present educational problems, we must create productive learning relationships that are at the same time both compatible with the individualism and pluralism that have been our hallmark as a society and supportive of the loyalties that bind family, neighborhood, and organizations together and provide the base for individuals' values and integrity. These goals, although involving tensions between them, are interrelated. Partnerships require partners, and we cannot have a vital interaction between active, independent learners and their schools unless *both* have a strong base and unless school-home relations foster such a base.

The question of reconstructing an educational system along these lines is not simple. Formulas such as "getting the government off our back" or programs to subsidize mediating structures are not the automatic answers. Redefining educational policy means redefining the role of government, bureaucracy, and professionalization in a number of fundamental aspects.

This is a tall order. One obviously cannot discount the difficulties of such a reorientation of ideology and institutions; yet the task may not be impossible for several reasons. In the first place, American education has traditions and values that can serve as the basis for reorienting policy along the lines suggested. Second, recent trends point in the same direction, increasingly recognizing the problems of overbureaucratized education. Last, and perhaps most important from a political perspective, dissatisfaction with present conditions is reaching levels that will force change of one kind or another; the only issue is what kind of changes will win out.

Let us see how, in each of the areas—government, bureaucracy, and professionalization—both longstanding traditions and recent trends offer hope for change in the direction of education through partnership based on voice, choice, and loyalty.

REDEFINING GOVERNMENT'S ROLE

Government today has become a bugaboo—the source of oppression, intrusion, usurpation, and disempowerment of parents and defenseless citizens. Some of the backlash and fears are clearly justified; there are too many cases of oppressive governments, including the domestic bureaucratic variety. It is, however, a mistake to imagine only the modern centralized state as "usurping" the responsibility of educating children. In all societies throughout human history, children have been essential links in the continuity of tribe or society, and their socialization into the customs and technology of the social group has been a responsibility of the whole group, many of its members besides the natural parents playing important roles in their education. The "right to make a world for one's children" has not been a traditional right of individual parents.

Furthermore, it is not always easy to decide when government is "usurping" and when it is "assisting" family functions. When a village digs a community well, it may displace the responsibilities of each family to send its members down to the river for water. When a town establishes a public fire department, it may displace the volunteer fire squad. When a city fluoridates its water supply, it preempts the decisions of each family on how it wants to take care of its children's teeth. In each case the society is both assisting families *and* displacing family functions.

Displacing family educational functions cannot be seen only in a negative light. Most families do not feel capable by themselves of providing their children with the education they need for modern society, and they do not feel they are being displaced when schools are provided to do the job, as long as the schools operate to their satisfaction. Yet in a certain sense families are weakened; if they had to provide their children's education, families would certainly be more honored as important institutions than they are now.

Policy questions about the role of government in education cannot be answered simply by ruling all state action illegitimate. The important question is not whether government should be involved in education, since it is bound to be. The question is *how* it is involved. If the government operates schools, do the schools act as *partners* of the home or as its displacer? What kind of partners are they? How do they fulfill their roles and functions in the partnership? How do they relate to the voice, choice, and loyalty of parents and students as partners? How do they relate to the values of other groups claiming the loyalty of parents and students?

Unlike tribal society, the modern state can alienate; it separates public and private life. Individuals and families have a consciousness of their own private worlds apart from the government; so they can feel that "I" or "we" might want something different from what "they" or "it"—the government—wants. This is what makes tension a normal expectation in a society as individualistic and as pluralistic as ours. To relate the public and private worlds in education, families must be partners in the educational enterprise, and government must appreciate that partnership with families requires both respect for families and policies that enable them to play their roles as partners.

This may not be as difficult as some suppose, once policy attention is directed to achieving such a shift in institutional values. Powerful and deeply entrenched as educational bureaucracy has become, its more extreme manifestations are a relatively recent phenomenon—recent enough that they are still looked upon as violations of traditional norms rather than as the status quo to be overthrown.

Most parents and citizens do not think of their local schools and classrooms as "big government." They are, on the contrary, likely to resent encroachments by the state or federal government that interfere with "their" schools.[4] Even in the large cities, where educational bureaucracy reaches such heights of lunacy, there is sometimes great loyalty to individual neighborhood schools and their staffs. For most parents, public education means the particular public school their children attend, not the system as a whole.

For all their problems, local schools are more often seen and felt to be extensions of families and communities than are other public agencies. Teachers and principals often work in a particular school for long periods and become known in the community. With most of a neighborhood's children spending six hours a day and nine months a year, for six to eight years, in a neighborhood institution, local schools are far closer to people than, for example, a state department of motor vehicles or the Internal Revenue Service.

Not only are there strong traditional feelings about education that run counter to the "megastructural" trends of recent years, but a number of specific recent policy trends may already be redefining government's role in education.

Voice and choice, for instance, are becoming increasingly important concepts in public education. New opportunities for voice, as pointed out in Chapter 9, are more readily accepted by public school officials in devices such as parent advisory councils and school site planning groups. The idea of choice has also been gaining ground, even though public school forces have thus far successfully resisted proposals for vouchers and tuition tax credits. As Evans Clinchy and Elisabeth Cody point out in a perceptive article, "the wall seems covered with large and legible handwriting." Modern parents want more say in the education of their children; they are aware that "there is no single, uniform, widely agreed-upon indisputably 'right' way to educate all children," and they are, therefore, "asking for more . . . educational diversity and choice." Educators are beginning to recognize that

> the existing structure is obsolescent, if not downright obsolete. It is not a structure that can easily or genuinely respond either to the legitimate educational demands of its clients or to the legitimate professional needs of its most important employees, the teachers. It is therefore not a structure that can easily adapt to or long survive the threat posed by the tuition tax credit and the enhanced attractiveness of the non public schools.[5]

Many commentators, including Clinchy and Cody, doubt that vouchers are the way to reform the system, but no less an opponent of vouchers than Albert Shanker, even while sharply attacking a California voucher proposal, points out that "there's no reason why you can't have different types of schools within a system and give parents the right to choose schools that would emphasize the 3 R's, and so forth."[6]

One can reasonably expect to see more "diversity and choice," either through increased incentive to choose private schools or through greater choice within and among public school programs. While voucher advocates correctly argue that there is a great difference between choice in a totally free market and choice within a public system, the availability of options within public schools significantly changes government's role; it signals a retreat from "the one best system" and places substantial responsibility on parents to judge whether a particular school or program is effective for their child. Even if parents "choose not to choose" a school different from the one their child attends, increased emphasis on choice in public policy would move education away from the megastructural and monopolistic trends of the recent past.

Judicial decisions have shown signs of moving in this same direction. In the *Yoder* case, involving Amish children, the Supreme Court recognized parental rights to choose religious schools that do not meet all state requirements, and it offered an approving description of Amish education. The Court implied that the Amish approach seems at least as successful as that of the public schools, thus under-cutting the legitimacy of the state's effort to restrict the Amish parents' choice.[7] More recent decisions pertaining to small Christian schools in several states strike a similar theme, upholding parents' rights to schools of their own choosing, free from undue state inter-ference as discussed more fully in chapter 21.

Recent school finance reform, while not advocated in terms of a redefinition of governmental role, may also provide an opportunity for new thinking, since its emphasis is on the redistribution of re-sources as separate from the bureaucratic control of educational processes. The public may be feeling its way toward a more sophisti-cated delegation of functions to the various levels of government. Providing resources and making sure they are equitably distributed might be viewed as a legitimate government function at the state or federal level. This need not mean, however, that the *operation* of schools must be similarly governed. It may be that "he who pays the piper calls the tune," but since the public ultimately pays the piper, why should it not call for different tunes from different levels of government, one level raising and distributing funds and another operating schools and making educational decisions for children?

The "family choice" concept carries this principle still further. Centrally raised funds would be equitably distributed through vouchers, and decision making would be decentralized down to the family level. One need not delegate all the way down to the family level, however, to separate fund raising and distribution from fund expenditure. State delegation of school functions to local districts already sets a precedent for such separation; the same principle can be used to increase opportunities for voice, choice, and loyalty at the school and classroom levels.

In summary, it is clear that if education is to emphasize partner-ships based on the voice, choice, and loyalty of the partners, govern-ment's role in education will have to be modified. While it might remain or become more centralized for functions such as financing and output standards, it will have to become more decentralized in operation. More decision making will have to be made where the essential partners—the students, teachers, and parents—can create and maintain effective learning partnerships. Whether such relationships are established through increased parental choice or through com-munity, parent, or student voice, it is these relationships, rather than governmental and bureaucratic relationships, that will have to be seen as the essential building blocks of successful and legitimate education.

One aspect of this shift from governmental forms to educational partnerships will have to be a change in the public's attitude toward accountability. The present policy framework stresses accountability through the political process and the bureaucratic chain of command. Experience has shown that this approach leads away from educational partnerships and toward increased bureaucracy, as upper echelon public representatives try to hold school system staffs accountable down through the ranks. The alternative is more direct, personal accountability among students, teachers, parents, and local communities. To achieve this, modifications in the bureaucratic structure are required.

REDEFINING THE BUREAUCRACY

Harvard sociology professor Talcott Parsons has said that bureaucracy is "the most effective large-scale administrative organization that man has invented and there is no direct substitute for it."[8] Perhaps that is true on Thursdays in a world overlooking Harvard Yard; yet the very institution within whose walls he developed his theories shows that there are alternatives. Professor Parsons would not for a moment allow the president of Harvard to tell him how to teach his classes or conduct his research. There may be more bureaucracy at Harvard than its professors want, but the governance and operation of education at its best are not bureaucratic. Harvard is not so much a bureaucracy as a collection of many smaller-scale, often collegial, operations.[9]

If there is a natural tendency to bureaucratize large-scale operations, one way to avoid the excesses of bureaucracy is to avoid large size. "Decentralization" probably does not adequately express this, since the term is sometimes used for merely rearranging bureaucratic control. What is needed is a different value system, and this is often not possible unless one is willing to give up some of the control mechanisms of large-scale organizations.

Where bureaucracy is desirable—and it sometimes is—there are many variant bureaucratic styles that substantially influence the degree to which bureaucratic values dominate an organization. A critical variable in this is the nature and quality of management.

"Leadership" rather than "bureaucracy" must be the watchword in schools or school systems built on partnerships. On the individual school level, what is needed is a principal who can bring out the best in teachers, respecting their individuality and nurturing their freedom to build strong classroom partnerships while maintaining high standards of academic performance and personal conduct. Such a principal is to be preferred to one who is seen as the agent of a centralized accountability system.

On the issue of leadership, too, we have both tradition and exemplary current practice to build on. The description above applies to the best principals in schools today as in the past. These principals may not fit the bureaucratic mold—they are indeed usually under siege in bureaucratic systems—but they are not a new invention that will have to await years of research to create. We need only make up our minds that such leadership is desirable, appropriate, and necessary for running effective schools. This is the judgment generally made by parents when they choose private schools for their children. It will also have to be what the "voice of the people" demands in public systems if they want their schools to be effective. In public school systems, the selection of principals is the function above all others that must be watched by school boards, since bureaucrats tend to pick other bureaucrats as subordinates.

The value systems of schools and classrooms must also change as a policy of partnership replaces a policy of bureaucracy. Christopher Jencks is right in saying a school must be seen as a "family" rather than a "factory."[10] If a school is not a direct extension of existing mediating institutions, such as a church or small, homogeneous community, it must develop within itself the kind of mutual goals and loyalty that make for personal accountability among the participants. A school operated on this basis will look—and feel—very different from one run on a bureaucratic basis: common goals rather than common procedures will be the basis for cohesion, and an integration of personal and institutional loyalties, rather than rules and supervision from above, will be the primary motivation for behavior.

Projecting goals commonly agreed upon by the Rockbilts, Joneses, and Choys sounds old-fashioned, especially if these are real goals and not, as is too often the case, bureaucratic procedures freshly dressed as parents' goals. It *is* old-fashioned—just like democracy. Joseph Featherstone lists schools along with families among the "countermodern institutions" on which Americans have relied over the years "to act as communal counterweights to the anarchy and ruthlessness" of American society.[11] Schools, as Hope Leichter points out, can "mediate" family experience, as well as vice versa.[12] Some new variations may be needed, but the basic concept of schools mediating a community's educational goals and aspirations is hardly a strange new idea, only an increasingly rare phenomenon in today's bureaucratic systems.

Creative leadership and a mediating structures approach at the school and classroom levels require changes in district and state educational bureaucracies as well. The overarching purpose of all structures above the school level must be to nurture learning partnerships "down there," in particular schools and classrooms. In a voucher system, the functions of centralized authorities can be limited to distributing funds equitably and enforcing whatever standards are agreed to for participating institutions. Very little else is needed when schools are publicly operated; district, state, and federal educational agencies should be sharply restricted to a very few functions beyond those. Every proposed function of a higher bureaucratic level should be measured against this test: will it facilitate learning partnerships in school and classroom? If not, it should be sustained only if it carries out a clear and important public purpose. This approach would allow superintendents, like principals, to become leaders, not administrators, and would save millions of dollars in reduced central staffs.

The present educational bureaucracy is antilearning; it must be turned upside down to redirect education to its primary purposes and to let teachers resume their lofty roles as partners in the discovery and stimulation of minds and talents, instead of continuing them in the ignoble role of bureaucratic functionaries. Teachers will have to be seen as the most important links in the educational process—next in importance to the real producers of learning, the students themselves. This will entail redefining professionalism.

REDEFINING PROFESSIONALISM

In partnership learning, emphasis must be on the leadership role of teachers and on mutual accountability among partners in the learning process, rather than on professional power and exclusiveness.

For the past several decades it was thought that power was the route to increased teacher satisfaction and effectiveness. Now there are growing doubts whether power by itself is enough. We hear of "burnout" and "combat neurosis" among teachers in small systems as well as large. Teachers feel they are not "part of a team" and that "no one cares about their welfare."[13] Power has been useful for gaining increased pay and job security; it was also a natural response to bureaucratized education, which has disempowered teachers along with parents and students.[14] Bureaucratic and political power, however, does not guarantee either teacher effectiveness or job satisfaction.[15] If wrongly handled, in fact, it reinforces the bureaucratic rigidities of centralized rules and procedures and interferes with productive learning by alienating teachers still further from students and parents and by obstructing the kinds of personal commitment and relationships that have always been at the heart of successful teaching.

As explained in Chapter 5, the drive for power has been closely related to the effort to base professionalism on an "expert body of knowledge" presumed to provide a scientific procedure for teaching.

A good teacher certainly needs expertise, and expertise commands respect. But teaching expertise is more an art than a science, and authority derived from presumed scientific expertise is leagues away from authority derived from actual competence and the loyalty of students, parents, and a community.

Partnership requires a different orientation of professional accountability, one in which teachers could be far more powerful than they are today. Teachers in real partnership with students and parents gain authority—so much so that they are often seen as threats by bureaucratic principals who, if they understand little else, can quickly sense the power of any loyalties not under their control. Only principals who realize that their job is to foster productive learning relationships will not be threatened by powerful teachers and strong student-teacher-parent partnerships.

The professional authority derived from educational partnerships is different from bureaucratic or political power. Teachers in partnership with parents are accountable to them for guiding the learning of their children. They gain authority from this relationship, and they need not be bashful about using it, as long as it genuinely reflects parents' values rather than professional values and interests clothed in the name of "the best interest of the child."

Teachers also gain power from their partnership role with students. Students are not equal partners; they are dependent on teachers for both knowledge and direction. Students should be thought of as partners not because they share an equal status with teachers but because they must assume responsibility for their own learning; they must become the real producers of learning. Since teachers cannot "deliver" education to students on behalf of parents and communities, students must be active participants rather than passive recipients. But they need teachers to lead them, and those who lead always gain power—a legitimate power derived from their leadership role, not from institutional or political domination.

Increased power for teachers in the partnership model also comes from the autonomy teachers need to make partnerships work. They have no such autonomy in bureaucratic systems. In assessing the ineffectiveness of many American classrooms, Urie Bronfenbrenner has commented that the teacher "must be perceived by the pupils as a person of status who has control over resources. . . . Teachers who are poorly paid, treated as subordinates, and given little freedom and autonomy by the school administration cannot help but reflect their true position and reduce their influence in the pupil's eyes."[16] For learning partnerships to work, teachers must be enabled to play their leadership role.

Much confusion accompanies the debate about whether "leadership" implies "authoritarian" or "democratic" behavior. Some professional experts have advocated the latter, and many frustrated parents and critics long for the former. This argument misses a more salient point, however: there are effective and ineffective teachers of both types. Insofar as the *structure* of the relationship is concerned, the important question is not a teacher's personal democratic or authoritarian style, but whether he or she acts as a bureaucratic functionary or a successful leader. The bureaucrat has been defined by Peter Berger as one who "is not concerned with the individual in the flesh before him but with his 'file.'"[17] A teacher with a file, even though he fulfills his job description and obeys all the rules, thus pleasing his bureaucratic superiors, is not teaching. The teacher, on the other hand, who is dealing "with the individual in the flesh before him," successfully motivating learning, can have a variety of successful styles.

Emphasis on the teacher as leader means that respect must be shown for the humanity of teachers, for their values and desires. Leaders in the classroom cannot be faceless bureaucrats. The voice, choice, and loyalty of teachers are important. Good teachers believe in what they are doing. Choice in assignments and voice in the management of their schools enhance their commitment and motivation. Granted, for a school to be successful teachers must work as members of a team to reinforce school values; yet they must do this as autonomous professionals rather than merely as employees following rules and directives. Providing opportunity for the exercise of leadership by teachers is the responsibility of principals; it tests their own leadership. To the principal falls the task of creating the possibility of partnership and cooperation among committed, active individuals.

The type of professionalism described above not only is respected by most parents and citizens but may also be preferred by teachers over the role now given them in many public schools. Professor Dan Lortie, who has made perhaps the most exhaustive recent study of teacher values and aspirations, has confirmed an NEA finding that the chief attraction of teaching is the "desire to work with young people." The second most powerful attraction is the "opportunity for rendering important service."[18] Most successful teachers are not comfortable with bureaucratic education, and the finest ones close their doors to its values and encourage their own learning partnerships inside their classrooms, where the voice, choice, and loyalty of the participants in the learning process come to the fore and bureaucratic rules and regulations of the system recede into the background.

Professionalism redefined in terms of learning partnerships is likely to be more satisfying to all concerned than the present dead end of power plays and conflict. A redefined professionalism can be integrated with redefined roles for government and bureaucracy to promote educational partnerships and make educational institutions both more effective and more legitimate than our present public schools.

20 LEARNING PARTNERSHIPS

Today in the inner city and suburbia alike, a wild manchild who is without a supportive culture raises hell in our schools. Uprooted, he cannot be shaped. Only a community of friends, family and others in whom he recognizes his economic and emotional dependence can provide the soil for his education.

Malcolm Provus, "In Search of Community"

The last chapter discussed both old traditions and new trends that would provide a base for restructuring public educational ideology and the role of government, bureaucracy, and profession in terms of the voice, choice, and loyalty of educational partners. But how likely is it that such a reorientation will take place? Might not the traditions be merely memories, leftover vestiges of an older, more personalized education, and the new trends merely the exotic visions of a few mavericks, exceptions to an otherwise unstoppable bureaucratic juggernaut?

There is no way to tell for certain. Public school systems may or may not reorient themselves away from bureaucratic values toward effective learning partnerships. But there are examples that show it can be done—schools or programs that exemplify small scale; more voice and choice for students, teachers, or both; more opportunity for student responsibility; more opportunity for teacher initiative; more parent involvement; more emphasis on the school or learning group as a "family"; and more emphasis on mutual goals, respect, and loyalty among the participants. These examples represent a move away from the typical patterns of school bureaucracies. Let us look at some of them to see if they have potential for helping to change public education.

SCHOOL-LEVEL COUNCILS

In bureaucratic thinking, factors such as control, accountability, uniform procedures, and economy of scale are the dominant values. The system, through its hierarchical organization and system-wide policies and procedures, is supposed to translate these values into efficient and effective operation. There is a growing recognition, however, that these formulas do not work in education and that the individual school, rather than the system, is the key unit in developing productive learning relationships. No matter how large or carefully organized, bureaucracy cannot substitute for a school as a *social organism* with internal values and loyalties that make the difference between success and failure.

The movement toward renewed emphasis on the individual school has names such as "school-level management," "school-based management," "school site management," and "local school development."[1] Whatever the label, the underlying assumptions are similar: the people in the school and their relationship to each other are what count. The procedures used in such programs also speak to the same point; these include discussions (that is, opportunity for voice) among the school participants—teachers, parents, administrators, and sometimes students and community representatives.

Although some schools and school systems have operated on the principles of school-level management for years, the trend for most of this century has been in the other direction—toward more centralized administration and consolidation of small districts to gain the presumed benefits of larger systems. By the late 1970s, however, increasing attention began to be paid to school systems such as the one in Monroe County, Florida, which began experimenting with reversing the trend and putting more emphasis on the school level.[2] Three states—Florida, California, and South Carolina—have recently adopted programs to sponsor school-level planning from the state level.[3] In 1979 New York City, under the leadership of the New York Urban Coalition, launched its Local School Development program, experimenting with school site participatory planning in over thirty schools.[4]

While planning and participation at the school level may seem simple and natural, the contrast between these approaches and the values that prevail in our school systems is shown in the testimony of participants, who report on the difference planning and participation make in school life. Members of the school family often realize how little they have communicated with each other, let alone worked together, under the centralized, bureaucratic systems. Sometimes the increased communication by itself is enough to change attitudes and improve learning. "Good things can happen in a city school—attitudes can change," reported Ruth Wilson, for thirteen years a public school teacher in New Haven, Connecticut, who had participated in a school-level planning process at the Martin Luther King school in that city. But she also reported on how much work and effort it took to overcome the distrust and mutual suspicion that had prevailed in the school before the process began.

Dr. James Comer of the Yale Medical School, who developed the program at the King school, has written an important book on the trials and tribulations—but also the great rewards—of partnership approaches at the school level. He talks of the importance of "shared perspectives" and "trust and mutual respect among participants," but he also outlines the special strategies that had to be devised to break down the normal bureaucratic attitudes and to "bring parents and teachers together so that they could know one another as personalities rather than as role-figures."[5] He was so impressed with the results of the new relationships that he called his book *School Power* to demonstrate that, with the proper approach, no school need live with the failure and defeatism that afflict so many city schools. After the changeover from a typical urban school run on bureaucratic principles to one based on partnership principles, the King school, which had been one of the lowest achieving schools in the city, became a school that has virtually eliminated the normal patterns of urban school failure that confront tens of thousands of today's city youngsters as they reach adolescence, incompetent in their own eyes as well as in the eyes of their teachers and prospective employers. The mission of successful learning had become the *personal* mission of the participants in the school, and the rules of the system had become less important than the mutual accountability the participants felt in achieving this goal.

School-level participatory planning represents the expanded use of voice and loyalty at the school level, not the voice of citizens operating through the formal political process but the voice of participants in a common enterprise. Those involved in the process usually already have a relationship with one another because they are related to the same institution as staff, students, or parents. Sometimes the school family proper is expanded to include community representatives, such as a businessman who hopes to reduce vandalism, a youth worker who wants to link the school to community activities, or a local artist who hopes to interest students in learning experiences outside the school.

The exercise of voice opens the school to ideas and plans that can help it enhance its quality or solve its problems. More important, it opens the possibility that people will begin to care about one another. Willingness to listen to another person's concerns, ideas, and values means "I care about you, even if I disagree with you." The exercise of voice by the individual enhances his own self-worth; listening to one another's voices enhances the group's sense of mutual loyalty.

In some cases the effort fails, and communications break down. Views and values are too divergent for the group to hold together. Sometimes the threat to bureaucratic power or "professional" self-image is too great.[6] But when it works, school-level management can transform a school from a failing collection of individuals to a successful learning community.

The Institute for Responsive Education (IRE) in Boston, which has studied parent and citizen participation in education across the country, reports that the necessity for school-community collaboration is becoming "more and more apparent to school people and citizens alike" and that "the school council is beginning to emerge as the dominant mechanism" for such collaboration.[7] As of 1976 at least 3,000 such councils were estimated to be in existence, and many hundreds more have been developed since then.[8] A council in which the various elements of the school family can meet and plan on a sustained basis provides the basis not only for parent, teacher, student, and citizen voice but also for the development of loyalty to each other and to the school as an institution. As was seen in the New Haven experiment discussed above, one should not underestimate the effort it sometimes takes, and the obstacles that often lie in the path, when new, collaborative relationships are introduced into systems with deeply ingrained habits of bureaucratic service delivery and client anger or apathy. Nevertheless, the IRE reports that school councils tend to move the participants "toward collaboration rather than confrontation" and therefore "hold great potential as one option for future directions in school/community activity."[9]

SCHOOLS OF CHOICE

While some people are taking the route of increased voice at the school level, others, as seen in the last chapter, are turning to choice as the mechanism for connecting the school's participants in productive learning relationships. Even though full voucher plans remain controversial, the practice of providing greater choice among schools is gaining ground. Two major public systems—in Minneapolis and Indianapolis—have adopted choice plans that have attracted attention in recent years.

As reported in one of the most widely read professional journals, *Phi Delta Kappan*, the Minneapolis program, which began in 1971 in one part of the city as an experiment, "has now been adopted as the basic structure of the entire Minneapolis school system,"

> with parents and teachers offered a choice among four different kinds of elementary schools.
>
> Before this experiment was put into effect, a poll of the parents indicated that only about 35% of them were "satisfied" with what the school system was then offering them. After four years of diversity and choice, the parent satisfaction level reached 85%. . . . What is perhaps even more impressive is that the offering of education options is being used to desegregate the schools in that city. Each optional school has racial quotas guaranteeing that at no time can the minority enrollment in an option exceed that of the school system as a whole. Since this approach to desegregation appears to be working without all the furor and turmoil that normally accompanies desegregation, the parents in Minneapolis, even if they have to put their children on buses, evidently feel that the educational benefit their children receive at the end of the bus ride is well worth the rigors of the trip.[10]

Indianapolis began its program with an intensive planning process in which some fifteen hundred parents and teachers took part in designing the options to be offered. They selected six options, including a "back-to-basics" school and a Montessori-type school, as well as a seventh that permitted parents to choose to stay with whatever kind of schooling their children were currently receiving. While school authorities expected at least 90 percent of parents to choose the "no change" option in the first year, 22 percent (or the parents of more than 6,000 students) chose one of the new options. Furthermore, "each of the first six options was selected by equal numbers of white and minority parents, . . . powerful evidence to support the idea that there are no racial preferences for particular kinds of schooling—at least in Indianapolis."[11]

In Lagunitas, California, a system of choice was adopted only after the community had torn itself apart trying to arrive at a consensus through voice. After much debate and hotly contested school board elections over the relative merits of "open" versus traditional schooling, it became evident that compromise was "clearly impossible"— the community was too sharply split to be able to develop loyalty to the open, the traditional, or the standard schooling that had been provided. The solution "seemed to emerge, as if from necessity": "Why not try all three kinds of education in our system, and let parents choose the program they want?" someone suggested, and the idea was tried, apparently with great success. Not only did each separate group of parents develop strong loyalties to the program they believed was best for their own children, but in some cases parents found that the type of program that was right for one child might not be right for another, and they chose according to their children's needs and learning styles rather than preconceived ideology. In at least one case an "open education" parent was met with her child's own voiced opinion": "I don't care for this kind of thing. I like to be told what I'm going to do." The child's voice led to choice of the regular program, and choice led to loyalty: "He loves it."[12]

Mario Fantini, who in the 1960s was an advocate of community control, has published two books advocating "schools of choice,"[13] and many other educators are beginning to look favorably on the idea. The trend represents a clear shift from the "one best system" approach that has dominated public education policy for a hundred years.

MINISCHOOLS AND PROGRAMS

While school-level management and schools of choice try to help whole schools develop a sense of purpose and social cohesion through voice or choice, some educators have concluded that many schools are too large for the development of family-type values. They have turned, therefore, to smaller units, either by forming mini-schools or subschools within larger schools or by establishing separate, smaller alternative schools, many of which are based on non-bureaucratic values.

Alum Rock

In Chapter 14 it was pointed out that the so-called voucher experiment in Alum Rock, California, failed to establish a free market for educational choice. What *did* happen, however, though apparently not anticipated by those whose main goal was vouchers, was the growth of a sense of autonomy and authority for teachers in a number of the minischools that parents were allowed to choose. Although this could be interpreted as a further example of professional domination, there was a significant difference in the kind of teacher power exercised in the Alum Rock minischools. Instead of collective power of a teacher organization wielded system-wide to affect bureaucratic decisions that applied to all schools, this was a case of classroom teachers exercising power in their own programs. The authority of Alum Rock's minischool teachers did not reinforce bureaucratic rigidities; rather it challenged bureaucracy's traditional, hierarchical control. At the same time, because parents could choose among the different minischools, the teachers' power was not coercive. Not surprisingly, after a while, the principals, and eventually the school hierarchy grew less enthusiastic about the experiment, and curtailed the teachers' autonomy.[14]

PROVE High School

While the Alum Rock program allowed parental choice and teacher initiative, the PROVE High School in Proviso Township outside Chicago emphasizes teacher *caring* and opportunities for students to give voice to their concerns and feelings within a tough, authoritarian environment. The school is designed for "incorrigibles"—boys in trouble with the law and beyond the control of their families or of regular schools. Students are sent to the schools either by their parents' choice ("We'd practically given up," said one father) or by a juvenile court. While choice can be involved, it is not often the students' choice. Nevertheless, attendance is nearly 95 percent daily. Why? "Well, the teachers—all male—drive the buses and often go into the students' homes with the parents' permission, if they don't come out. If that doesn't work a return visit is paid by school officials. In one case where they talked to a reluctant student for an hour, the mother said, 'I don't know how they had the patience.'"[15]

"Patience is indeed an important quality in all of PROVE's teachers, for sheer patience often forces a boy to capitulate." The aim is communication. Many of the boys are psychologically isolated. They lack self-confidence and a positive self-image. If patience does not work, confrontation is used—in extreme cases, physical confrontation—in which a boy is wrestled under control until he finally says what is bothering him. "Most of these boys never have had the opportunity to express their anxiety and frustration verbally, as you and I do, because they don't know how. This gives us a situation where a kid can physically vent—and afterwards feel comfortable enough to talk and listen," reported the school's headmaster. After-school "consequence time," with no set limits, is equally unorthodox; teachers are prepared to spend the night if necessary to get to the bottom of a behavior problem.[16]

Most schools, public or private, would have difficulty getting approval for such methods, and they would certainly be dangerous in the wrong hands. In the case of PROVE, the secret may be the intense sense of caring expressed by the school staff—caring for each and every student, no matter how "bad" or "incorrigible." The group activities of the school, including Outward-Bound-type wilderness trips, provide opportunities for both group and individual responsibilities. Personal behavior is graphically seen and felt as consequential both for the self and for others. The caring "often initiates the kind of interpersonal bonds all but lacking in the boy's life."[17]

This kind of intensive school experience obviously is not appropriate for most young people, but there are many students in schools today who feel the lack of "interpersonal bonds" in their educational experience either at home or at school. The spirit of PROVE seems to be, "We'll do whatever it takes to make a connection." Emphasis on human connection—the opportunity for voice and loyalty—rather than merely the carrying out of bureaucratically defined functions seems to be a common thread of many of the mini and alternative schools.

The Bedford-Stuyvesant Street Academy

The Bedford-Stuyvesant Street Academy was started as a private school by the New York Urban League and is now a part of the New York City public school system, with continuing private sponsorship through the Public Education Association. The school is attached to Boys and Girls High School, a regular city high school in Brooklyn, from which from two hundred to five hundred "problem" students are sent to the street academy each term, usually for a one-term period. The school provides an interesting synthesis of voice, choice, and loyalty.[18]

Student voice is emphasized in the orientation period, usually lasting six weeks, at the beginning of each term; at that time a new group is given intensive group counseling sessions in which the values of the school are made clear but in which students are also encouraged to voice their own feelings about school, themselves, and their future. Techniques from drama—the "line" and the "circle"—are used to help students voice their feelings. After the formal orientation period is over and academic classes resume, students are encouraged to express their feelings and concerns in daily counseling sessions, to staff members, or in constructive ways during classes.

While the voice of individual students is a key feature of the program, the "voice of the community" is also present, in the emphasis not only on black pride (the school is nearly all black) but also on broader community values. The goals of the school are explicit; students are told what behavior and achievement is expected of them.

When New York state's minimum competency requirements became effective in 1979, an even broader community voice took on institutional expression: The fact that the "community" of the entire state was expecting a certain level of achievement from all students was used by the school to help bring the goals of the academic program into clearer focus.

Choice is an aspect of the school because students need not go to the academy if they or their parents object. There has been some shift in policy over the years on whether students "opt in" or only have the freedom to "opt out" once assigned, but in either case students are not there against their will. Even more important, great stress is placed on choice once a student is part of the school. The lesson is drummed home over and over again: "This is your life; it is your choice as to what you make of it."

Like PROVE High School, the street academy staff puts great

emphasis on caring about what choices the students make, but there is recognition that in the end it is the students, not the staff, who make the choices. Since the students are adolescents who have been in trouble either academically or personally, there is also an awareness that the parents will have little power to make the necessary choices; the reality is that the students have their lives in their own hands, and the school tries to make them conscious of that.

Loyalty as a value permeates the school. As in many alternative schools, both staff and students speak of the school as a family. The six-week orientation is consciously used to encourage a sense of mutual respect and cohesion among the school's participants. The result is that even in the academic classes, evaluators from Teachers College

> saw numerous instances of students correcting one another in a natural, uninhibited way that brought no retaliation. . . . In class, students urged others to be quiet, not to hassle the teacher when asked to get a late pass, and so on. On one occasion, one student said to another, "You're not respecting Miss _____," when the second student was arguing with the teacher.

"Respect" is an important word in the values of the school—respect for self and respect for others—and respect has to go in all directions, not only among students but also between staff and students.

Professor Joseph Grannis, who conducted the evaluation and compared the academy's value structure to that of the regular parent high school, Brooklyn's Boys and Girls High, concluded that such mutually supportive behavior is a major contributor to the academy's effectiveness:

> At the Street Academy, students contributed substantially to the success of classes, whereas at the High School, success of classes (where it was obtained) depended more exclusively on the teachers. A teacher who was less than outstanding could still be effective in the positive environment of the Street Academy, but at Boys and Girls High School the more negative peer culture often turned this situation into disorder.

The street academy, in addition to trying to create a familial atmosphere within the school, also makes a conscious effort to "connect" with the families of the students. The school's director, Thom Turner, insists on meeting as many parents as possible and asks them during their own orientation what kind of behavior they want from their children at home; he then tells them that the school respects these family values and will apply the same standards of behavior to students while they are in school. The object is to make the parents feel the school is operating *on their behalf* and as an extension of the family, even if the family has lost control over the child. Staff members often pay home visits to help cement this relationship.

THE COOPERATIVE CLASSROOM

To some educators even a minischool is too large to be the starting point for group loyalty. They opt for the classroom as the key unit in achieving mutually supportive family-type values. This approach does not contradict the idea of school as the crucial context in which productive classroom relationships flower. School and classroom philosophies must be complementary. A growing body of evidence, however, supports the significance of classroom climate as a key determinant of learning.[19]

One result of such thinking is a move toward the cooperative approach to group achievement goals in classrooms, as opposed to competition among students. While competition is a time-honored American value, linked to individualism, it is often misused within the classroom. It makes no sense to encourage children to play winner-loser in learning to read or do arithmetic; the goal should be mastery of these skills by *all* children in a class. William Glasser, a physician concerned about the destructive aspects of American schooling, argues persuasively in *Schools without Failure* that school failure could be substantially reduced by shifting to a cooperative approach in which a whole class works toward the common goal of everyone's learning what needs to be learned.[20] This does not preclude competition beyond basic expected levels of achievement for all students; it does, however, set up classroom dynamics that motivate students to help one another learn rather than put all their efforts into individual achievement, with the expectation that some will succeed and others fail.

Urie Bronfenbrenner, in his *Two Worlds of Childhood,* recommended similar approaches: "group commitment," "teams, cooperative group competition, organized patterns of mutual help."[21] Educators at the Johns Hopkins University are attempting to hone these ideas by means of their "teams games tournaments," a technique that reduces individual competition by structuring the competitive spirit into subgroups within the class.[22]

All these approaches have the effect of promoting effective learning partnerships and making the classroom a mediating structure where mutual goals and closer human relationships in achieving goals become the dominant values.

ONE-TO-ONE TUTORING

The most basic learning partnership is one-to-one tutoring, an effective teaching-learning approach since the time of earliest recorded human activity. This venerable heritage is given little place, however, in many modern bureaucratic school systems.

An effort to revive and spread the use of one-to-one tutoring was begun by the Public Education Association with the establishment in 1956 of the School Volunteer Program in New York City and a project funded by the Ford Foundation to help develop the program nationally. It is now a regular part of public school systems not only in New York but also in dozens of other cities, with a reported 6 million volunteers now working in schools throughout the country. It has now gained a foothold in national educational policy through amendments to the Elementary and Secondary Education Act.[23]

Experience in one-to-one tutoring leaves no doubt that learning is a partnership enterprise. In a classroom a teacher can be deceived into thinking education is the "delivery" of bureaucratically defined "services." In tutoring nothing happens unless student and tutor work together, with a clear understanding that the student does the learning. One of the reasons why tutoring is so effective is that the tutor can give concentrated attention to the student's voiced concerns about either the substance of the lesson or any problems that may be interfering with his learning it. The student also has much less opportunity to play a passive role than in most classrooms, especially when a beleagured teacher is only too glad to have a few students tune out of the proceedings.

Tutoring is antibureaucratic and is therefore seldom used by bureaucratic schools and school systems, despite its effectiveness. Because tutors are usually not trained or licensed professional teachers, they violate the "professionalization" of education. Teachers may feel a direct threat to their jobs, their status, and their competence. The personal bonds that often develop between tutor and student can also be a threat but they can usually be a strong motivating factor in successful learning.

The spread of tutoring is a hopeful sign that many ordinary citizens understand that schools cannot by themselves "deliver" education and that many children need extra "mediation" in the learning process. Even more important, it is a sign that some teachers and educational officials also understand this and are willing to lay aside bureaucratic models of schooling and professionalism.

Tutoring proved its mettle during the "competency crisis" in 1979 when New York State's new graduation requirements threatened to deny diplomas to hundreds of high school seniors who had not been able to pass competency examinations. The teacher's union, although it has an official statewide policy opposing school volunteers, agreed not to object to the use of tutors for dealing with the "emergency." On very short notice, 400 New Yorkers gave their time to help students overcome deficiencies that had developed over many years. After six weeks of tutoring, over 90 percent of those tutored passed and received their diplomas.[24]

Peer tutoring—by students either of the same or of somewhat older age than those being tutored—can be even more effective than tutoring by adults, and the tutors need not be limited to "good" students. As one of the early antipoverty initiatives of the 1960s, Mobilization for Youth established a peer tutoring program whose evaluation showed even more startling learning gains for the tutors than for those receiving the tutoring—reading gains averaging more than three years after seven months of tutoring.[25] Stimulated by these positive results and by other peer programs sponsored by the National Commission on Resources for Youth, programs were operating in at least 60 cities by 1969 and in over 400 by 1971. Evaluation again shows significant learning gains for both tutors and students.[26]

In the summer of 1980, a group of tutors was selected for a project sponsored by the Public Education Association (PEA) in the Bedford-Stuyvesant section of Brooklyn who themselves had difficulty with basic math competence. With minimal but carefully planned training and counseling on the job, the tutors gained one month in math skills for each week they tutored. They not only learned more math, but in a questionnaire given at the end of the program, 87 percent of them either "agreed" or "strongly agreed" with the statement, "I like mathematics more than I used to."[27]

Peer tutoring is only one example of a movement toward programs in which youths assume more responsibility both for their own educational development and for that of others. The National Commission on Resources for Youth has assembled information in *New Roles for Youth* on fifty exemplary programs that "provide opportunities for youth to take initiative and to carry on activities that are socially constructive and productive and for which young people can take the major responsibilities."[28] The book describes programs in which young people set up and operate projects in which they help peers cope with academic problems as well as general adolescent problems, such as "alienation from adults, running away from home, drug abuse, need for recreational facilities, need for appropriate peer and adult models with whom they can identify, need for development of self-esteem and a sense of personal direction, and need for gainful employment." Underlying this is the assumption of a "young person's need to be needed," a perspective that is lost when a program's aim is to "deliver" services to young people.

Urie Bronfenbrenner has said that "surely, the most needed innovation in the American classroom is the involvement of pupils in responsible tasks on behalf of others within the classroom, the school, the neighborhood and the community."[29] The importance of this, as James Coleman points out, is not just to "rescue" a few students from their peer culture of "irresponsibility" and "hedonism," but to enable the whole peer group to "buy into" the educational process by becoming involved as responsible partners.[30] If we want to escape what Grace and Fred Hechinger once called "teen-age tyranny," one solution is to assure opportunities for young people to be responsible learners and citizens.

In addition to opportunities for young people to assume responsibility, one of the characteristics of peer programs is the chance it gives them to voice personal views and values, "to raise questions, help identify problems, contribute ideas, plan for action, make decisions." In a "Spark" program in New York City, a student reports, "I used to feel that when I said something I wouldn't be listened to, and people would laugh." The counselor "helped me to talk to others and not be shy." The result of such opportunity to voice feelings and personality "is to build trust within the group."[31] In the PEA's 1980 peer tutoring project in Bedford-Stuyvesant, one tutor, echoing the comments of many others said, "I learned how to express myself, to communicate better with others, to express anger, and to have maturity and patience."[32]

Since the young people in the peer programs have usually volunteered to be involved and since their commitment to the programs is a major element in their success, such programs provide good examples of the combination of voice, choice, and loyalty.

SMALL IS BEAUTIFUL

A common element of all the new approaches discussed above is smallness, at least something smaller than a "system." Small size is relevant because it allows for face-to-face communication, personal loyalty, and the sharpening of nonbureaucratic values. Bureaucracy asks for loyalty to the rules and procedures of the system and to higher officials who embody bureaucratic authority. What develops in small groups is loyalty to other group members as human beings because of mutual caring and because members want to maintain relationships with one another.

For these reasons, the "little red schoolhouse" is reemerging as more than a romantic educational setting from the past. A recent federally sponsored study found that much of the presumed advantage of consolidating small rural schools into larger, "more efficient" and modern ones is illusory. It now seems that the people from the hills and hollows who resisted consolidation were not simply ornery and backward as portrayed by "forward-thinking" school administrators. They were, in important respects, right to cling to "their schools."[33]

A parent in Shiloh, Michigan, which has one of the few remaining one-room schools, commented about the effect of the school on its students: "I just think they learn more." The teacher at the school "acknowledged that one-room school houses cannot offer modern science equipment, varied electives, large libraries, athletics and other programs readily available at large schools. But she said she believed that country schools excelled at giving children the opportunity to be independent and to feel secure with basic mathematics, reading, and writing." In state reading scores, *all* of the children from Shiloh's old-fashioned school scored above average, and *all* scored between 75 percent and 100 percent in mathematics. Caring about the success of each individual student can create a "school without failure."[34] In another rural school, when a school board member was asked what was done with children who fail, he replied, "I go visit the parents to see what is wrong."[35] In some cases it is the teacher who pays the visit; in others it might be one of the older children who brings a problem to the attention of the parents.

Testimony from the Shiloh school also reveals the important link between group cohesion and independence: "They know they aren't going to be led by the hand through things," said the teacher, and yet care is taken to make sure that every student learns: "You have to be very loyal and ready to put forth many hours. You have to have the willingness to do everything, from being a janitor to a nurse."[36]

Coons and Sugarman, in arguing for family control, refer to the European political concept of "subsidiarity," which holds that "responsibility for dependent individuals should belong to the smaller and more intimate rather than the larger and more anonymous communities to which the individual belongs." The small group "is more likely to listen to and respect constituent voices, to know individual interests, and to be motivated to serve them—particularly when it is so structured that all members are affected by its decision about any member."[37]

The family, according to Coons and Sugarman, is the social unit most likely to fill the need of subsidiarity. The small school environment shows some of the same characteristics, however. The fact that a class typically stays together for a term or a year can engender some of the same mutual respect and group processes that exist in the family. For this reason, some argue that in urban conditions, where so little else is stable, students should be kept together as a group with the same teacher for two or more years at a time.

What is especially significant is both the group cohesion that can develop among individuals in the school group and the approach to the individuals as real human beings, in all their particularities, including those brought as members of families and communities outside the school. The teacher at the Shiloh school reports that involvement among parents, children, and the teacher is greater than at a larger school. "I have parents coming in all the time—before school, after school—they want to know how their child is doing." As a result, parents and citizens often develop fierce loyalty to the school. One commented, "It's just our way, and we'll be here until the state forces us to close."[38]

Research increasingly shows the importance of a close home-school relationship. McDill and Rigsby point out the importance of "institutions in which parents and school officials have mutual respect and are engaged in concerted efforts to develop and maintain school environments in which students are strongly encouraged to value and strive for academic success and are socially rewarded for such behavior . . . schools with normative climate in which teachers and students heavily invest their energies"—in which there is "mutual trust and accountability, common responsibility for determination of educational goals and procedures." Good, Biddle and Brophy also stress the importance of "the development of close relationships with parents; the provision of opportunities for parents to have input in the program and to participate in it."[40]

Nicholas Hobbs speaks of the importance of a "shared responsibility between family and school" and sees this as an "emerging new pattern."[41] He cites as examples developments such as the community school movement and new approaches to special education for the handicapped, both of which call for heavy parent or community involvement and both of which have been endorsed in federal legislation.

Small size is a prerequisite of all these benefits of relationships within the school setting and between the school and the broader educational community. Whether we are dealing with the family as a small human group with the advantages of "subsidiarity," or the one-room school, or the classroom within a huge urban school system, respect for the value of the small human group and the loyalties it can engender are necessary for successful and legitimate education.

LARGE CAN BE BEAUTIFUL TOO

We do not live in a world of little red schoolhouses—or of tiny hamlets, well-knit families, or robust churches. Smallness enhances a sense of partnership and hence of effective learning; but the megastructural world is a reality, too, which will not go away; it brings too many benefits. Modern life is impossible without large social, economic, and political structures. Educational policy cannot be built on escapism or romantic longing for the presumed glories of bygone days. It must be based first of all on preserving and encouraging human voice, choice, and loyalty *within* a megastructural world; next, on using the megastructures themselves to enhance educational values; and, finally, on infusing the larger structures with the values of the smaller ones, so that even city, state, and national educational enterprises develop a sense of partnership.

Why close a small school like the one in Shiloh, Michigan, if it is working and people are happy with it? Is not its human and educational effectiveness more important than bureaucratic abstractions about efficiency? One citizen whose neighborhood school was threatened with closing said, "It's more than a school to us; it's the focal point of our neighborhood."[42] The value expressed in this statement will not appear in the tables and charts of the state educational bureaucracy, but it is the kind of attitude that must be taken into account in public policy planning if loyalty and institutional effectiveness are to be preserved in modern society.

The kinds of programs and policies described earlier in this chapter give only a few examples of what could be a vast expansion of human-scale educational partnerships if educational policy were turned in this direction.

State minimum competency requirements are an expression of large-group norms that should be seen for their social as well as academic purposes. When "we the people" of Oregon decide that all young people in the state should learn survival skills, there is an effort to develop a sense of community on a statewide scale. Although this can be seen as oppressive from one point of view ("Where does the state come off telling me my children have to learn to swim?"), it can provide for a certain social strength ("We're proud that here in Oregon we ensure that every young person can swim)." When all members of a society can read, there is a possibility of a greater common bond among them. If the standards go beyond basic skills and require all students to have some grounding in science, history, literature, and the arts, they can also help to create a sense of common culture.

Television and modern commerce already provide a common culture of sorts. The Superbowl and Coca Cola have become the common property of vast numbers of Americans. Although little of this experience is thought of as "educational," some television programs, such as "Roots," can be seen as a mass educational experience. More could be made of the potential of television if it were seen as an important instrument for common culture beyond the levels of *Dallas* and Alka Seltzer.

Television is an interesting medium because, while it clearly carries megastructural values, it has also become a part of the family life of millions of Americans.[43] Teachers can take advantage of this by having students watch productions such as "Roots" and invite their parents to watch with them, then join in a family discussion of what they have seen. If this worked with "Roots," it might carry over to family participation around televised performances of "Hamlet" or the Alvin Ailey Dance Company. If we become more ingenious in using the opportunities for large-group common educational experiences, we might be less threatened by concurrent policies for encouraging more small-group experiences and programs of choice.

Professionalism also, if properly conceived, has a legitimate megastructural function that can enhance education. Teachers who are merely the functionaries of bureaucracy can violate human values, but teachers who, as individuals, represent a broader culture and more universalistic values than their students are one of the reasons for schooling. The teacher has the sublimely delicate task of marrying the small-group loyalties necessary for productive learning to the large-group loyalties of the broader community and of universalistic principles. This is why teachers must be leaders. They are leading students from one world to the other. How a balance is struck and a synthesis achieved varies at different levels of education and with different types of students and communities. Eugene Litwak, for instance, suggests that some parents are already too oppressively involved in their children's education and have to be fended off so that the child can make his own relationships in school, while other parents are too "distant" and must be brought closer to the educational process.[44] It is possible that teachers in small towns and rural areas would benefit from greater independence, whereas teachers in urban areas need to be brought more in touch with their students' lives.

The educational policy goal in integrating mediating and megastructural worlds must be to infuse the larger institutions with the values developed in human-scale learning partnerships, rather than the other way around, as is now the case. Instead of classrooms being the lifeless creations of central bureaucracies, school policies and structures above the classroom level should be the result of the values, energy, and devotion flowing out of many thousands of effective learning partnerships at the base of the enterprise. If this is done, even statewide and federal educational programs can be learning partnerships, and the people involved thought of as "we" rather than "they."

21 BUSING, BOOK BURNING, AND BILINGUALISM

Controversy is the basis of change.

James Noll, *Taking Sides*

One might also say that change is the basis of controversy. American Society—indeed, the whole human race—is going through cataclysmic change. It should be no surprise that there are controversies as people sort out what to save, what to modify, and what to create anew. Educators complain that they have no time for educational policy because they are preoccupied with controversies that have nothing to do with education—controversies over busing, censorship, ethnic politics, and sexual values. But such issues have everything to do with education, since they represent the friction points of a changing society, and the education of the next generation is one of the ways societies change.

How might a new policy framework based on partnership help with these controversial issues? The policy framework proposed in this book will not provide simple cookbook answers. A partnership approach can lead to quite different answers to controversial issues depending on the circumstances and values of the policy makers. The proposed framework can, however, provide a more constructive way to approach many of these problems. Controversies become heated because they involve deeply held but conflicting values. A bureaucratic service-delivery framework often ignores these important value differences or obscures them by redefining them as managerial or professional issues. This often only exacerbates the

235

controversy, since it provides no way for the real issues to be identified and dealt with. When they finally break into the political arena, they are often so explosive that they can be handled only through the most rough-and-ready patchwork solutions, leaving the problems festering for future controversy.

Although each of the issues discussed in this chapter deserves more discussion than this book can provide, a brief look at some of them will give a sample of how a partnership approach based on voice, choice, and loyalty might provide a better framework for dealing with some controversies currently plaguing American education.

RACIAL INTEGRATION

When, in 1954, the Supreme Court decided to outlaw the segregation of children by race in public schools, it opened up an epochal question about the nature of American society, a question that clearly could not then, and cannot now, be left to the values and practices of individual local communities. Yet it is an issue that also involves the most sensitive and intimate values of families, neighborhoods, and local schools. It is hard to imagine a policy area that presents more difficult problems for educational partnerships and the voice, choice, and loyalty of educational partners.

The most fundamental problems about racial integration are questions about loyalty. Until 1954 it was the official policy of seventeen states and the unofficial practice and attitude of much of the rest of the country that "we the people" means "we white Americans"—blacks were "they" or "them." What began in 1954 and is by no means yet completed was a struggle for America's soul, to see if "we" can mean "we Americans," black as well as white.

It is an awesome struggle. Such a change in fundamental group loyalties is unprecedented in the history of human societies. It is a struggle that has produced bloodshed in the past and will almost certainly produce more before it is over. It will take all the ingenuity and resourcefulness of American culture to resolve. For this very reason it is an issue that calls for sensitivity as well as courage, understanding as well as persistence.

Those who complain that the government's enforcement of desegregation is an illegitimate use of the schools for social purposes forget that the establishment of separate schools for black and white children was one of the most extensive acts of governmental social engineering ever undertaken. The vast machinery of state and local school systems was a key element in the Jim Crow system for institutionalizing second-class citizenship for blacks, for teaching them that they were unfit to associate with whites, and for teaching white children that theirs was a superior race.[1]

By 1954 the habit of segregated schools was so deeply engrained that they seemed "natural" in those areas where they existed; organizing schools without separation by race seemed, and was, a revolutionary change. There was no way the change in America's loyalties could take place without ending this massive machinery of government-sponsored cultural conditioning. Even many of those who fought hardest to retain segregated school systems now admit that the changes had to be made and that making them required federal intervention.

Where does this lead us with regard to the busing controversy that is still with us in the 1980s? The struggle to make "American" mean more than "black" or "white" is certainly not over, but the situation has changed.

One of the changes has been the ending of official segregation and the dismantling of the extensive machinery of dual school systems, segregated rest rooms, drinking fountains, restaurants, and hotels, and exclusionary voting procedures. Many people discount the importance of these changes because in many areas there is more segregation now than before 1954 and because other forms of discrimination have grown up to replace those struck down. But the ending of official segregation is vastly important. As was argued in the original desegregation cases, segregation laws placed a *governmentally sponsored* mark of inferiority on blacks; it made racial discrimination official and legitimate. Black children who had an inclination to consider themselves equal to their fellow white citizens had to overcome a heavy burden of psychological pressure telling them that to do so was a breach of loyalty to their society, which decreed their inferiority as a condition of membership. Many blacks managed to overcome this burden—some, indeed, by abrogating their loyalty to American society and some by subtle forms of dual loyalty to America and their own subculture. But many also accepted membership on the terms offered, including acceptance of their own inferior status. Such is the nature of racism; it is one of the ways the oppressed internalize their own oppression. Racism can and does operate without governmental sanction, and the effects of official segregation are long lasting even after it has ended, but it is much more difficult to maintain the psychology of inferiority without the help of official sanctions and symbols and much easier to escape it for those who struggle to be free.

A second change flows from the first: many more minority people have freed themselves from the psychology of inferiority. Although discrimination continues, many fewer are willing to accept it. The "black is beautiful" movement symbolized this change in psychology. Social science has started to pick up indications of the change—"a clear shift to more positive racial self-esteem."[2] Whites who have associated with blacks before and after the changes have not needed social science to detect the differences.

A third change related to the second has been an increasing split in the black community and within individual blacks between wanting to assume full first-class citizenship in American society and wanting to form a new "separate and equal" (or perhaps separate and superior) black identity to replace the "separate and inferior" image being cast aside. It is not necessarily unhealthy for these tendencies to coexist, but their coexistence has implications for educational policy.

Add at least two more complications before considering a simple little problem like busing: the process of integration has become more difficult, and the resistance to it has increased in many areas. Back in the days when black children were being bused dozens of miles past white schools to segregated black schools, and vice versa, it cannot be said that changes were easy; shots were fired into children's homes and civil rights workers were killed to prevent them. Nevertheless, once governmental policy had been made clear and was being enforced, the injustices of legalized segregation, not to mention its inconvenience and expense, did much to help people accept the changes. Now, even in the South, segregation is much more often of the urban and suburban variety so prevalent in the North, with large areas inhabited by few members of "the other" race. The balance of inconvenience has shifted to the integration side. In addition, there are no longer any official segregation laws for whites to feel guilty about. It is much easier, even if unjustified, for whites to say, "We've given them equality and stopped discrimination; that's enough."[3]

Putting these various changes together leaves many black parents saying "to hell with integration." If integration means busing their child halfway across town to a school full of hostile whites and the disruption of their efforts to create a strong community school in their own neighborhood, their feelings are understandable. Nor can these feelings be equated with the reluctance of many black parents to have their children be the "pioneers" in the first desegregation cases. That reluctance was often connected with acquiescence in second-class citizenship, whereas the new reluctance is often connected with a growing sense of racial security and first-class citizenship, of either the assimilationist or the dual-loyalty variety.

With such a complex set of factors, there are few absolutes that make much sense. One of the few is *never* to treat "busing" as a single policy or program that one can be for or against. It makes about as much sense as asking if someone is for or against factories (yes, in an industrial park; no, in a residential neighborhood) or for or against highways (yes, in some circumstances; no in others).

There are successful busing programs that have brought effective desegregation. And there are horrible busing programs that have made educational partnerships impossible and resulted in more segregation than existed before they began. There are still many segregated schools that can and should be integrated, but there are also many places where no one has yet found a way to produce healthy integration.

While mandates are clearly needed in some cases, it is also possible that choice could play a greater role in promoting integration at this stage of the struggle. In the earlier periods "free choice" was almost always a scheme for maintaining segregation. Now that more blacks are asserting their equality, choice may have more legitimacy. Magnet schools in Boston, Chicago, Detroit, Houston, and New York are drawing students of both races. A number of advocates of integration point out that integration by choice can provide reasonably healthy race relations in a generally unhealthy overall social context.[4] In many cases choice can still lead to segregation instead of integration, but policy should be alert to opportunities where it can work productively.

Voice is also important. This is a time for Americans to listen to one another carefully and sensitively on this issue. That does not mean "caving in" to extremists on either side, or encouraging resistance when enforcement is necessary, but the problems are too complex to be solved by simple slogans. The real values in the interests of all parties should be expressed and laid on the table in coming to answers that will have a chance of working.

Finally, we come back to loyalty. The key issue in this struggle is creating an America in which "we" means all Americans and where pluralism does not mean that some groups are inferior to others. Even where schools are still segregated, much can be done to help students and their parents understand the nature of this struggle—its past history and its crucial importance to our future. Creating effective learning partnerships within classrooms and between schools and communities can do much to provide the new generation of Americans with the academic and moral skills needed to meet the challenge of this problem and move it to its next stages of resolution.

BILINGUAL EDUCATION

Like racial integration, bilingual education raises basic questions of loyalty and the nature of American society. For some, any bilingual education is a threat to American society. They cannot be satisfied except by removing all traces of teaching in any language other than English, even though this leaves thousands of students floundering with instruction they cannot understand. For others, bilingual education is the necessary instrument of a new cultural pluralism, essential to the internal loyalty of cultural subgroups and the self-concept of their members. They cannot be satisfied except by mandating bilingual education for all children with non-English-speaking backgrounds, even though many of them are doing well with all-English instruction and their parents vigorously object to bilingual instruction.[5]

Passions on this issue have been smoldering beneath the surface for years. Some inkling of their depth was revealed by the outpouring of outraged opposition to the proposed federal bilingual education regulations in the fall of 1980. Most of the major educational organizations, including the National School Boards Association and the American Federation of Teachers, testified strongly against the proposed new rules, and both houses of Congress passed amendments to block their implementation. Some of the opposition took the form of objection to federal control, but much of it clearly reflected a deep fear that the regulations were the harbinger of new cultural patterns and a shift from the assimilationist policy that has dominated public education for a hundred years.[6]

The proposed regulations ostensibly dealt only with children's legal right to bilingual instruction. As Education Secretary Shirley Hufstedler said in issuing them, "A child cannot learn subjects taught in a language he or she cannot understand." But it is clear from the debate that the issue goes beyond the constitutional issue to one of language and cultural policy. Those who favor accepting the shift to a more multilingual and multicultural society see bilingual education as a way for those with non-English-speaking backgrounds to maintain and strengthen their competence in their native language (so-called maintenance bilingual education), as well as for English-speaking students to gain knowledge of a second language. Those who are opposed to such a shift are willing to agree, at most, to only a minimal amount of bilingual instruction while students are given intensive instruction in English so that they can shift out of bilingual instruction as soon as possible (so-called transitional bilingual education).

The Supreme Court, in the landmark case of *Lau v. Nichols* in 1974, did not settle the differences between these two points of view. It only dealt with children's right not to be excluded from the benefits of educational programs because of English-language deficiencies. This mandate can be met with transitional bilingual instruction, but it does not preclude maintenance bilingual programs, which might continue long after the student is able to learn in all-English classes.[7] Which approach is better is a matter of policy—and therefore of politics—not of constitutional law.

What policy would best facilitate educational partnerships? There is no question that for many families bilingual education helps to maintain a bond of trust, a nexus of meaning, and a sense of mutual respect between home and school. For many children, the experience of receiving instruction only in English does not just mean falling behind in their subjects; it is also a denial of self-worth—a "put-down" of their cultural background—that creates negative school experiences and a very high rate of failure. As one judge put it, "the policy of using English exclusively in the Texas public schools must be seen, not as neutral or benign, but rather as one more vehicle to maintain these children in an inferior position."[8]

In many urban areas, only 25 percent of Hispanic youngsters finish high school. At the same time, some parents are strongly opposed to bilingual education and prefer to have their children experience "total immersion" in intensive English lessons and all-

English instruction in their subjects. They feel that this is the best and quickest way for their children to enter the mainstream of American society. They may have alternative means of helping their children maintain their original language and culture, or they may not be interested in having them do so. In short, there are divergent views among parents about what they think will best serve their children's needs.

Why not choice, then, as the primary means of dealing with the bilingual education dilemma? With parents differing on what they want and experts split on what is best, this would seem to be an area preeminently suited to parental choice. Since a sense of trust is particularly important and often hard to develop between school and non-English-speaking families, giving parents options would be more likely to signal to them that the school is sensitive to their values and feelings and will allow the child to attend the program in which they can have the greatest confidence. When parents have chosen a program, they are more likely to give their child the psychological support that is especially important for the non-English-speaking student.

The only clear public policy that should be maintained in offering such choices is to insist that all options enable students to master English, as well as their school subjects, through whatever kind of bilingual or other program is chosen. This legitimate public goal coincides with the wishes of virtually all parents, yet today is all too often not fulfilled in either bilingual *or* all-English programs. In the muddled pulling and tugging between various professional groups who want to increase or limit the number of children in bilingual programs, thousands of children are falling between the cracks; they are not getting good instruction of either kind. If public policy would concentrate on the primary public interest—mastery of English and successful learning of subject matter—and leave the choice of bilingual or alternative programs to the parents, it is more likely that both public and family interests would be served.

Safeguards would be needed in any optional approach to ensure that parents have real choices and the information necessary to make them intelligently. There is great suspicion among non-English-speaking groups that the hostility of many school people to bilingual education leads them to discourage parents from applying and to implement bilingual programs with such inferior standards that parents would not wish to choose them. Legal enforcement should concentrate on making sure that high-quality bilingual education, including strong English instruction, is available for those who want it.

Admittedly, a choice approach would not settle the issue of overall language policy for the country. Whether the United States should encourage multilingualism is an important question that has received insufficient public debate. Given the changes in the world and in the technology of communication and travel, there is strong justification for shifting from what has until now been a basically monolingual language policy. But it will take time before a social and political consensus can develop on a policy for the future. The backlash antibilingual vote in Miami indicates that patience, as well as time, will be needed to work out a new formula. Meanwhile, for children going to school in the immediate future, parental choice may be the best policy. Interestingly, where choice is available, some English-speaking families are choosing bilingual programs for their own children. They see bilingual education as superior to the traditional monolingual approach as a way to prepare their children for the world they will live in.[9] Perhaps parental choice will help show the way to a future in which multilingualism is the norm for all Americans.

MINIMUM COMPETENCE TESTING

The controversy over testing children's achievement in the basic skills of reading, writing, and arithmetic does not compare with busing or bilingual education in emotional content, but it is shaping up as an important educational issue. Minimum competence testing is "moving like a 'grass fire' through state capitols catching many educators in a web of controversies."[10] Legislative battles are being fought, editorials written, and bitter words exchanged over it. At least part of the heat aroused by the minimum competence debate may be explainable by the thesis of this book: it represents a serious challenge to an important element of the professional-bureaucratic hegemony in public education.

For years one of the ways in which professional bureaucracies have been able to run public schools without regard to the "voice of the people" has been to take advantage of the pluralism and complexity of American society to keep the goals of public schools comfortably vague. Slogans such as "equal educational opportunity" or "educating all children to their fullest potential" sound grand in school systems' goal statements, but they permit the widest possible levels of achievement, including a substantial degree of educational failure. As long as the educational bureaucracy is "delivering educational services" according to the proper bureaucratic rules and procedures, the failure of large numbers of students to learn can be, and has been, explained by the presumed lack of potential of the children. There have been no established educational achievement standards against which to measure their achievement. Furthermore, the doctrine of "social promotion," introduced as part of the new professional science of education, allowed school systems to pass children along from grade to grade whether or not they learned, thus further easing the educational bureaucracy along its merry way, paying salaries and preserving jobs regardless of educational achievement.

The minimum competence movement represents a grass-roots rebellion against this form of unaccountability. Educators complain bitterly that the requirements for basic skills testing are coming from politicians, not educators—who presumably know better because of their superior scientific expertise. It does not seem to occur to these professional pundits that the "politicians" are responding to the voices of none other than their employers, the public.

It is true that "back to basics" can take on a know-nothing, regressive form that would dismiss the arts and critical thinking as frills and limit schooling to boring drills of the three R's. But this is more of a caricature than a fair description of this widespread popular movement, which has now brought minimum competence testing to two-thirds of the states.[11] For the most part, it represents no animus at all against solid liberal education, but merely a strong consensus that at least some learning goals can be widely agreed upon as basic for all children and must be achieved, regardless of the barrage of double-talk from the professional educators.

One of the strongest jeremiads against minimum competence testing is a book-length essay called *Legislated Learning* by Arthur E. Wise of the Rand Corporation. His overall thesis parallels that of this book in many ways, coming out strongly against the bureaucratization of education. Wise, however, mistakenly identifies state-mandated competence tests as a form of increased bureaucratization. He sees them as a way to "reduce" educational goals "to the basic skills alone"—a form of "hyper-rationalization" that "requires replacing the exercise of administrative discretion either with rules or

procedures."[12] But there is no evidence that the purpose of competence tests is to limit the goals of education; their purpose is to ensure that at least a minimum is achieved by all children (and schools).
This definition of minimum "output" standards actually represents
a major change from the bureaucratic trends of the last century,
which have prescribed increasingly detailed bureaucratic means for
achieving ever more vaguely defined ends.

Wise assumes that decisions made at a higher level of government
are necessarily more bureaucratic than those made at lower levels.
They usually are, but he forgets that some of the most oppressive
bureaucratization of schooling occurs at the district, school, and
even classroom levels. Sometimes decisions made at higher levels
of government represent the voice of people who have been closed
out of educational policy decisions at lower levels. The minimum
competence movement is an example of this. Parents, business
people, and concerned citizens who see thousands of high school
seniors graduating from high school without the most elementary
school skills have been ignored by local school bureaucracies, which
are so entrenched in their comfortably unaccountable systems that
they cannot hear the voice of common sense. The widespread concerns of the public have finally found a hearing in state boards of
education and legislative halls.

Wise is correct in warning that state achievement standards could
open the door to increased state bureaucratic control in the hands
of aggressive state officials. All they need do is follow the "output"
standards with more state "input" standards, telling local school
districts in detail *how* they are to run schools to achieve the desired
levels of learning. But this need not be the result. Because minimum
competence standards are output rather than input standards, they
could pave the way for greater autonomy at the local level. Those
who oppose the debilitating effects of overbureaucratization could
use the new competence standards as a basis for urging states to
permit local districts and individual schools to deviate from present
state requirements, as long as they produce the desired results.[13]

It is ironic that Wise, who sees so well the disabilities of educational bureaucracy, nevertheless accepts the classic bureaucratic
definition of the problem of attaining basic levels of competence for
all children as "more technical than political." It is a technical problem only so long as education is defined as a technological process.
Within that framework it is true that school systems "do not know"

how to educate large numbers of these students—it is "beyond the bounds of knowledge" (technological, scientific knowledge, that is).[14] The remedy, of course, within this framework, is more research, more technology, and probably more staff and overhead. But it is not beyond the professional skill of the many teachers and principals who prove every day that virtually all children can be taught basic school skills. The problem is far more political than technological. It is political, first, in requiring reassertion of a legitimate public goal that many school systems have lost sight of in their technocratic-bureaucratic myopia, and it is political, second, in requiring political action to intervene in the bureaucratized system to assure achievement of the goal.

Minimum competence standards, in short, could represent just such a debureaucratizing trend in public education. They can help reestablish the sense of community and common purpose so sorely lacking in school systems that have lost sight of their ends in their increasingly bureaucratic means. It is perverse to think that minimum standards are intended as maximum goals. They should instead be seen as goals that all can agree on, that benefit all children (since all suffer from the many alienated students who now fail to achieve them), and that all can work together to achieve. They can reunite schools and families, school systems and communities, and teachers and students in a common endeavor. They not only give effective voice to the many families and community groups concerned about their children's educational failure but also open up the possibility of much stronger educational partnerships for ensuring educational success far beyond minimum standards.

SEX EDUCATION

While some Americans are concerned about the three R's, others are concerned about teenage pregnancies, illegitimate births, and the spread of venereal disease. Some people assume that the obvious remedy for these problems is sex education in the schools.

The concern is understandable, but the remedy is fraught with problems. Sex education programs vary so greatly in purpose and in implementation that generalizations are dangerous, but hysterical puritans are not the only ones who question the appropriateness and efficacy of much that is done in the name of helping school children develop "healthy sexuality."[15]

The main problem, of course, is that what to one person is healthy sexuality is to another the most heinous perversion and a threat to religious and family values. As a result, a firestorm of opposition is gathering across the country against sex education in the schools. The National Education Association estimates there are some three hundred organizations now working to oppose sex education, and they are growing more organized and effective day by day.[16]

Some analysts view this as a fight between the great majority of Americans who favor sex education in schools (with 80 percent reported supporting it in the polls) and "a tiny but vociferous minority" who use misinformation and scare tactics in an attempt to abolish the programs. What is needed from this point of view are counter tactics to "make sure the media get on our side" so that the majority view can prevail.[17]

From the point of view of partnership there are problems with this approach, quite aside from one's views of the merits of sex education. If public schools are to be for all children, and if a bond of trust and sense of mutuality are important for the effectiveness and legitimacy of the enterprise, it is not enough for a majority to win out on such an issue, whichever side the majority may be on. The partnership approach introduces another element into the equation in addition to one's views of the merits of sex education, namely, concern for the relationship between families and schools.

In a governmental service-delivery approach to education sex education may seem a straightforward enough remedy for teenage pregnancies. If there is a problem let the "system" provide professionalized services to deal with it. Those who object can be brushed aside as backward people trying to stand in the way of enlightened, scientific progress; they obviously do not know what is good for their children. An article in the Reader's Digest advocating sex education, for instance, cites gruesome statistics about "a million teen-age pregnancies a year," abortion clinics "flooded with girls, some as young as 12," and gonorrhea doubling in a decade. The article then jumps, without further argument, to the conclusion that therefore, sex education in the schools is of course "imperative." The only reason it has not been implemented more widely, according to this article, is because of pressure from "small but well-organized lobbying groups."[18] If one cares, however, about the quality of the relationships between homes and communities there are good reasons, even for those who favor sex education for their own children, to hesitate before taking governmental action that is so frightening to some parents.

Some advocates of sex education argue that this problem can be dealt with by permitting families who object to opt out of the program. But the problem is not so simple. Quite aside from the pressure this puts on the objectors' own children, this approach avoids the real issue, which is that there is a sharp clash of values and assumptions as to what is best for children and for society as a whole. Parents can read, not just in right-wing journals or religious tracts but in the *New York Times,* about sex educators who "have developed curriculum designed not only to warn of the dangers of sex, but also, unprecedentedly, to promote its pleasures," and who think they should promote "an appreciation for the wide range of sexuality . . . not limited to heterosexual, genital intercourse."[19] The values-clarification techniques used in many programs openly proclaim that their purpose is to help young people make up their own minds how they want to govern their sex lives, while many parents feel that family and religious values should prevail.

The situation is just the reverse, in other words, of the community-building potential of the minimum competence movement. In that case, there is widespread public agreement on the learning goals and the schools' role in promoting them, and a potential for developing a sense of partnership in achieving them. In sex education, on the contrary, there are passionate disagreements about what should be taught (if anything), fierce controversy over the role of the schools in teaching it, and every potential for community conflict and the destruction of trust. From the point of view of educational partnerships, it is better to concentrate in public schools on those areas where there is a reasonable consensus both about ends and about means. Sex education is clearly not such an area in many communities.

It is a free country, and therefore Planned Parenthood, the Catholic Church, Playboy International, and the Moral Majority are all free to promote whatever view of healthy sexual behavior or new sexual utopia suits their outlook on life. This does not mean, however, that a public school is the best arena into which to toss these contending views, much less for any one of them to be selected as the official, government-sponsored view on sex. To do so only increases the conviction of many that public schools are not appropriate institutions for a pluralistic society.

How, then, to deal with the concerns about increasing teenage pregnancies and unwanted births? The lessons of educational bureaucracy indicate that a healthier approach may be to use and support the mediating structures that can deal with these issues within a value framework—not only such traditional structures as families and churches but also newer mediating structures, such as peer groups and self-help programs, which often show promise in establishing the relationships necessary for helping young people work their way out of self-destructive behavior. At present there is little funding for such programs because funding is preempted by social service bureaucracies, which, until now, have managed to persuade the public that the only available response to ineffective programs is more money, more services, more research, and more bureaucracy.

It will take ingenuity to find ways to use mediating structures without strangling them in red tape. This is, however, the right place to apply social invention. In many cases it may prove more productive than trying to get public bureaucracies to undertake tasks for which they are as inherently ill suited as they are for teaching young people how to deal with sex.

BOOK BANNING

Banning books from schools can lead to controversies at least as heated as those over sex education. Indeed, different sexual values are often the source of the heat.

In West Virginia thousands of people were involved in passionate combat over whether certain books used in the public schools are harmful to students. Fierce political campaigns have been waged and school boards wrenched violently over this issue.[20] In Warsaw, Indiana, in 1978, the banning escalated into burning. A senior citizens' group, jubilant over its success in getting books it opposed removed from the schools, piled up the offending books in a local parking lot and set them on fire. It is not clear whether they were aware of the symbolism of their act or chose it exactly because they knew it would strike revulsion into the hearts of every civil libertarian. The whole community was afflicted with what one observer called "a massive seizure of anti-intellectualism," which led to firing of teachers, business boycotts, and bitter family feuds.[21]

Such cases usually start when someone in the community claims that various books used in the schools are "offensive," "obscene," "objectionable," "immoral," "subversive," "un-American," or otherwise unfit for schoolchildren. Sometimes the books are quietly removed, and the issue ends. But if the school authorities decide to retain the books, and those who object to them escalate their pressure, the stage is set for a battle royal.

On one side are ranged those who want to "defend the morals of our children." They brandish selections from the offending books before their fellow citizens, showing passages with curse words, lurid descriptions of sexual perversions, examples of moral relativism, criticism of America's foreign policy, or ungodly theories of evolution. They argue that it is outrageous to have "our" schools, paid for by "our" hard-earned taxes to educate "our" children, teaching these odious values and ideas.

On the other side are usually a variety of forces. The largest group may be those who are so turned off by the extreme tactics of the "book burners" that they support the school authorities just because they do not want to be identified with the "kooks." There are also the school authorities and professional leaders, who argue that they cannot carry out their professional duties if their judgments are second-guessed "by every crackpot in the community." After all, have they not studied child development, curriculum, and library science for years so that they would know more than the ordinary citizen about what books are good for educating children? Why are their professional judgments not trusted?

Backing up the school authorities are usually the civil libertarians, who are passionately commited to free speech and the free exchange of ideas. Sometimes their leadership comes from the local community, sometimes from regional or national organizations that join the fray because of the "momentous issues that go to the heart of our democratic system of government."[22] They argue that children should be exposed to many different ideas as they grow up, that "protecting" people from dangerous or "bad" ideas is the very essence of a closed society, and that book banning is the first step down the slippery path to totalitarianism.

Such controversies are not limited to the heartland. In 1976 the school board in Island Trees, Long Island, voted to withdraw "objectionable" books from its schools, including *The Naked Ape, Slaughterhouse Five,* and *Soul on Ice.* Bitter community controversy erupted; school board campaigns were fought over the issue (thus far vindicating the book-banning school board members who have stood for reelection). Civil liberty and professional education groups joined forces to overturn the decision of the local school board in court.[23]

The state of the law on this issue is far from clear. Some courts have ruled that the withdrawal of "objectionable" books from school libraries or curriculums violates First Amendment guarantees of free speech; others have upheld the school authorities. The dilemma in these cases is exemplified in the saga of Jody Caravaglia's poem, written while Jody was a high school student in New York City. The poem describes vividly how lecherous men were always after her body. The poem was printed in a book called *Male and Female under Eighteen,* which was selected for the high school library in Chelsea, Massachusetts. One of the great champions of free speech, Nat Hentoff, in his book *The First Freedom,* describes how James McCarthy, father of a fourteen-year-old Chelsea high school student, called the chairman of the local school committee, "about to explode": his daughter had borrowed *Male and Female under Eighteen* from the school library "and had become so distraught" from reading the poem that he was "on the verge of going down to the high school and punching out the headmaster." "I pay $2,012 in taxes to this city," roared the father, "and I just can't believe this kind of poem is available to my child." At the discussion before the school committee, the chairman, Arthur Quigley, asked, rhetorically, has a father "no right to protect his daughter from contamination by the 'slime' . . . in this poem?"[24]

Apparently the librarian and her allies thought not, for the school committee was brought into court to have the book returned to the school library.

As Hentoff tells the story, at the six-day trial "a number of experts in adolescent literature testified to the poem's bracingly educational value. The other side pointed out, however, that none of these so-called experts lived in Chelsea. Were the educational wishes of this working-class community to be wholly ignored because *outside* specialists thought filth was good for Chelsea school children?" "Look," Chairman Quigley said after the trial, "they were *all* outsiders. . . . They're floating free thinkers is what they are.

And there's nothing wrong with that in places like Newton and Marblehead, where the parents are the same way. But it doesn't go in Chelsea, nor should we be forced to accept it if this is a democracy."[25]

Judge Joseph Tauro thought otherwise and ordered the book back in the school library. He said the school board had shown "no evidence at the trial that the poem could cause any damage at all" and "no substantial and legitimate government interest" in banning the book—only "their outraged tastes." In reaching his decision, Judge Tauro relied on the precedent of the *Minarcini* case, which had also overturned a school board's decision to remove books on the ground that the decision "related solely to the social or political tastes of the school board members."[26]

Clearly, a book-banning mentality—the idea that a community can impose an orthodoxy and suppress unwanted views—is a threat to the right of everyone to have, and to express, their own values and ideas and not just those of the majority or the government. But these are also the very rights that are violated when school authorities presume to decide which values are "best for children" over the objections of their parents. They are violated, that is, as long as children are seen as *members of families* and not just individuals whose family values can be disregarded. The fact that children and families are involved makes these cases different from issues of free speech in the marketplace.

In 1975 the school board in Drake, North Dakota, ordered that copies of Kurt Vonnegut's *Slaughterhouse Five* be burned. The teacher who assigned the book lost his job. In defending himself he said that he was only trying "to get the kids to think clearly about current problems. . . . A few four letter words in a book is no big deal. . . . I've always thought the purpose of school was to prepare these people for living in the 'big, bad world,' but it evidently isn't so."[27] Many parents and educators would applaud this teacher's approach. For other parents, however, the use of four-letter words and a tolerant attitude toward them by those hired as role models for their children are indeed a "big deal." Are differences of opinion over four-letter words, sexual deviance, or obscenity purely questions of professional expertise, or are they questions of value? If the latter, then school authorities who presume to answer them solely on professional grounds without regard to parental values run a high risk of jeopardizing relationships of trust between schools and families.

In these cases there is usually evidence that in withdrawing the books, the school board members assume they are carrying out the wishes of the community they represent. They are, in other words, heeding the voice of their constituents. From the point of view of educational partnership, the "legitimate government interest" at stake is not the personal tastes of the school board members, but the relationship of trust between parents and schools. School boards have not only a right but also a responsibility to foster such relationships. The basis of this responsibility is not prudery, or any particular morality or ideology, but the effective education of children, which cannot operate properly except in a context of trust.

Book banning is bad business, without question. It stirs up passions of bigotry and narrow-mindedness. As Supreme Court Justice Brennan said in one case, it casts "a pall of orthodoxy" over a community;[28] and it suppresses the voice of both citizens and teachers. But it is often the school authorities themselves, through their lack of sensitivity to the varied values of a diverse constituency, who stimulate these bigoted responses. From the offended parents' point of view, it is the school officials who are trying to create a "pall of orthodoxy"—an orthodoxy of values they do not agree with —when they insist on using materials the parents feel are harmful to their children. Such action repudiates parental responsibilities and tells parents that their concerns are of no account. It violates the very essence of voice, choice, and loyalty.

The cause of free speech is not well served when parents are told that, in the name of free speech, the state can cram whatever it wants down their children's throats or that professional educators or the courts have a constitutional right to override the decisions of their elected representatives in deciding what is best for their children. This constitutes a grievous violation of voice. There is nothing very liberal about a powerful government agency's violating families' most deeply held values.

How can both sets of values—free speech and the rights of families to their own values—be reconciled in a public school system? Education by partnership requires respecting the values of parents and families, even if they are in disagreement with those of professional educators or, for that matter, the majority of the community.

Obviously, there are limits to this. Parents who believe Shakespeare is an instrument of the Devil and want all his works banned from the school can properly be advised to seek a private school where their children will not be exposed to the immoral bard. But if some of the parents in a community say they are offended by the use of *Little Black Sambo* because it insults blacks, or the *Merchant of Venice* because it stereotypes Jews, or *The Naked Ape* because they do not want its explicit descriptions of sexual intercourse presented to their children, why is it a violation of the First Amendment—or even of the spirit of the First Amendment—for the school authorities to select other books that would be equally valuable as literature or social science and would not offend the values of the families whose children are in their care?

A school is not a public marketplace.[29] Children are involved, and so are family values. The issues are by no means easy, and some books and parental values present borderline cases. Parents should be educated to the difference between political and moral orthodoxy and between books assigned in class and books in the school library. But they are more likely to accept such distinctions and trust school officials to use their judgment about what should be given to children at different ages if the school is sensitive to parents' values and respects them.

One way to do this is to have committees of teachers and parents of various backgrounds consider these questions before they reach the level of community controversy, so that there is greater opportunity to take into account both professional concerns and family values.

Partnership requires respect—not just respect for those one agrees with, not just lip service that says school officials will respect families by doing what the professional staff thinks is best for their children over the objection of their wrongheaded parents—but real respect, which listens to the voices and honors the choices that reflect parents' real values. Some professional groups seem blind to this. The National Council of Teachers of English, the National Council for the Social Studies, and the Speech Communication Association, in their brief in the *Island Trees* case, asserted that in deciding what books to discard from a school library, "in no circumstances, we submit, may the choice merely be the product of an official's views as to the 'basic values of the community.'"[30] Such a contemptuous attitude toward the values of the community does not foster the trust and loyalty necessary for effective education to develop. If that means not using every book that a teacher or curriculum expert fancies, that is not too high a price to pay for creating a sense of partnership with parents. Nor does it in any way preclude equipping students with the intellectual skills and moral commitments needed for participating in the free exchange of ideas and the democratic process. On the contrary, it teaches that the spirit of free speech means respecting the views of others, even if one does not agree with them.

CORPORAL PUNISHMENT

If sex fails to stir up a community, perhaps child beating will. From listening to those who want legislatures or courts to prohibit corporal punishment, one would think the only question is whether one is for or against child abuse. Indeed, there certainly are cases in which corporal punishment constitutes child abuse that presumably all decent people would condemn. But there is another issue often overlooked in this debate: What levels or techniques of government should be used to deal with the question?

The concept of educational partnerships has something to tell us about this. It tells us to be wary of the simple formula that says if something is bad, pass a law against it. The normal consequence of passing the law is the establishment of a bureaucracy to enforce it; and the proliferation of governmental bureaucracy is one of the enemies of educational partnerships. It may in the end cause more harm than it was set up to prevent.

In New York City, where I have lived and worked for the past thirteen years, I favor the current rule against corporal punishment. There is too much risk of abuse, too much alienation between school authorities and the communities they serve, too much chance that parents will see corporal punishment as aggression against their children rather than as an extension of their own parental care and authority. What about a small rural community, however, where corporal punishment has been school policy for years, where it is rarely used and never abused, and where parents and citizens view it, perhaps more symbolically than operationally, as an important part of their school policy? Such people may be misguided, and I would not for a moment stifle efforts educators or citizens might want to make to persuade them to change their policies. But if we want to foster a sense of partnership between schools and families, there is at least a question about the wisdom of having a distant state government tell the people of such a community what they may or may not do with their own children in their own schools. To say that the values and beliefs of the people in the local community should not be considered if they are so misguided as to allow corporal punishment is, to that extent, to tell them that the schools are not "their" schools—and the process of alienation between parents and schools is under way, all in the name of "the best interests of the child."

The New York State Board of Regents debated this issue recently and adopted a policy prohibiting corporal punishment throughout the state. The new policy will probably be of no great moment either way insofar as the actual use of corporal punishment is concerned. There is relatively little corporal punishment in the schools of New York State, and some of the worst of it occurs in New York City, where it is already supposedly prohibited. But the issue became symbolic. Local communities saw yet one more area taken out of their decision-making control. Not only are communities disempowered in deciding whether to authorize corporal punishment and if so under what conditions and how, but the jurisdiction over each individual case will now shift to the state bureaucracy, and the local people will be continually reminded of their disempowerment. Any time a teacher restrains a student from committing mayhem can be the occasion for state authorities to step in and tell the local people what to do.

Would the Republic fall to pieces if this issue were left to local communities? Real cases of child abuse could still be dealt with through the courts or state educational authorities. Those who believe that corporal punishment is bad under all conditions would still be free to wage a campaign to persuade communities to abandon it. Meanwhile, however, the people in local communities would retain some sense of control over their own destinies, and the state policy machinery would remain free to deal with issues that more urgently require policy making beyond the local level.

THE CHRISTIAN SCHOOLS

There is hardly a problem in American society more fraught with complexities than the relationship between church and state, and there is no opportunity here to examine all of them. The partnership approach to educational policy can be sampled in an aspect of this problem that has recently become more controversial—the issue surrounding the so-called Christian school movement.

Two contradictory trends have helped to bring this issue to the fore: a sharp increase in the number of the small, fundamentalist schools in many parts of the country and increased governmental activity trying to regulate nonpublic schools.[31] Perhaps the two phenomena are linked; public education authorities may feel threatened by the exodus of families to nonpublic schools, which, since 1975, have had increasing enrollments while public school enrollments have been declining. Whatever the reasons, there is a potential for increasing conflict as parents exercise their right to choose private schools, and government follows after to limit the scope of their choice.

Governmental supervision of the Christian schools usually comes in the form of actual or threatened state regulation of curriculum, personnel policies, library standards, etc. The schools do not object to many of these requirements; they are willing to meet what they view as reasonable curriculum requirements and health and safety standards, but they claim that the amount and detail of state regulation go far beyond any reasonable level, to the point of harassment.

In a series of recent court cases, the independent schools have won a number of significant victories, which have enabled them to escape from unwarranted governmental regulation and interference. One judge went so far as to conclude:

> The State is unable to demonstrate that its regulatory scheme applied to the *public* schools has any reasonable relationship to the supposed objective of advancing educational quality; not only is that unfortunate truth apparent in this case, but more ominously, it has become apparent to the taxpaying Kentucky citizens who support the educational apparatus. Plaintifs, on the other hand, have shown that without benefit of the State's ministrations their educational product is at least equal to, if not somewhat better than, that of the public schools, in pure secular competence.

He found, in addition, "not the slightest connection between teacher certification and enhanced educational quality in State schools, nor is there generally any such requirement in private schools."[32]

A more difficult issue arose in the late 1970s over an attempted federal regulation of independent schools through the Internal Revenue Service. The problem faced by the IRS was serious: many private schools had sprung up during the course of desegregation to help white families escape from integrated public schools. Civil rights groups pressured the federal government to deny tax exemption to these "segregation academies." As Clarence Mitchell, then lobbyist for the National Association for the Advancement of Colored People, put it, "Every school that's been started to evade desegregation has called itself Christian. That's not my idea of being Christian."[33]

The remedy proposed by the IRS, however, was a blanket regulation requiring all private schools formed or expanded since desegregation had begun to adopt affirmative action plans, unless they could show that they already had a significant number of minority students, defined as at least 20 percent of minority school-age population in the community. The affirmative actions required included the institution of scholarships for minority students, the recruitment of minority staff, and the appointment of minority members to the governing board, requirements that were clearly impractical for many of these small schools run by and for religious congregations. The proposal created a storm of protest and a backlash in the Congress, which put a halt to the IRS plans.

What is one to make of this? To the extent that people were trying to protect segregated havens, some of the heat could be attributed to old-fashioned American racism. But the segregationist forces were able to gain many allies because the IRS regulation touched another raw nerve with deep roots in American traditions—the threat of heavy-handed governmental control over private schools—and religious schools to boot. The IRS reaped some of the animus that had already been building because of efforts by state educational bureaucracies to interfere with these schools.

While "segregation academies" clearly require government attention, there are also legitimate Christian schools whose origins can be traced more to parents' objections to the "secular humanist" values of the public schools than to race. Peter Skerry, in his "Christian Schools versus the IRS," reports on his visit to a number of these schools in North Carolina and concludes that "skepticism toward the religious orientation of these schools is altogether unwarranted, and . . . the effort to reduce their emergence to a matter of racism is a gross oversimplification."[34]

Skerry also makes a strong argument that the legal basis for the IRS regulation is shaky at best, since it equates tax exemption with government subsidy, thus triggering the regulatory requirements that accompany federal aid. Since one of the most important reasons for the tax-exempt status of churches is to *prevent* governmental entanglement with religion, it is ironic to have that status used as a justification for governmental regulation.

What concerns us, however, is not so much the legal theory as the educational policy. An educational policy framework that views education as a matter of bureaucratic service delivery will have no problem justifying the most detailed governmental regulation of schools. The concerns and values of individual parents can be relegated to a position of irrelevance, if not illegitimacy. Within such a framework it is much easier to lump all private schools together and subject them all to the same set of regulations—much easier, and much more convenient for bureaucratic administration. If, however, one looks at education in a free society as necessarily involving partnerships with families and respect for the mediating structures people choose for themselves, then policies to deal with the problem of "segregation academies" must be more sensitive. This does not tell us how to solve this sticky problem, but it tells us how not to try to solve it, that is, through blanket bureaucratic policies showing no regard for parental values that do not violate legitimate federal laws and policies. If the IRS had been sensitive to a mediating structures approach, perhaps it could have made more progress in dealing with the legitimate needs for federal intervention.

In general, a mediating structures approach to private schools would be one of minimal interference. Even for public schools we have seen that a sense of partnership at the local level calls for minimal bureaucratization and rationalization of state-wide educational systems. For private schools, where people have declared their independence from the state system, it is even more important to respect the autonomy of individual schools.

CONCLUSION

If we did not have a public school system, many of the problems discussed in this chapter would not exist. As advocates of voucher plans point out, the great variety of views among Americans over such issues as sex education, bilingual instruction, corporal punishment, and the proper books for children could all be accommodated by letting parents choose schools that conform to their values. Providing vouchers large enough to permit real choices would therefore be one way of dealing with these issues. Vouchers would maximize choice and promote relationships of *loyalty* and partnership. The lesson for public education, if it wants to survive, is also to offer more scope for choice and loyalty. Since common enterprises by definition limit choice, however, public schools must also offer their constituents more voice in order to maintain their sense of ownership and loyalty to the enterprise.

Admittedly, giving voice to so many divergent voices causes complications, and respecting the myriad values of American citizens means that there are no simple solutions to questions of value conflict in public schools. But no one ever said democracy was easy. It is, after all, one of the highest purposes of our public education system to help develop a sense of community in a diverse population. If the task is difficult, there is no alternative except to try harder if we want to succeed. One thing is certain: trying to steamroller over these issues with an insensitive service-delivery system is no solution. A public school system that continues on its present path of over-governmentalization, bureaucratization, and professionalization will not much longer endure.

EPILOGUE

In the end we must come back to the question: Can it be done? Can the policy framework and practices of public education be shifted from bureaucracy to partnership, and from service delivery to empowerment of students, families, and communities?

The answer lies in the political will of the American people. We will have to decide what we want in the way of education for our children and their future, and then take the appropriate political action to get it.

The first step is to decide how dissatisfied we are with the present system. As this book goes to press, the media report hopeful statements about increased reading scores and school improvements. Are the assumptions about the system's failure premature or invalid?

Failure is a relative term—and so is success. The reported improvements are in relation to the abysmal levels of achievement that have prevailed up to now. They still leave us with tens of thousands of young people arriving at adulthood without the most minimal educational preparation, and many thousands more with a mediocre education at best.

The failure is in relation to the levels of education needed to survive and prosper in today's world—and tomorrow's. The debate as to whether schools are doing better than they did fifty or a hundred —or five—years ago is beside the point. The urgent question is

261

whether they are doing well enough for now and the future. It is on this score that we must remain dissatisfied with the present system.

Our children are learning much less than they should be learning and much less than they could be learning. It is clear that it will take political action to bring about the changes needed, just as it has taken political action to bring about even the small improvements achieved thus far. For better or worse, education in the United States is once again squarely in the political arena. Much folly can be expected to flow from this, but the system established by previous generations is no longer functional, and in a democracy responsibility to find new paths properly reverts to the political process.

There are at least two kinds of political action that might be taken. One is to work for the establishment of a voucher system, by which public money would flow directly to families so they could exercise direct control over their children's education. Although there would be many problems with this route, and certainly strong opposition, it represents a relatively "quick fix." If it could be adopted at the state or federal level, either through legislation or referendum, and at a sufficient level to pay the full costs of a good education, the dynamics of the educational system would be instantly, and probably permanently, changed. Specific political action to change the policies and practices of public schools and school systems would become less important.

The other kind of political action is much more diffuse. It requires the conversion of present systems, district by district, school by school, and classroom by classroom, from a sterile bureaucratic approach to an active partnership which draws on the voice, choice, and loyalty of all involved. Such a shift can be facilitated by leadership at the state and national levels, both lay and professional, but it cannot be achieved without the countless efforts of parents, teachers, administrators, and community leaders in local school districts all across the country.

The unlikelihood of the slower approach ever happening is what makes many people see a voucher system as the only answer. They may be right. The present policy framework may be so deeply embedded in people's minds and behavior patterns that, without some radical departure such as vouchers, the present system is destined to slide to its inevitable self-destruction or to wallow in a perpetual crisis of dissatisfaction and piecemeal reform that will keep it stumbling indefinitely, but inadequately, into the future.

The quick fix, however, is not always the best one. Nor is it necessarily as practical an avenue for political action as may at first appear. One advantage of the slower approach is its feasibility, right now, in any school, community, or state where enough people want to undertake it. It is already being undertaken to some degree in individual schools where principals or community leaders have taken initiative, or in special programs such as the Local School Development Program in New York City, the National Partnership for Successful Schools, or the family choice systems developed in the Minneapolis and Indianapolis public schools. I have no question but that any community wanting to can create a collaborative relationship between teachers, parents, students, and citizens that will produce educational results far in excess of what we are now achieving. And this can be done despite the present fiscal constraints. Indeed, the effort to create such a collaboration can help to overcome past polarizations and generate enough support to provide whatever resources are needed.

A major purpose of this book is not to prove that there is only one path to educational partnerships, but to point out the complexity, as well as the urgency, of the problem. We must begin in earnest the political dialogue about which way to turn. It took many years to build the present system, and much of that process involved developing a political consensus about the kind of educational system we wanted as a nation. Now that it is clear that the present system will not, and cannot, achieve our purposes as a nation, we will have to go through the same kind of consensus-building anew to decide where we go from here. While this book does not provide easy answers, it is hoped that it provides both a stimulus, and a useful framework, for seeking them.

THE MEDIATING STRUCTURES
PROJECT

This volume is an important part of a three-year study of "mediating structures" directed by Peter Berger and myself and sponsored by the American Enterprise Institute. We readily acknowledge that the controlling concept, mediating structures, is not entirely new with us. Although called by different names, the concept is rooted in nineteenth and twentieth century social theory addressing the problems of modernity and, particularly, the role of the modern state in social change. What is new is the effort to refine the concept and explore its implications with specific reference to contemporary American public policy in the fields of education, housing, criminal justice, welfare, child care, and health.

By mediating structures we mean those institutions that stand between the individual in the solitariness of his or her private life and the megastructures of society (big government, big labor, big corporations, and the like). The mediating structures about which we are chiefly concerned are the family, the neighborhood, the church, and voluntary associations. Other institutions may be defined as mediating structures if in fact they do mediate in the sense suggested above. Mediating structures are "people sized" and have about them a face-to-face quality through which people can both feel empowered and be empowered to control the decisions most crucial to their own lives. (For a more detailed explanation of the mediating structures concept, see our *To Empower People*, published by the American Enterprise Institute.)

In advancing this concept and spelling out its policy implications we hope to sustain the best of the policy approaches generally associated with the New Deal. We are not opposing the positive or affirmative state. We believe, however, that the policies of the welfare state have been grievously, perhaps fatally, flawed by one key and fundamentally wrong-headed assumption. That assumption is that public responsibilities must be exercised chiefly or exclusively through governmental action. We do affirm a broad definition of what are public responsibilities. But we are convinced that most of those responsibilities can be more effectively and more economically fulfilled through the imaginative use of mediating structures—more effectively and more economically and, it must be quickly added, more democratically fulfilled.

Just complaints about "big government" are not directed so much at a comprehensive notion of what human needs should be of concern to government but at the government's intrusion into people's lives by imposing its own answers about how such needs are to be met. Our premise is that in almost all instances, the people most directly affected best understand their needs. Public policies should aim at being supportive and ancillary to people's vision of their own good. Obviously, such vision is largely shaped by the values to which people subscribe. This is especially true in the area of education. Whatever else education may be, it is a process by which people seek to transmit their world—and most particularly their values—to their children. It is a primary strength of mediating structures that they are value-generating and value-bearing institutions. This is especially true of family, church, and voluntary associations.

The frequently well-intended policies of the welfare state have tended to undercut rather than to strengthen mediating structures. In the field of education and elsewhere, the project involved a "minimalist" and a "maximalist" proposition. The minimalist proposition is that, wherever possible, public policies should be changed so that they do not weaken mediating structures. The maximalist is that, wherever possible, public policies should be devised that utilize the strengths of mediating structures.

We are grateful to David Seeley for accepting the assignment to examine the concept of mediating structures in the field of education. The authors involved in each of the five policy areas examined what public policies have been and what alternative policies have been proposed, always asking the question of how they weaken or reinforce mediating structures, thus empowering or disempowering people. It is hoped that each volume in the series also breaks new ground in exploring public policy designs that can enhance the freedom and well-being of Americans.

This study on education comes at a time when many observers believe that the United States is in political retreat from social problems and especially from urban problems. While this study encompasses many other aspects of education, there is of necessity a strong focus on urban education and education for the urban poor. While the problems of urban education are acute and manifest, the core issues of defining the educational process and the role of values within it are as urgent in Galesburg, Illinois, as they are in the Williamsburgh section of Brooklyn, New York.

Mr. Seeley's experience has been largely in urban education, but his work over the years has involved the most careful examination of the key ideas that have shaped the educational enterprise in our society. It is noteworthy that during the time of this study, Mr. Seeley directed the Public Education Association, itself a voluntary, New York–based organization that has, since the late nineteenth century, played a central role in defining and promoting the ideology of the public school. Although unimaginative and fearful defenders of the public education establishment may interpret some of the project's recommendations as hostile to the public school, that is not the case. Certainly some vested interests of the establishment may legitimately feel threatened. But far from being directed against the public school, this project is aimed at redefining what is meant by "public" in public education. Education is "public" that serves and is accountable to the relevant public for which it is devised. The proper distinction, therefore, is not between public education and private education but between government schools and voluntary schools. With reference to the poor, the goal is to *empower* them with an ability to choose similar to the ability already enjoyed by the more affluent.

The mediating structures project and this part of it are offered in the confidence that ours need not be a time of fearful retreat and simple-minded retrenchment on social programs. Rather, it is a time to ask first-principle questions about the possibilities and limitations

of government in a free society. It is a time to reconceptualize—
sometimes radically—and we are heartened that the mediating structures approach has been welcomed by policy planners on both the
left and right of the political spectrum. We believe ours is a time not
so much for cutting back (although in some areas, cutting back is
clearly required) as it is for cutting *through* the liberal-conservative
polarizations that have blinded us too often to what is actually happening in people's lives.

Now and in the years immediately ahead, it appears that those
who call themselves conservative will be in the policymaking saddle.
Conservatism has often been identified with negative reaction to the
apparent mistakes and illusions of its opposition. But this can be
the moment for testing whether conservatives have the nerve and
imagination to advance the best in the humane intentions that
liberals have claimed. The hope we propose is that the affirmative
state need not be the oppressive state, that public policy is not a
zero-sum game, that the prudent exercise of governmental power
need not be at the price of disempowering those whom government
is to serve.

Richard John Neuhaus

NOTES

CHAPTER 1: INTRODUCTION

1. Ivan Illich, *Deschooling Society* (New York: Harper & Row, Harrow Books, 1970).
2. Peter L. Berger and Richard John Neuhaus, *To Empower People: The Role of Mediating Structures in Public Policy* (Washington, D.C.: American Enterprise Institute, 1977).

CHAPTER 2: THE ROOTS OF EDUCATIONAL FAILURE

Epigraph from Ray Rist. *Restructuring American Education* (New Brunswick, N.J.: Transaction Books, 1972), p. 2.

1. Jonathan Kozol, *Prisoners of Silence* (New York: Continuum Publishing Corp., 1980), p. 1.
2. Lawrence A. Cremin, ed., *Horace Mann on the Education of Free Men* (New York: Teachers College Press, 1957), p. 8.
3. James S. Coleman, Ernest Q. Campbell, et al., *Equality of Educational Opportunity* (Washington, D.C.: U.S. Department of Health, Education, and Welfare, 1966), p. 218: "Studies of school achievement have consistently shown that variations in family background account for far more variation in school achievement than do variations in school characteristics."

269

4. Thomas Good, Bruce Biddle, and Jere Brophy, *Teachers Make a Difference* (New York: Holt, Rinehart & Winston, 1975), p. 22.
5. For a general overview and exhortation for more studies of these factors, see Donald A. Erickson, "Research on Educational Administration: The State of the Art," invited address, 1978 Annual Meeting, American Educational Research Association, Toronto, Ontario, March 27, 1978. For outstanding examples of research along these lines, see Micheal Rutter et al., *Fifteen Thousand Hours: Secondary Schools and Their Effects on Children* (Cambridge, Mass.: Harvard University Press, 1979); and Jean B. Wellisch et al., "School Management and Organization in Successful Schools (ESAA In-Depth Study Schools)," *Sociology of Education,* vol. 51, no. 3 (July 1978), pp. 211-26.
6. Many scholars have made this point. Two of the most notable, working from different perspectives, are Benjamin S. Bloom, *Human Characteristics and School Learning* (New York: McGraw-Hill, 1976), and Lawrence A. Cremin, *Public Education* (New York: Basic Books, 1976).
7. This is, in simplified form, much like Bloom's position in *Human Characteristics.* See also Good, Biddle, and Brophy, *Teachers Make a Difference.*

CHAPTER 3: GOVERNMENTAL SCHOOLING

Epigraph is from Lawrence A. Cremin, ed., *Horace Mann on the Education of Free Men,* (New York: Teachers College Press, 1957), p. 19.

1. David B. Tyack, *Turning Points in American History* (Waltham, Mass.: Blaisdell Publishing Co., 1967), p. 120.
2. Cremin, *Horace Mann,* p. 19.
3. Carl F. Kaestle, *The Evolution of an Urban School System, New York City, 1750-1850* (Cambridge, Mass.: Harvard University Press, 1973), p. 170.
4. L. Harmon Zeigler and M. Kent Jennings, with G. Wayne Peak, *Governing American Schools: Political Interaction in Local School Districts* (North Scituate, Mass.: Duxbury Press, 1974). See also David B. Tyack, *The One Best System: A History of American Urban Education* (Cambridge, Mass.: Harvard University Press, 1974); and Harmon Zeigler, "How School Control Was Wrested from the People," *Phi Delta Kappan,* vol. 58 (March 1977), pp. 534-39.
5. Diane Ravitch, *The Great School Wars, New York City, 1805-1973* (New York: Basic Books, 1974), chaps. 1-7.
6. Michael B. Katz, *Class, Bureaucracy, and Schools,* expanded ed. (New York: Praeger Publishers, 1975), p. 37; and Richard John Neuhaus, "No More Bootleg Religion," in Dwight Allen, ed., *Controversies in Education* (Philadelphia: W.B. Saunders Co., 1974), pp. 72-86.

7.   This is most obvious when one considers those cases in which there is a
     clear disagreement between family values and what is taught and expected
     in schools. The break of the Catholics from the Protestant-dominated
     school system in the nineteenth century, which is discussed in Ravitch
     The Great School Wars, is the most obvious example, but the rapid growth
     of "Christian schools" in the past ten years indicates not only that parents
     want values taught in school (a point corroborated by recent Gallup polls)
     but that if values are not taught, parents will actively do something about
     it. On discontinuities in value codes and in language codes, see J.W. Getzels,
     "Socialization and Education: A Note on Discontinuities," in Hope
     Jensen Leichter, ed., *The Family as Educator* (New York: Teachers College
     Press, 1974), pp. 44–51. McDill and Rigsby suggest that "alienation (re-
     flecting feelings of inefficacy and inability to master one's environment or
     control one's destiny) acts as an impediment to learning by depressing
     motivation and ability to act with confidence;" in Edward McDill and Leo
     C. Rigsby, *Structure and Process in Secondary Schools: The Academic
     Impact of Educational Climates* (Baltimore: Johns Hopkins University
     Press, 1973), pp. 122–23. See also Sara Lawrence Lightfoot, *World's
     Apart: Relationships between Families and Schools* (New York: Basic
     Books, 1978).

8.   Zeigler et al. *Governing American Schools,* p. 7. Blau and Scott developed
     a typology of organizations, which includes commonweal organizations,
     service organizations, and mutual benefit organizations. See Peter Blau
     and W. Richard Scott, *Formal Organizations* (San Francisco: Chandler
     Publishing Co., 1962).

9.   Zeigler et al. *Governing American Schools.* William Lowe Boyd, "The
     Study of Educational Policy and Politics: Much Ado about Nothing?"
     Teachers College Record, vol. 80, no. 2 (1978), p. 261, makes the same
     point and goes on to argue that since the people who work in the system
     are often its chief beneficiaries, the schools may also operate as mutual
     aid organizations.

10. Zeigler et al., *Governing American Schools.* Blau and Scott, *Formal
     Organizations,* p. 65: "The issue posed by commonweal organizations is
     that of external democratic control—the public must possess the means
     of controlling the ends served by these organizations. While external
     democratic control is essential, the internal structure of these organiza-
     tions is expected to be bureaucratic, governed by the criterion of effi-
     ciency, and not democratic. The challenge facing these organizations, then,
     is the maintenance of efficient bureaucratic mechanisms that effectively
     implement the objectives of the community, which are ideally decided
     upon, at least in our society, by democratic methods."

272   APPLICATIONS

CHAPTER 4: BUREAUCRATIZED EDUCATION

Epigraph from Robert Merton, "Bureaucratic Structure and Personality," in *Social Theory and Social Structure* (New York: Free Press, 1957), p. 196.

1. Carl F. Kaestle, *The Evolution of an Urban School System, New York City, 1750-1850* (Cambridge, Mass.: Harvard University Press, 1973), p. 161. See also David B. Tyack, *The One Best System: A History of American Urban Education* (Cambridge, Mass.: Harvard University Press, 1974), pt. 2, pp. 28-77.

2. Kaestle, *Evolution of an Urban School System*, pp. 164-66.

3. Tyack, *One Best System.*

4. Seymour Sarason, *The Culture of the School and the Problem of Change* (Boston: Allyn & Bacon, 1971); Philip Jackson, *Life in Classrooms* (New York: Holt, Rinehart & Winston, 1968); Ray Rist, *Restructuring American Education* (New Brunswick, N.J.: Transaction Books, 1972).

5. Kaestle, *Evolution of an Urban School System*, p. 178.

6. Peter Berger, Brigitte Berger, and Hansfried Kellner, *The Homeless Mind* (New York: Vintage Books, 1974), p. 55.

7. Benjamin S. Bloom, *Human Characteristics and School Learning* (New York: McGraw-Hill, 1976), p. 14.

8. David Kirp, "Schools as Sorters: The Constitutional and Policy Implication of Student Classification," *University of Pennsylvania Law Review*, vol 121, no. 4 (1973), pp. 705-97.

9. John Ogbu, "Racial Stratification and Education: The Case of Stockton, California," Institute for Urban and Minority Education, Teachers College, Columbia University, *IRCD Bulletin*, vol. 12, no. 3 (1977), p. 13.

10. This problem is neither new nor unique to New York City. Several writers have noted how, historically, "professional" interests and bureaucratization have gone hand in hand with questionable results for learning relationships. See Jacob Michaelsen, "Revision, Bureaucracy, and School Reform: A Critique of Katz," *School Review*, vol. 85, no. 2 (1977), pp. 229-49.

11. Bloom, *Human Characteristics and School Learning.* Ray Rist, "On Understanding the Processes of Schooling: The Contributions of Labeling Theory," in Jerome Karabel and A.H. Halsey, eds., *Power and Ideology in Education* (New York: Oxford University Press, 1977), pp. 292-306; Barry Anderson, "Socio-Economic Status of Students and School Bureaucratization," *Education Administration Quarterly*, Spring 1971, pp. 12-23.

12. Raymond Callahan, *Education and the Cult of Efficiency* (Chicago: University of Chicago Press, 1962).

13. Berger et al., *The Homeless Mind*, p. 59.

CHAPTER 5: PATHOLOGICAL PROFESSIONALISM

Epigraph from John Dewey, *The Public and Its Problems* (Chicago: Gateway Books, 1946), p. 125.

1. "Preliminary Report of the New York State Education Commissioner's Task Force on Teacher Education and Certification," Albany, New York, July, 1976. "Recommendations of the Commissioner's Task Force on Teacher Education and Certification," April 1, 1977, Albany, New York, New York State Department of Education.

2. Dan C. Lortie, *Schoolteacher* (Chicago: University of Chicago Press, 1975).

3. W. Timothy Weaver, "In Search of Quality—The Need for New Talent in Teaching," keynote address, National Association of State Directors of Teacher Education and Certification, Annual Conference, Boston, Massachusetts, June 17, 1980, and Frank Riessman, *The Inner City Child* (New York: Harper & Row, 1976), p. 75.

4. Riessman, *Inner City Child;* and Sara Lawrence Lightfoot, *Worlds Apart; Relationships between Families and Schools* (New York: Basic Books, 1978).

5. John Ogbu, "Racial Stratification and Education: The Case of Stockton, California," Institute for Urban and Minority Education, Teachers College, Columbia University, *IRCD Bulletin*, vol. 12, no. 3 (1977), p. 2.

6. National Committee for Citizens in Education (NCCE) newsletter, *Network*, February 1978.

7. Gilbert Highet, *The Art of Teaching* (New York: Alfred A. Knopf, 1950), pp. vii, viii.

8. Rist, *Restructuring American Education*, p. 2.

9. William Ryan, *Blaming the Victim* (New York: Vintage Books, 1971), p. 62. See also Charles A. Valentine, "Deficit, Difference, and Bicultural Models of Afro-American Behavior," in *Challenging the Myths: The Schools, the Blacks, and the Poor*, Reprint Series no. 5, Harvard Educational Review, 1971, pp. 1–21.

10. Ryan, *Blaming the Victim*, pp. 31ff; Riessman, *Inner City Child;* Valentine, "Deficit, Difference, and Bicultural Models"; and Ray Rist, "On Understanding the Processes of Schooling: The Contributions of Labeling Theory," in Jerome Karabel and A.H. Halsey, eds., *Power and Ideology in Education* (New York: Oxford University Press, 1977), pp. 292–306.

11. Ogbu, "Racial Stratification and Education," p. 13.

12. Riessman, *Inner City Child*, p. 75.

13. Ogbu, "Racial Stratification and Education," p. 13.

14. Jacques Maritain, *Education at the Crossroads* (New Haven, Conn.: Yale University Press, 1943), p. 3.

15. Myron Lieberman, *Education as a Profession* (Englewood Cliffs, N.J.: Prentice-Hall, 1956), Cf., however, his current revised views in *Public-Sector Bargaining: A Policy Reappraisal* (Lexington, Mass.: Lexington Books, 1980) and in "Eggs That I Have Laid: Teacher Bargaining Reconsidered," *Phi Delta Kappan*, vol 60, no. 6 (1979), pp. 415-19.

16. Statement of David Selden, past president of the American Federation of Teachers, quoted in Mario Fantini, *What's Best for the Children* (Garden City, N.Y.: Doubleday, Anchor Press, 1974), p. 68.

17. Charles Cheng, *Altering Collective Bargaining: Citizen Participation in Educational Decision Making* (New York: Praeger Publishers, 1976); Fantini, *What's Best for the Children*, pp. 57-150; Bert Shanas, "Albert Shanker: The Politics of Clout," *New York Affairs*, vol. 5, no. 1 (1978). Shanas reports that when Shanker, president of the American Federation of Teachers, was told that money could be found to clean up disasters, he thought, "That's when we decided to become a disaster." See also Stephen Cole, *The Unionization of Teachers: A Case Study of the UFT* (New York: Praeger Publishers, 1969).

18. Albert Shanker, "Where We Stand," *New York Times*, September 3, 1972, paid advertisement.

19. Ronald Corwin, *Militant Professionalism* (New York: Appleton-Century-Crofts, 1970); Fantini, *What's Best for the Children*, pp. 100–101, is also sympathetic with this analysis. Others would argue that, historically, bureaucratization and self-seeking professionalism have gone hand in hand; see Jacob Michaelsen, "Revision, Bureaucracy, and School Reform: A Critique of Katz," *School Review*, vol. 85, no. 2, (1977), pp. 229–49.

20. A point made by Fantini, *What's Best for the Children*, pp. 82, 139. For a more scholarly look at the general phenomenon, see James Coleman, "Loss of Power," *American Sociological Review*, (1973), vol. 38, no. 1.

21. "Shanker's Great Leap," *New York Times Magazine*, September 9, 1973. See also Shanas, "Albert Shanker: The Politics of Clout."

22. Fantini, *What's Best for the Children*, p. 65; and Lortie, *Schoolteacher*, pp. 221–25.

23. John H. Marvin, "What Comes after Collective Bargaining?" Maine Education Seminars, Maine Teachers Association, September 14, 1979.

CHAPTER 6: THE ONE WORST SYSTEM

Epigraph from Jonathan Messerli, *Horace Mann: A Biography* (New York: Alfred A. Knopf, 1972), p. 216.

1. The irony in this is that the "professionals" are far from convincing in their claims of expert knowledge. See Dale Mann, "Public Understanding and Education Decision-Making," *Educational Administration Quarterly*

vol 10, no. 2 (1974); and National Committee for Citizens in Education, *Public Testimony on Public Schools* (Berkely: McCutchan Publishing Corp., 1975).

2. Mario Fantini, *What's Best for the Children?* (Garden City, N.Y.: Doubleday, Anchor Press, 1974), p. 139. See also Dan C. Lortie, *Schoolteacher*, (Chicago: University of Chicago Press, 1975), pp. 225 ff.

3. Jacob Michaelsen, "Revision, Bureaucracy, and School Reform: A Critique of Katz," *School Review*, vol. 85, no. 2 (1977), pp. 229–49; Myron Lieberman, "Eggs That I Have Laid: Teacher Bargaining Reconsidered," *Phi Delta Kappan*, vol. 60, no. 6 (1979), pp. 415–19; Douglas and E. Mitchell, "The Impact of Collective Bargaining on Public and Client Interests in Education," *Teachers College Record*, vol. 80, no. 4 (1979).

4. L. Harmon Zeigler and M. Kent Jennings, with G. Wayne Peak, *Governing American Schools: Political Interaction in Local School Districts* (North Scituate, Mass.: Duxbury Press, 1974); and David B. Tyack, *The One Best System: A History of American Urban Education* (Cambridge, Mass.: Harvard University Press, 1974), pp. 126–76.

5. Zeigler et al., *Governing American Schools*, p. 4.

6. Michaelsen, "Revision, Bureaucracy, and School Reform," p. 236.

7. Fantini, *What's Best for the Children?* p. 68; see also Mann, "Public Understanding."

8. Lortie, *Schoolteacher*; Amitai Etzioni, *The Semi-Professions and Their Organization* (New York: Free Press, 1969), in the preface offers one argument for why this should continue to be the case.

9. Charles S. Benson, *Education Finance in the Coming Decade* (Bloomington, Ind.: Phi Delta Kappa, 1975), pp. 24–25; Jonathan P. Sher and Rachel B. Tompkins, "Economy, Efficiency, and Equality: The Myths of Rural School and District Consolidation," in Sher, ed., *Education in Rural America: A Reassessment of Conventional Wisdom* (Boulder, Colo.: Westview Press, 1977), esp. pp. 46 ff.

10. Michael B. Katz, *Class, Bureaucracy, and Schools*, expanded ed. (New York: Praeger Publishers, 1975), p. 37; David Tyack, "The Perils of Pluralism: The Background of the Pierce Case," *American Historical Review*, vol. 74, no. 1 (1968), pp. 74–98.

11. J.W. Getzels, "Socialization and Education: A Note on Discontinuities," in Hope Jensen Leichter, ed., *The Family as Educator* (New York: Teachers College Press, 1974), pp. 44–51; and James McPartland and Edward McDill, ed., *Violence in Schools: Perspectives, Programs, and Positions* (Lexington, Mass.: Lexington Books, 1977).

12. Ray C. Rist, "On Understanding the Processes of Schooling: The Contributions of Labeling Theory," in Jerome Karabel and A.H. Halsey, eds., *Power and Ideology in Education* (New York: Oxford University Press, 1977), pp. 292–306.

13. Michael Rutter et al., *Fifteen Thousand Hours: Secondary Schools and Their Effects on Children* (Cambridge, Mass.: Harvard University Press, 1979).

14. Charles A. Valentine, "Deficit, Difference, and Bicultural Models of Afro-American Behavior," in *Challenging the Myths: The Schools, the Blacks, and the Poor,* Reprint Series no. 5, Harvard Educational Review, 1971, pp. 12–13.

15. Valentine, "Deficit, Difference, and Bicultural Models," pp. 18–19. See also Rist, "On Understanding the Processes of Schooling."

CHAPTER 7: THE LOSS OF LEGITIMACY

Epigraph from Leonard J. Fein, "Community Schools and Social Theory: The Limits of Universalism," in Henry M. Levin, ed. *Community Control of Schools* (Washington, D.C.: Brookings Institution, 1970), p. 94.

1. Many Anne Raywid, "The Novel Character of Today's School Criticism," *Educational Leadership,* vol. 36, no. 3 (December 1979), p. 201.

2. Lawrence A. Cremin, ed., *Horace Mann on the Education of Free Men* (New York: Teachers College Press, 1957), p. 8.

3. Henry J. Perkinson, *The Imperfect Panacea: American Faith in Education, 1865–1965* (New York: Random House, 1968), p. 145.

4. Henry J. Perkinson, *Two Hundred Years of American Educational Thought* (New York: David McKay Co., 1976), p. 45.

5. David B. Tyack, *The One Best System: A History of American Urban Education* (Cambridge, Mass.: Harvard University Press, 1974), pp. 56–59.

6. Tyack, *One Best System,* pp. 56–59; and Michael B. Katz, *Class, Bureaucracy, and Schools,* expanded ed. (New York: Praeger Publishers, 1975), pp. 41ff.

7. John Gardner, *Excellence* (New York: Harper & Row, 1961).

8. Benjamin S. Bloom, "New Views of the Learner: Implications for Instruction and Curriculum," *Educational Leadership,* vol. 35, no. 7 (April 1978), p. 564. This idea is explained and developed in great length throughout Bloom's *Human Characteristics and School Learning* (New York: McGraw-Hill, 1976).

9. Alfredo Casteneda, "Persisting Ideological Issues of Assimilation in America," in Edgar G. Epps, *Cultural Pluralism* (Chicago: National Society for the Study of Education; Berkeley, Calif.: McCutchan Publishing Corp., 1974), p. 57. See also William Greenbaum, "America in Search of a New Ideal," *Harvard Educational Review,* vol 44 (August 1974).

10. Nathan Glazer, "Public Education and American Pluralism," in *Parents, Teachers, and Children: Prospects for Choice in American Education*

(San Francisco: Institute for Contemporary Studies, 1977), pp. 85–110, esp. pp. 91, 92.

11. Glazer, ibid., suggests John Higham's proposal for a "pluralistic integration." See Higham, "Ethnic Pluralism in Modern American Thought," in *Send These to Me: Jews and Other Immigrants in Urban America* (New York: Atheneum, 1975).

12. Vincent P. Lannie, *Public Money and Parochial Education, Bishop Hughes, Governor Seward, and the New York School Controversy* (Cleveland: Press of Case Western Reserve University, 1968); David Tyack, "Onward Christian Soldiers: Religion in the American Common School," in Paul Nash, ed., *History and Education: The Educational Uses of the Past* (New York: Random House, 1970), pp. 212–55; David Tyack, "The Kingdom of God and the Common School: Protestant Ministers and the Educational Awakening in the West," *Harvard Educational Review*, vol. 36, (Fall 1966), pp. 447–69.

13. Richard John Neuhaus, "No More Bootleg Religion," in Dwight Allen, ed., *Controversies in Education* (Philadelphia: W. B. Saunders Co., 1974), pp. 72–86.

CHAPTER 8: EDUCATION AS PARTNERSHIP

Epigraph from Mario Fantini, *What's Best for the Children,* (Garden City, N.Y.: Doubleday, Anchor Press, 1974), p. xi.

1. John Holt, introduction to Roland Betts, *Acting Out* (Boston: Little, Brown & Co., 1978), p. ix.

2. See Robert Merton on "goal displacement" in bureaucracy, *Social Theory and Social Structure* (New York: Free Press, 1957), pp. 199ff. Scholars have observed this at all levels within the schools. See Philip Jackson on the "hidden curriculum" in "The Student's World," in Melvin Silberman, Jerome Allender, and Jay Yanoff, eds., *The Psychology of Open Teaching and Learning: An Inquiry Approach* (Boston: Little, Brown, & Co. 1972), p. 81; Michael B. Katz, *Class, Bureaucracy, and Schools,* expanded ed. (New York: Praeger Publishers, 1975); for case study, David Rogers, *110 Livingston Street: Politics and Bureaucracy in the New York City School System* (New York: Vintage Books, 1969), esp. pp. 267–68; and Seymour Sarason, *The Culture of the School and the Problem of Change* (Boston: Allyn & Bacon, 1971).

3. Eugene Litwak and Henry J. Meyer, *School, Family, and Neighborhood: The Theory and Practice of School-Community Relations* (New York: Columbia University Press, 1974), on the necessity of combining uniform and nonuniform knowledge in the schools.

4. *Roget's Thesaurus* (New York: Grosset & Dunlap, 1937).
5. Council for Advancement and Support of Education, *Currents,* July 1979, p. 6.
6. Although there is increasing research support for this contention, much more work needs to be done. See Lawrence A. Cremin, *Public Education* (New York: Basic Books, 1976), p. 58; Donald A. Erickson et al., *Characteristics and Relationships in Public and Independent Schools* (An Interim Report of the "Baseline Survey" as aspect of COFIS—A Study of Funding Independent Schools in British Columbia), (San Francisco: University of San Francisco, Center for Research on Private Education, and Vancouver: Educational Research Institute of British Columbia, February 1979); Hope Jensen Leichter, ed., *Families and Communities as Educators* (New York: Teachers College Press, 1979); and Edward McDill and Leo C. Rigsby, *Structure and Process in Secondary Schools: The Academic Impact of Educational Climates* (Baltimore: Johns Hopkins University Press, 1973).
7. Albert O. Hirschman, *Exit, Voice, and Loyalty: Responses to Decline in Firms, Organizations, and States* (Cambridge, Mass.: Harvard University Press, 1970).
8. Others have begun to deal with this area using Hirschman's theory. See R.B. Freeman, "Individual Mobility and Union Voice in the Labor Market," *American Economic Review,* vol. 66, no. 2 (1976).

CHAPTER 9: VOICE

Epigraph from Ray Rist, *Restructuring American Education* (New Brunswick, N.J.: Transaction Books, 1972), p. 8.
1. David B. Tyack, Michael Kirst, and Elisabeth Hansot, "Educational Reform: Retrospect and Prospect," *Teachers College Record,* vol 81, no. 3 (1980), pp. 253–69.
2. Michael Novak, *The Rise of the Unmeltable Ethnics* (New York: Macmillan Co., 1971).
3. This was, of course, a basic point in John Dewey's classic, *Democracy and Education* (1916; reprint ed., New York: Free Press, 1966).
4. A similar point is made by Evans Clinchy and Elisabeth A. Cody, "If Not Public Choice, Then Private Escape," *Phi Delta Kappan,* vol. 60, no. 4 (1978).
5. Many scholars have written about this. See especially L. Harmon Zeigler and M. Kent Jennings, with G. Wayne Peak, *Governing American Schools: Political Interaction in Local School Districts* (North Scituate, Mass.: Duxbury Press, 1974); and David B. Tyack, *The One Best System: A*

History of American Urban Education (Cambridge, Mass.: Harvard University Press, 1974).

6. Tyack, *One Best System*, p. 77.

7. Donald A. Erickson, *The New "Public" Schools* (Wichita, Kans.: Center for Independent Education, 1977), p. 3.

8. See, for instance, Henry J. Perkinson, *The Imperfect Panacea: American Faith in Education, 1865-1965* (New York: Random House, 1968); and Tyack, *One Best System*.

9. Don Davies et al., *Patterns of Citizen Participation in Educational Decision-making* (Boston: Institute for Responsive Education, 1978), vol.1 p. 9.

10. Ibid.

11. Ibid., p. 103. See also R. Weatherley and M. Lipsky, "Street-Level Bureaucrats and Institutional Innovation: Implementing Special-Education Reform," *Harvard Educational Review*, vol. 47 (May 1977), pp. 171-97.

12. Even some of the outspoken critics of the present situation and advocates of increased participation fall into the trap of seeing parents as clients. For an otherwise excellent article, see Harmon Zeigler, "Creating Responsive Schools," *Urban Review*, vol. 6, no. 4 (1973).

13. Molly Ivins, "A Radical Plan Puts Everybody in Charge," *New York Times*, March 20, 1979, p. C1.

14. Willian Greenbaum, "American in Search of a New Ideal," *Harvard Educational Review*, vol. 44 (August 1974). National Committee for Citizens in Education (NCCE) newsletter, *Network*, February 1978, and National Committee for Citizens in Education, *Public Testimony On Public Schools* (Berkeley: McCutchan Publishing Corp., 1975); also issues of *Citizen Action in Education*, esp. vol. 5, no. 1 (1978), the newsletter of the Institute for Responsive Education.

15. José P.V. Ambach, Civil Action #79C270 (E.D.N.Y. 12/14/79) 3EHLR 551:412 (Clearinghouse #25,934).

16. David Kirp and Mark Yudof, *Educational Policy and the Law* (Berkeley: McCutchan Publishing Corp., 1974); Clifford B. Hooker, ed. *The Courts and Education, The Seventy-seventh Yearbook of the National Society for the Study of Education, Part 1* (Chicago: National Society for the Study of Education, 1978); and Leroy J. Peterson, Richard A. Rossmiller, and Marlin M. Volz, *The Law and Public School Operation*, 2d ed. (New York: Harper & Row, 1978).

17. Raoul Berger, *Government by Judiciary: The Transformation of the Fourteenth Amendment* (Cambridge, Mass.: Harvard University Press, 1977); Alexander M. Bickel, *The Supreme Court and the Idea of Progress* (New Haven, Conn.: Yale University Press, 1978), pp. 130-39; Nathan Glazer "Towards an Imperial Judiciary," *Public Interest*, Fall 1975; and Tyll van Geel, *Authority to Control the School Program* (Lexington, Mass.: Lexington Books, 1976).

18.   See sections on *in loco parentis* in Richard D. Gatti and Daniel J. Gatti, *Encyclopedic Dictionary of School Law* (West Nyack, N.J.: Parker Publishing Co., 1975), and in Peterson et. al., *Law and Public School Operation*, pp. 346–47.

19.   This is especially noticeable lately in regard to procedures dealing with the handicapped. See Lawrence Kotin and Nancy Eager, *Due Process in Special Education: A Legal Analysis* (Cambridge, Mass.: Research Institute for Educational Problems, February 1977); and Weatherley and Lipsky, "Street-Level Bureaucrats."

20.   *New York Times*, September 22, 1980, p. A14.

21.   Council for Basic Education, *Basic Education*, March 1979, p. 5.

22.   John Holt describes a similar situation in *How Children Fail* (New York: Delta Books, 1964), pp. 12–13.

23.   See especially Benjamin S. Bloom, *Human Characteristics and School Learning* (New York: McGraw-Hill, 1976).

24.   See James S. Coleman, Ernest Q. Campbell, et al., *Equality of Educational Opportunity* (Washington, D.C.: U.S. Department of Health, Education, and Welfare, 1966), pp. 320–21.

25.   Private schools, small schools, and schools with a high percentage of involvement in extracurricular activities apparently have advantages because of this. See R. G. Barker and P. V. Gump, *Big School, Small School: High School Size and Student Behavior* (Stanford, Calif.: Stanford University Press, 1964); Donald A. Erickson, Testimony, U.S. Congress, Subcommittee on Taxation and Debt Management, Senate Finance Committee Hearings, 95th Cong., 2d sess. January 18, 19, 1978; William G. Spady, "Status, Achievement, and Motivation in the American High School," in Donald A. Erickson, ed. *Educational Organization and Administration* (Berkeley, Calif.: McCutchan Publishing Corp., 1977), pp. 88–109.

26.   Jonathan Kozol, *Children of the Revolution* (New York: Delacorte Press, 1978).

27.   Albert O. Hirschman, "'Exit, Voice, and Loyalty': Further Reflections and a Survey of Recent Contributions," *Social Science Information*, vol. 13, no. 1 (1974), p. 8.

28.   B.D. Anderson, "Bureaucracy in the Schools and Student Alienation," *Canadian Administrator*, vol. 11 (1971), pp. 9–12; and Donald J. Willower, "Schools and Pupil Control," in Erickson, *Educational Organization and Administration*, pp. 296–310.

CHAPTER 10: CHOICE

Epigraph from Denis Doyle, "The Politics of Choice: A View From the Bridge" in *Parents, Teachers, and Children: The Prospects for Choice in*

American Education San Francisco: Institute for Contemporary Studies, 1977), p. 245.

1. Albert O. Hirschman, *Exit, Voice, and Loyalty: Responses to Decline in Firms, Organizations, and States* (Cambridge, Mass.: Harvard University Press, 1970), p. 4 and chap. 2.

2. The centrality of choice in modern experience and consciousness is discussed by Peter Berger, *The Heretical Imperative* (Garden City, N.Y.: Doubleday, Anchor Press, 1979), pp. 11–17.

3. Hirschman, *Exit, Voice, and Loyalty*, p. 106.

4. David Tyack, *"Governance and Goals,"* in Don Davies, ed., *Communities and Their Schools* (New York: McGraw-Hill, 1981), p. 14.

5. John E. Coons and Stephen D. Sugarman, *Education by Choice: The Case for Family Control* (Berkeley and Los Angeles: University of California Press, 1978); Mario Fantini, *Public Schools of Choice* (New York: Simon & Schuster, 1973); Christopher Jencks et al., *Education Vouchers: A Report on Financing Elementary Education by Grants to Parents* (Cambridge, Mass.: Center for the Study of Public Policy, 1970); and *Parents, Teachers, and Children: Prospects for Choice in American Education* (San Francisco: Institute for Contemporary Studies, 1977).

6. Donald A. Erickson, Richard Nault, and Bruce Cooper, "Recent Enrollment Trends in U.S. Nonpublic Schools," in S. Abromowitz and Stuart Rosenfeld, eds., *Declining Enrollments: The Challenge of the Coming Decade* (Washington, D.C.: National Institute of Education, March 1978); Otto F. Kraushaar, *American Nonpublic Schools: Patterns of Diversity* (Baltimore: Johns Hopkins University Press, 1972), esp. chaps. 8, 11; U.S., Congress, Senate, Committee on Finance, *Tuition Tax Relief Bills: Hearings on S.96, S.311, S.834, S.1570, S.1781, S.2142,* 95th Cong., 2d sess., January 18, 19, and 20, 1978.

7. Evans Clinchy and Elisabeth A. Cody, "If Not Public Choice, Then Private Escape," *Phi Delta Kappan,* vol. 60, no. 4 (December 1978). See also note 6, this chap.

8. In addition to evidence from experiments within the public schools, see Richard Nault, "The School Commitments of Nonpublic School Freshmen Voluntarily and Involuntarily Affiliated with Their Schools," in Donald A. Erickson, ed., *Educational Organization and Administration* (Berkeley, Calif.: McCutchan Publishing Corp., 1977), pp. 264–95.

9. Charles E. Bidwell, "Students and Schools: Some Observations in Client-Serving Organizations," in W.R. Rosengren and M. Lefton, eds., *Organizations and Clients: Essays in the Sociology of Service* (Columbus, Ohio: Charles E. Merrill, 1970), pp. 37–70; Benjamin S. Bloom, *Human Characteristics and School Learning* (New York: McGraw-Hill, 1976), p. 8 and throughout; Sarane Boocock, *Sociology of Education: An Introduction,* 2d ed. (Boston: Houghton Mifflin Co., 1980), p. 154; Richard O. Carlson,

"Environmental Constraints and Organizational Consequences: The Public School and Its Clients," in D.E. Griffiths, ed., *Behavioral Science and Educational Administration*, pt. 2 (Chicago: University of Chicago Press, 1964), pp. 262–76; and Robert Dreeben, "The School as a Workplace," in R. Travers, ed., *Second Handbook of Research on Teaching* (Chicago: Rand McNally, 1973), pp. 450–73.

10. Boocock, *Sociology of Education*, p. 152.

11. R. Weatherley and M. Lipsky, "Street-Level Bureaucrats and Institutional Innovation: Implementing Special-Education Reform," *Harvard Educational Review*, vol. 47 (May 1977), pp. 171–97.

12. Peter W. Doe v. San Francisco Unified School District, 60 Cal App. 3d 814, 131 Cal. Rptr. 854 (1976); Donohue v. Copiague Union Free School District, 408 NYS 2d 584 (1977).

13. Sarane Boocock, "The Social Organization of the Classroom," *Annual Review of Sociology*, vol. 4 (1978), pp. 10–11; and John Ogbu, *The Next Generation* (New York: Academic Press, 1974), pp. 164–69.

14. James Wellington, "American Education: Its Failure and Its Future," *Phi Delta Kappan*, vol. 58, no. 7 (March 1977), p. 528. This is true for reasons suggested in recent research; see overview in Boocock, *Sociology of Education*, pp. 160–62.

15. For a discussion of the general phenomenon, see Jethro K. Lieberman, *The Tyranny of the Experts* (New York: Walker & Co., 1970), chap. 12. An extreme case is *The Navajo Nation: An American Colony* (Washington, D.C.: 1975), U.S. Commission on Civil Rights, pp. 77–88. Two cases in which parents removed their children from the New York City public schools because they were not being educated and in which the parents were subsequently prosecuted include *Matter of Skipwith*, 14 Misc. 2d 325 (Domestic Relations Court, NYC, 1958) and *Matter of Baum*, no. N 204–75 (Family Court).

16. William Raspberry, "Does 'Apathy' Deserve All the Blame?" *New York Times*, May 5, 1978. Historians and other social scientists have shown that the effort to get local influences out of the schools in the name of increased efficiency and professionalism is an old story. See, among others, Diane Ravitch, *The Great School Wars* (New York: Basic Books, 1974), and the Introduction to L. Harmon Zeigler and M. Kent Jennings, with G. Wayne Peak, *Governing American Schools: Political Interaction in Local School Districts* (North Scituate, Mass.: Duxbury Press, 1974).

17. Statement of Association of California School Administrators, *Phi Delta Kappan*, vol. 60, no. 10 (June 1979), p. 763.

18. Nancy St. John, *School Desegregation: Outcomes for Children* (New York: John Wiley & Sons, 1975), pp. 94–95; and Boocock, *Sociology of Education*, pp. 71–74.

19. Bob Herbert, "Where You Live Equals How You'll Do," *Daily News,* March 8, 1979, p. 5.

20. For descriptions of this process, see Sara Lawrence Lightfoot, *World's Apart: Relationships between Families and Schools* (New York: Basic Books, 1978), pp. 30–37; and Ogbu, *The Next Generation,* pp. 133–59.

21. Tyll van Geel, *Authority to Control the School Program* (Lexington, Mass.: Lexington Books, 1976), p. 355.

22. Ibid.

23. An opinion shared by David B. Tyack, Michael W. Kirst, and Elisabeth Hansot, "Educational Reform: Retrospect and Prospect," *Teachers College Record,* vol. 81, no. 3 (1980), pp. 253–69.

CHAPTER 11: LOYALTY

Epigraph from Jewish Theological Seminary, Twenty-fourth Annual High Holy Day Message, reprinted, *New York Times,* November 7, 1978, p. 39.

1. For arguments along this line, see John Dewey, *The Public and Its Problems* (Chicago: Gateway Books, 1946); Maxine Green, "The Predicaments of American Selfhood: A Response to the New Irrationalism," in her *Landscapes of Learning* (New York: Teachers College Press, 1978), pp. 7–21; Christopher Lasch, *The Culture of Narcissism* (New York: Warner Books, 1979); and William Carey McWilliams, *The Idea of Fraternity in America* (Berkeley and Los Angeles: University of California Press, 1973).

2. Recently a similar conclusion was reached by David B. Tyack, Michael W. Kirst, and Elisabeth Hansot, "Educational Reform: Retrospect and Prospect," *Teachers College Record,* vol. 81, no. 3 (1980), pp. 253–69.

3. Albert O. Hirschman, *Exit, Voice, and Loyalty: Responses to Decline in Firms, Organizations and States* (Cambridge, Mass.: Harvard University Press, 1970), pp. 76–105, quotation from p. 77.

4. Ibid., p. 78.

5. Ibid., pp. 100–101.

6. Ibid., p. 82.

7. This is also apparent in the commitment of many people to neighborhood schools and to parochial schools. On rural schools, see Jonathan P. Sher, ed., *Education in Rural America: A Reassessment of Conventional Wisdom* (Boulder, Colo.: Westview Press, 1977).

8. Leonard J. Fein, "Community Schools and Social Theory: The Limits of Universalism," in Henry M. Levin, ed., *Community Control of Schools* (Washington, D.C.: Brookings Institution, 1970), p. 91.

9. While students, parents, and the lay public in general are certainly not "rational" or even well informed about schooling, there is little evidence that educational professionals are any more so. Some view this as some-

what ironic; see Dale Mann, "Public Understanding and Education Decision-Making," *Educational Administration Quarterly*, vol. 10, no. 2 (1974).

10. E.F. Schumacher, *Small is Beautiful: Economics As If People Mattered* (New York: Harper & Row, 1973), p. 97.

11. This is the basic goal of the Mediating Structures and Public Policy Project. See Peter L. Berger and Richard John Neuhaus, *To Empower People: The Role of Mediating Structures in Public Policy* (Washington, D.C.: American Enterprise Institute, 1977). Among educators John Dewey was more aware of the complexities of the situation than most, especially in *The Public and Its Problems*. More recently, see Lawrence A. Cremin, *Public Education* (New York: Basic Books, 1976).

12. See Dewey, *The Public and Its Problems;* Peter Berger, "Reflections on Patriotism," in *Facing Up to Modernity* (New York: Basic Books, 1977), pp. 118–29; McWilliams, *Idea of Fraternity in America*.

13. J.W. Getzels, "The Communities of Education," in Hope Jensen Leichter, ed., *Families and Communities as Educators* (New York: Teachers College Press, 1979), pp. 95–118.

14. Berger and Neuhaus, *To Empower People;* Jean B. Quandt, *From the Small Town to the Great Community: The Social Thought of Progressive Intellectuals* (New Brunswick, N.J.: Rutgers University Press, 1970).

15. An example of this suspicion in Orlando Patterson, "Hidden Dangers in the Ethnic Revival," *New York Times*, February 20, 1978, Op. Ed. Page.

16. This totalitarian strain is inherently present in loyalty-promoting institutions like the public schools. See Hirschman, *Exit, Voice, and Loyalty*, pp. 92–93; and Lawrence A. Cremin, *The Genius of American Education* (New York: Vintage Books, 1965), pp. 15–17. Cremin writes; "In a sense, the whole modern concept of totalitarianism is fundamentally an educational idea, made possible by the theory and technology of 20th century communication."

17. This point has been observed repeatedly; see Berger, "Reflections on Patriotism"; Berger and Neuhaus, *To Empower People;* Dewey, *The Public and Its Problems;* and McWilliams, *Idea of Fraternity in America*. See also John H. Schaar, *Loyalty in America* (Berkeley and Los Angeles: University of California Press, 1957). See also note 2 this chapter.

18. Albert O. Hirschman, "'Exit, Voice, and Loyalty': Further Reflections and a Survey of Recent Contributions," *Social Science Information*, vol. 13, no. 1 (1974), pp. 7–26.

19. Jesse Jackson, *Christian Science Monitor*, September 12, 1978, p. 13.

20. Tyack, Kirst, and Hansot, "Educational Reform."

21. Hirschman, *Exit, Voice, and Loyalty*, pp. 120–28.

22. Ibid., pp. 92–93; Jacob Michaelsen, "Revision, Bureaucracy, and School Reform: A Critique of Katz," *School Review*, vol. 85, no. 2 (1977), pp. 229–49, makes a similar point.

CHAPTER 12: EQUALITY REVISITED

Epigraph from Jonathan Kozol, *Prisoners of Silence* (New York, Continuum Publishing Corp., 1980), p. 4.

1. The Coleman report found that "for most minority groups, then, and most particularly the Negro, schools provide no opportunity at all for them to overcome this initial deficiency; in fact, they fall farther behind the white majority in the development of several skills which are critical to making a living and participating fully in modern society"; see James S. Coleman, Ernest Q. Campbell, et al., *Equality of Educational Opportunity* (Washington, D.C.; U.S. Department of Health, Education, and Welfare, 1966), p. 21. Subsequent studies confirm this finding.

2. This characterization is from Michael Katz's review of Diane Ravitch's *The Revisionists Revised;* see Michael Katz, "An Apology for American Educational History," *Harvard Educational Review,* vol. 49 (May 1979), p. 263.

3. Actually what is and is not revisionist is hardly clear. One of the most renowned scholars of education, Lawrence Cremin, would call most contemporary writers in the field revisionist, including himself, because they depart from the type of educational scholarship that characterized most of this century. He would, however, distinguish his more "latitudinarian" revisionism from the revisionism that Ravitch decries. See Lawrence A. Cremin, *Traditions of American Education* (New York: Basic Books, 1977), p. 131ff.

4. Diane Ravitch, *The Revisionists Revised: A Critique of the Radical Attack on the Schools* (New York: Basic Books, 1978), p. 11.

5. Ibid.

6. Katz, "Apology for American Educational History." See also Joseph Featherstone's review of Ravitch's book in the *New York Times Book Review,* June 18, 1978, p. 9.

7. This "black box" effect has been noted by some educational researchers. See, for instance, Sarane Boocock, *Sociology of Education: An Introduction,* 2d ed. (Boston: Houghton Mifflin Co., 1980), p. 312. Over the past ten years there has been a clear move toward a more "grounded" approach, which looks at interaction inside the "black box" of the schools.

8. Harry C. Bredemeier, "Schools and Student Growth," *Urban Review* vol. 2, no. 8 (April 1968) pp. 21–24; and Edward McDill and Leo C. Rigsby, *Structure and Process in Secondary Schools: The Academic Impact of Educational Climates* (Baltimore: Johns Hopkins University Press, 1973), pp. 122ff.

9. Harvey A. Averch et al., *How Effective Is Schooling? A Critical Review and Synthesis of Research Findings* (Santa Monica: Rand Corporation, January 1972); Martin Carnoy and Henry M. Levin, *The Limits of Educational Reform* (New York: David McKay Co., 1976), pp. 3–4. On a more positive note, see *Compensatory Education Services: Final Report to*

Congress (Washington, D.C., National Institute of Education, U.S. Department of Health, Education, and Welfare, September 1978).

CHAPTER 13: COMMUNITY CONTROL

Epigraph from Erik Erikson, *Childhood and Society* (New York: W.W. Norton & Co., 1950), p. 101.

1. On the confusion between decentralization and community control, see Leonard J. Fein, *The Ecology of the Public Schools: An Inquiry into Community Control* (New York: Pegasus, 1971), pp. 22–24. Fein also points out how obtuse the press has been in failing to distinguish the different strands of the community control movement.

2. Ibid., p. 139.

3. Albert Shanker, "Cult of Localism," in Patricia Cayo Sexton, ed., *School Policy and Issues in a Changing Society* (Boston: Allyn & Bacon, 1971), p. 213.

4. On the debate over the success or failure of community control in New York City, see also Martin Schiff, "The Educational Failure of Community Control in Inner-City New York," *Phi Delta Kappan*, vol. 57, no. 6 (February 1976), pp. 375–78; Luis Fuentes, "Community Control Did *Not* Fail in New York: It Wasn't Tried," *Phi Delta Kappan*, vol. 57, no. 10 (June 1976), p. 695.

5. Fein, *Ecology of the Public Schools*, p. 139.

6. Leonard J. Fein "Community Schools and Social Theory: The Limits of Universalism," in Henry M. Levin, ed. *Community Control of Schools* (Washington, D.C.: Brookings Institution, 1970), p. 89.

7. Shanker, "Cult of Localism," p. 213. The "joke" is also on Horace Mann and other founders of the public school system who justified centralization on this ground. see Michael B. Katz, *Class, Bureaucracy, and Schools*, expanded ed. (New York: Praeger Publishers, 1975), pp. 28–29. On the other hand, central government (as opposed to bureaucratic administration on this ground. See Michael B. Katz, *Class, Bureaucracy, and Schools*, hearing at the local level.

8. Stokely Carmichael, "Power and Racism," *New York Review of Books*, September 22, 1966.

9. Fein, "Community Schools and Social Theory," p. 99.

10. Ibid., pp. 92, 95, 91, and Fein, *Ecology of the Public Schools*, p. 139.

11. An interesting historical example of this in the early days of the country was the policy of the newly formed United States government to deny land grants to national groups for local self-governing ethnic enclaves. See

Nathan Glazer, *Affirmative Discrimination: Ethnic Inequality and Public Policy* (New York: Basic Books, 1975), pp. 22ff.

12. Ira Glasser, *The Burden of Blame* (New York: New York Civil Liberty Union, 1968). and William Greenbaum, "America in Search of a New Ideal," *Harvard Educational Review*, vol. 44, no. 3 (1974).

13. George Gallup, "The First Ten Years: Trends and Observations," in Stanley M. Elam, ed., *A Decade of Gallup Polls of Attitudes toward Education, 1969–1978* (Bloomington, Ind.: Phi Delta Kappan, 1978), p. 1.

14. Diane Ravitch, *The Great School Wars: New York City, 1805–1973* (New York: Basic Books, 1974), pp. 251ff.

15. Myron Lieberman, *Education as a Profession* (Englewood Cliffs, N.J.: Prentice-Hall, 1956), and Myron Lieberman, *The Future of Public Education* (Chicago: University of Chicago Press, 1960). One should note that in the intervening years Lieberman has changed positions. See his "Eggs That I Have Laid": Teacher Bargaining Reconsidered," *Phi Delta Kappan*, vol. 60, no 6 (1979), pp. 415–19, and *Public-Sector Bargaining: A Policy Reappraisal* (Lexington, Mass.: Lexington Books, 1980).

16. National Committee for Citizens in Education, *Public Testimony on Public Schools* (Berkeley, Calif.: McCutchan Publishing Corp., (1975).

17. Mayor's Advisory Panel on Decentralization of the New York City Schools, *Reconnection for Learning: A Community School System for New York City* (New York: Ford Foundation, 1967).

18. Ibid., pp. 1, 2, 3.

19. Ibid., pp. 4, 10, 13, 13–14.

20. Coalition for Community Control, *Community Control Is Community Responsibility*, (New York, 1968).

21. Mayor John V. Lindsay to Governor Nelson Rockefeller, January 2, 1968, p. 2.

22. David S. Seeley, "Today's Most Important Educational Experiment," *Public Education Association Newsletter*, October 1970.

23. Benjamin S. Bloom, *Human Characteristics and School Learning* (New York: McGraw-Hill, 1976), Thomas Good, Bruce Biddle, and Jere Brophy, *Teachers Make a Difference* (New York: Holt, Rinehart & Winston, 1975), chap. 4; and Edward McDill and Leo C. Rigsby, *Structure and Process in Secondary Schools: The Academic Impact of Educational Climates* (Baltimore: Johns Hopkins University Press, 1973).

24. John Dewey, *The Public and Its Problems* (Chicago: Gateway Books, 1964), p. 127.

25. Jacob Michaelsen, "Revision, Bureaucracy, and School Reform: A Critique of Katz," *School Review*, vol. 85, no. 2 (1977), pp. 237, 240, 236, 244, 242.

CHAPTER 14: FAMILY CONTROL

Epigraph from Stephen Sugarman, *Where,* April 1979, as quoted in Albert Shanker, "Vouchers Would Pull Our Society Apart," *New York Times,* June 3, 1979, p. E9.

1. Jacob Michaelsen, "Revision, Bureaucracy, and School Reform: A Critique of Katz," *School Review,* vol. 85, no. 2 (1977), p. 236.

2. Adam Smith, *Wealth of Nations* (Chicago: Encyclopedia Britannica, Great Books Edition, 1952), p. 340. Quoted in John E. Coons and Stephen D. Sugarman, *Education by Choice: The Case for Family Control* (Berkeley and Los Angeles: University of California Press, 1978), p. 18.

3. Coons and Sugarman, *Education by Choice,* p. 17 ff; and George LaNoue, ed., *Educational Vouchers: Concepts and Controversies* (New York: Teachers College Press, 1972).

4. Milton Friedman, "The Role of Government in Education," in Robert A. Solo, ed., *Economics and the Public Interest* (New Brunswick, N.J.: Rutgers University Press, 1955), pp. 127–28. See also Milton Friedman, *Capitalism and Freedom* (Chicago: University of Chicago Press, 1962), chap. 6.

5. Christopher Jencks et al., *Education Vouchers: A Report on Financing Elementary Education by Grants to Parents* (Cambridge, Mass.: Center for the Study of Public Policy, 1970).

6. Doyle, "The Politics of Choice," p. 230.

7. Ibid., p. 232.

8. Ibid., p. 239.

9. Ibid., p. 240.

10. Rand Corporation, *Education Vouchers: The Experience at Alum Rock* (Santa Monica, Calif.: Rand Corporation for National Institute of Education, Health, Education, and Welfare, December 1973), p. 6.

11. Rand Corporation, *Education Vouchers,* p. 31.

12. Doyle, "The Politics of Choice," pp. 232, 244.

13. David Selden, "Vouchers: A Critic Changes His Mind," *Nations Schools and Colleges,* vol. 2, no. 6 (1975), pp. 44–46. For his earlier opposition, see David Selden, "Vouchers Unvouchsafed," *Educational Forum,* vol. 37 (November 1972), pp. 7–12.

14. Rand Corporation, *Education Vouchers.*

15. Ibid., pp. 24, 33.

16. Doyle, "The Politics of Choice," p. 233. See also "School Vouchers Rejected in Test; Six New Hampshire Districts Bar Experimental Plan," *New York Times,* April 11, 1976; and William Weber, "The Eclipse of Education Vouchers in America: The East Hartford Case," *Journal of Education,* vol. 159, no. 2 (1977).

17. Coons and Sugarman, *Education by Choice.*

18. John Coons, William Clune III, and Stephen Sugarman, *Private Wealth and Public Education* (Cambridge, Mass.: Harvard University Press, 1970).

19. For a similar argument, see Coons and Sugarman, *Education by Choice*, pp. 48ff.

20. J.W. Getzels, "Socialization and Education: A Note on Discontinuities," *Teachers College Record*, vol. 76, no. 2 (1974), pp. 218–25; and Robert A. Levine, "Western Schools in Non-Western Societies: Psychosocial Impact and Cultural Response," in Hope Jensen Leichter, ed., *Families and Communities as Educators* (New York: Teachers College Press, 1979), pp. 185–91 (first published in *Teachers College Record*, vol. 79, no. 4, 1978).

21. In the Netherlands, where choice is offered, 42 percent of the elementary schools are Catholic, 27 percent Protestant, and only 27 percent secular and government operated (*American School Policy Journal*, August 1978, p. 5).

22. Peter L. Berger and Richard John Neuhaus, *To Empower People: The Role of Mediating Structures in Public Policy* (Washington, D.C.: American Enterprise Institute, 1977). See also a strong plea for help to private schools by Senator Daniel P. Moynihan, "Government and the Ruin of Private Education," *Harper's*, April 1978.

23. Doyle, "The Politics of Choice," p. 237. He suggests that many Catholic school supporters felt that the OEO vouchers were too rich for them and increased the risks of court findings of illegal aid to religion. For another interesting perspective on the effects of government funding of religious schools, see Donald Erickson and Richard Nault, "Currency, Choice, and Commitment: An Exploratory Study of the Effects of Public Money and Related Regulation on Canadian Catholic Schools." (Research report submitted to the Spencer Foundation), January 1978. They found that a decrease in the commitment of parents, teachers, and students may occur with the influx of public money into Catholic schools.

24. Coons and Sugarman, *Education by Choice*, pp. 36, 45.

25. For a case study of what happened to one child left to face the school's bureaucratized professionals without parental defense, see Charles A. Valentine, "Deficit, Difference, and Bicultural Models of Afro-American Behavior," in *Challenging the Myths: The Schools, the Blacks, and the Poor*, Harvard Educational Review, Reprint Series no. 5, 1971.

26. Coons and Sugarman, *Education by Choice*, pp. 51, 58.

27. "To both Friedman and Jencks, choice was a device to reconnect students and schooling, to make each more accountable to the other." Doyle, "The Politics of Choice," p. 245. Many scholars feel that the compulsory affiliation between parties in the present system undermines productive, trusting relations. If this is so, choice offers great hope. On lack of trust in the schools brought about by lack of choice, see Charles E. Bidwell, "Students and Schools: Some Observations on Client-Serving Organizations," in W.R.

Rosengren and M. Lefton, eds., *Organizations and Clients: Essays in the Sociology of Service* (Columbus, Ohio: Charles E. Merrill, 1970), pp. 37-70.

28. Berger and Neuhaus, *To Empower People*, p. 21.

29. Ibid., pp. 21-23. E. Babette Edwards, "Why a Harlem Parents Union," in *Parents, Teachers, and Children: Prospects for Choice in American Education* (San Francisco: Institute for Contemporary Studies, 1977), pp. 59-66.

30. Thomas Vitullo-Martin, "New York City's Interest in Reform of Tax Treatment of School Expenses: Retaining the Middle Class in the City," *City Almanac*, vol. 13, no. 4 (1978).

31. Theodore R. Sizer and Phillip Whitten, "A Proposal for a Poor Children's Bill of Rights," *Psychology Today*, August 1968, p. 58.

32. Barbara Lerner, *Minimum Competence, Maximum Choice*, (New York: Irvington Publishers, 1980), pp. 39ff.

33. In the only voucherlike experiment evaluated, Alum Rock found vouchers "administratively feasible"; Doyle, "The Politics of Choice," p. 242.

34. William Cornog, "The Options Market in Education," in *Parents, Teachers, and Children*, pp. 149-64.

35. Coons and Sugarman, *Education by Choice*, p. 148f.

36. *New York Times*, December 1, 1978, p. A16.

37. R. Freeman Butts, "Once Again the Question for Liberal Public Educators: Whose Twilight," *Phi Delta Kappan*, vol. 58, no. 1 (September 1976), pp. 4-14. Albert Shanker, president of the United Federation of Teachers agrees; see "Vouchers Would Pull Our Society Apart," *New York Times*, June 3, 1979.

38. Coons and Sugarman, *Education by Choice*, pp. 35, 91.

39. Ibid., pp. 91, 96, 93, 95. See also the contrast piece to Butts, "Once Again the Question,": Theodore Sizer, "Education and Assimilation: A Fresh Plea for Pluralism," *Phi Delta Kappan*, vol. 58, no. 1 (September 1976), pp. 31-35.

40. Coons and Sugarman, *Education by Choice*, p. 109

41. Ibid., chap. 7, "The Issue of Racial Integration," esp. pp. 109-11.

42. Some opponents of the voucher idea argue, like Coons and Sugarman, for a separation of the public versus the private ends of education but come down much more heavily on the need to restrict parent choice in order to achieve certain "public" goals like a reduction of race and class stratification. See Henry M. Levin, "Educational Vouchers and Educational Equality," in M. Carnoy, ed., *Education in a Corporate Society*, 2d ed. (New York: David McKay Co., 1975).

43. Coons and Sugarman, *Education by Choice*, p. 93.

44. Ibid., pp. 95, 91-108.

45. Sugarman, *Where*. Coons and Sugarman, *Education by Choice*, discuss the issue at length, pp. 45ff.

46. Butts as quoted in Shanker, "Vouchers Would Pull Our Society Apart." See also Butts, "Whose Twilight" and *Public Education in the United States*. Butts interprets the views of liberty in the early days of the republic in a similar way: "Liberty was not so much conceived of as a private right of individuals to act in freedom from any governmental control; rather, it was seen as the right of the people collectively to exert political power free from the restrictions of royal power or officialdom or from a governmental authority in which the people did not participate" (*Public Education in the United States*, p. 9).

47. *Phi Delta Kappan*, vol. 60, no. 10 (1979), p. 763, reporting on statement of the Association of California School Administrators (ACSA).

CHAPTER 15: A PARALYSIS OF POLICY

Epigraph from Francis Bacon, *Advancement of Learning*, Book 1.

1. See, for example, Thomas Vitullo-Martin's testimony favoring tuition tax credits, U.S. Congress, Senate, Committee on Finance, *Tuition Tax Relief Bills: Hearing on S.96, S.311, S.834, S.1570, S.1781, S.2142*, 95th Cong., 2d sess., January 18, 19, and 20, 1978, p. 157, where he says that the option to pull out of public schools "is really the only kind of leverage that the people in the cities could have."

2. Theodore Sizer, former headmaster of Phillips Academy in Andover, Massachusetts, spoke of Andover as a "public" school for this reason.

CHAPTER 16: FAMILIES AS VICTIMS

Epigraph from Joseph Featherstone, "Family Matters," *Harvard Educational Review*, vol. 49 (Feb. 1979), p. 34.

1. Quoted in Christopher Lasch, *Haven in a Heartless World: The Family Besieged* (New York: Basic Books, 1977), p. 14.

2. Quoted in ibid.

3. Ibid.

4. Peter L. Berger and Richard John Neuhaus, *To Empower People: The Role of Mediating Structures in Public Policy* (Washington D.C.: American Enterprise Institute, 1977) p. 21.

5. Ibid.; and Lasch, *Haven in a Heartless World*, p. 18.

6. Lasch, *Haven in a Heartless World*, p. 13.

7. Sara Lawrence Lightfoot, *World Apart: Relationships between Families and Schools* (New York: Basic Books, 1978), p. 31.

8. Lee Rainwater and William L. Yancey, *The Moynihan Report and the Politics of Controversy* (Cambridge, Mass.: M.I.T. Press, 1967); includes

the full text of Daniel Patrick Moynihan, "The Negro Family: The Case for National Action."

9. Moynihan in Rainwater and Yancey, *Moynihan Report*, pp. 75, 93 (pp. 29, 47 of Moynihan text).

10. Rainwater and Yancey, *Moynihan Report*, chaps. 9, 10, 17. See also William

11. Lyndon Baines Johnson, "To Fulfill These Rights" speech at Howard University, June 4, 1965; found in Rainwater and Yancey, *Moynihan Report*, p. 130.

12. For an excellent overview of early criticism of the Moynihan report, see Rainwater and Yancey, *Moynihan Report*, 9, 10, 17. See also William Ryan, *Blaming the Victim* (New York: Vintage Books, 1972); Lightfoot, *Worlds Apart*, pp. 168, 175; Lasch, *Haven in a Heartless World*, pp. 160–66; Eugene Genovese, *Roll, Jordon, Roll: The World the Slaves Made* (New York: Pantheon, 1974); and Herbert Gutman, *The Black Family in Slavery and Freedom, 1750–1925* (New York: Pantheon, 1976).

13. Moynihan, in Rainwater and Yancey, *Moynihan Report*, p. 75 (p. 29 of Moynihan text).

14. Cf. Robert Staples, "Divorce, illegitimacy, and female-headed households are not necessarily dysfunctional except in the context of western, middle-class, white values"; quoted in Lasch, *Haven in a Heartless World*, p. 162.

15. Daniel P. Moynihan and Frederick Mosteller, eds., *On Equality of Educational Opportunity* (New York: Random House, 1972), pp. 3–66. For criticism of both Coleman and Moynihan, see Ryan, *Blaming the Victim.*

16. Mary Jo Bane, *Here to Stay: American Families in the Twentieth Century* (New York: Basic Books, 1976), p. 70.

17. Ibid., p. 143.

18. Kenneth Keniston and the Carnegie Council on Children, *All Our Children: The American Family under Pressure* (New York: Harcourt Brace Jovanovich, 1977), p. xiii.

19. Richard deLone, *Small Futures: Children, Inequality, and the Limits of Liberal Reform* (New York: Harcourt Brace Jovanovich, 1979), p. 93.

20. Lasch, *Haven in a Heartless World*, p. 18.

21. Ibid., p. xiv.

22. DeLone, *Small Futures*, pp. 42, 60–61, 78–112.

23. Keniston, *All Our Children*, pp. 15, 23.

24. Featherstone, "Family Matters," p. 35.

25. Keniston, *All Our Children*, p. 80.

26. DeLone, *Small Futures*, p. 199.

27. Advisory Committee on Child Development, *Toward a National Policy for Children and Families* (Washington, D.C.: National Academy of Sciences, 1976), pp. 12–13.

28. Keniston, Foreword to deLone, *Small Futures*, p. xiv.

29. Keniston, *All Our Children*, p. 46.

30. DeLone, *Small Futures*, pp. 11–12.

31. Lasch, *Haven in a Heartless World*, p. 160.
32. Ibid., pp. 164–65.
33. Ibid., p. 161.
34. Ryan, *Blaming the Victim*.
35. Cf. Fein, "Community Schools and Social Theory," p. 82. When we stop to think about it, it is not so surprising that the recent family studies have revived in their own way the thesis of how the problems of families interfere with schooling, because such a thesis bolsters their prime recommendations for improving the income and employment characteristics of families. From a political point of view, the public is more likely to accept reallocations of income and full employment policies if it can be convinced that having a breadwinner in each family (Keniston) and sufficient income to allow each family to manage its affairs (National Academy of Sciences, deLone, Bane) would increase the chances of children's succeeding in school. Helping the "unworthy poor" has never been popular, but helping children and opening "equal opportunity" for the next generation has always been inviting social policy. As Keniston points out, proposals for changing the economic system have been "few and unpopular, and one reason for their unpopularity is surely our alternative faith in the capacity of liberal reforms to improve our society by improving our children" (foreword to deLone). If this "faith" that education can improve the life chances of children can be deflated, there may be more chance of getting people to see the need for changes in the economic system.
36. DeLone, *Small Futures*, p. 160.
37. Ibid., p. 162.
38. Ibid., p. 161.
39. Ibid., p. 166.
40. Featherstone, "Family Matters," p. 40.
41. It must be presumed that neither deLone nor the Carnegie Council intends to encourage defeatism about what schools can do, although the effect of their argument is to do so. The Carnegie Council writes that, "It is a slander on any child to think that he or she cannot learn the skills needed to participate effectively in society. If the schools set this standard in what they demand for themselves and expect of children, they can increase the opportunities open to the excluded even if they cannot themselves guarantee complete equality of opportunity" (*All Our Children*, p. 47).
42. DeLone, *Small Futures*, p. 169.
43. Ibid.
44. Keniston, Foreword to deLone, *Small Futures*, p. xi.
45. Lasch, *Haven in a Heartless World*, p. 87.
46. DeLone, *Small Futures*, p. 177. DeLone does not "rule out the possibility that an extraordinarily influential individual (a teacher, a counselor, a peer) or an exceptional subsetting—a school, a family—can effect [a powerful intervention to counteract social class determinism]" (p. 177).

47. Ibid., p. 172.
48. James S. Coleman, Ernest Q. Campbell, et al., *Equality of Educational Opportunity*, (Washington, D.C.: U.S. Office of Education, 1966).
49. Erik Erikson, *Childhood and Society* (New York: W.W. Norton & Co., 1950), p. 245.
50. Keniston, Foreword to deLone, *Small Futures*, p. xii.

CHAPTER 17: FAMILIES AS PARTNERS

Epigraph from Sara Lawrence Lightfoot, *Worlds Apart: Relationships between Families and Schools* (New York: Basic Books, 1978), p. 38.
1. Hope Jensen Leichter, ed., *The Family as Educator* (New York: Teachers College Press, 1974).
2. Frank Riessman, *The Inner City Child* (New York: Harper & Row, 1976).
3. Lightfoot, *Worlds Apart*; Leichter, *Family as Educator*; Hope Jensen Leichter, *Families and Communities as Educators* (New York: Teachers College Press, 1979); Donald Erickson, U.S. Congress, Senate, Committee on Finance. *Tuition Tax Relief Bills: Hearing on S.96, S.311, S.834, S.1570, S.1781, S.2142*, 95th Cong., 2d sess., January 18, 19, and 20, 1978; Lawrence A. Cremin, *Public Education* (New York: Basic Books, 1976); and Benjamin S. Bloom, *Human Characteristics and School Learning* (New York: McGraw-Hill, 1976).
4. Lightfoot, *Worlds Apart*, p. 12.
5. Mary Jo Bane, *Here to Stay: American Families in the Twentieth Century* (New York: Basic Books, 1976), p. 142.
6. J.W. Getzels, "Socialization and Education: A Note on Discontinuities," in Leichter, *Family as Educator*, pp. 44–51.
7. Lawrence A. Cremin, "Family-Community Linkages in American Education: Some Comments on the Recent Historiography," in Leichter, *Families and Communities as Educators*. Cremin comments on Tyack's work and on the work of others who find such a "growing dissonance," p. 695. See, generally, David B. Tyack, *The One Best System: A History of American Urban Education* (Cambridge, Mass.: Harvard University Press, 1974).
8. Lightfoot, *Worlds Apart*, p. 22. Others have made similar points. See, for instance, Talcott Parsons, "The School Class as a Social System," *Harvard Educational Review*, vol. 29 (Fall 1959), pp. 297–318.
9. Lightfoot, *Worlds Apart*, pp. 26, 34.
10. The literature and examples are vast. See, among others, George Hillocks, Jr., "Books and Bombs: Ideological Conflict and the Schools—A Case Study of the Kanawha County Book Protest," *School Review*, vol. 86, no. 4, (1978), pp. 632–54; *New York Times*, "Iowa Takes a Breather in Dis-

pute over Theories of Human Origins," June 3, 1979; *Kanawha County West Virginia: A Textbook Study in Cultural Conflict* (Washington, D.C.: National Education Association, 1975). Connaught Coyne Marshner, *Blackboard Tyranny* (New Rochelle, N.Y.: Arlington House Publishers, 1978); anything on the conflict between the Amish and public educators, for instance, Albert N. Keim, ed., *Compulsory Education and the Amish: The Right Not to Be Modern* (Boston: Beacon Press, 1975); and, for historical perspective, the documents reprinted in Herbert M. Kliebard, ed., *Religion and Education in America: A Documentary History* (Scranton, Pa.: International Textbook Co., 1969). See also recent court decisions: State of North Carolina v. Columbus Christian Academy, #78 CVS 1678; and Rev. C.C. Hinton, Jr., et al. v. Kentucky State Board of Education, Franklin Circuit Court (Ky.), Civ. Action No. 88314, Division 1.

11. Horace Mann, *Tenth Annual Report, 1846*, in Lawrence A. Cremin, *Horace Mann on the Education of Free Men* (New York: Teachers College Press, 1957), pp. 63, 71, 75. On Mann and subsequent development of this perspective, see Lawrence A. Cremin, *The Transformation of the School: Progressivism in American Education, 1876-1957* (New York: Vintage Books, 1964).

12. Peter L. Berger and Richard John Neuhaus, *To Empower People: The Role of Mediating Structures in Public Policy* (Washington, D.C.: American Enterprise Institute, 1977) p. 21. See also the classical case in this area, Pierce v. Society of Sisters, 268 U.S. 510 (1925).

13. Bane, *Here to Stay*, p. 143.

14. Erik Erikson, *Childhood and Society* (New York: W.W. Norton & Co., 1950), pp. 383-84. See also Rosalie H. Wax, "The Warrior Dropouts," in Donald Erickson, *Educational Organization and Administration* (Berkeley, Calif.: McCutchan Publishing Corp., 1977), and U.S. Commission on Civil Rights, *The Navajo Nation: An American Colony* (Washington, D.C., 1975).

15. Getzels, "Socialization and Education," comments on this generally.

16. Peter L. Berger and Thomas Luckmann, *The Social Construction of Reality* (Garden City, N.Y.: Doubleday, Anchor Books, 1967), pp. 133-34; George Herbert Mead, *Mind, Self, and Society* (Chicago: University of Chicago Press, 1974, originally published in 1934), pp. 154ff.

17. James Bryant Conant, *The Child, the Parent, and the State* (Cambridge, Mass.: Harvard University Press, 1959), p. 18.

18. Kenneth Keniston and the Carnegie Council on Children, *All Our Children: The American Family under Pressure* (New York: Harcourt Brace Jovanovich, 1977), pp. 17ff.

19. Richard deLone, *Small Futures: Children, Inequality, and the Limits of Liberal Reform* (New York: Harcourt Brace Jovanovich, 1979), pp. 199ff.

20. Keniston, *All Our Children*, p. 18.

21. DeLone, *Small Futures*, p. 200.

22. Edward B. Fiske, "Jesse Jackson Builds Up Support in a Drive for Student Discipline," *New York Times*, March 4, 1979, pp. 1, 38. See also Mayor's Advisory Panel on Decentralization of the New York City Schools, *Reconnection for Learning: A Community School System for New York City* (New York: Ford Foundation, 1967), p. 13.

23. John E. Coons and Stephen D. Sugarman, *Education by Choice: The Case for Family Control* (Berkeley and Los Angeles: University of California Press, 1978), pp. 82, 83; see especially chap. 5, "Autonomy as the Goal: A Personal View," pp. 71–88.

CHAPTER 18: NOT ALL IN THE FAMILY

Epigraph from Hope Jensen Leichter, "Families and Communities as Educators: Some Concepts of Relationship," *Teachers College Record*, vol. 79, no. 4 (1978), p. 567.

1. Ibid.

2. Ibid.

3. Peter L. Berger and Richard John Neuhaus, *To Empower People: The Role of Mediating Structures in Public Policy* (Washington, D.C.: American Enterprise Institute, 1977), pp. 7, 2. Robert Nisbet expresses similar views in *Community and Power* (New York: Oxford University Press, 1962).

4. Leichter, "Families and Communities as Educators," p. 596; Hope Jensen Leichter, ed., *The Family As Educator* (New York: Teachers College Press, 1974), pp. 30–41.

5. Richard deLone, *Small Futures: Children, Inequality, and the Limits of Liberal Reform* (New York: Harcourt Brace Jovanovich, 1979), p. 138.

6. James S. Coleman, "Academic Achievement and the Structure of Competition," in A.H. Halsey et al., *Education, Economy and Society* (New York: Free Press, 1961), p. 377.

7. Frederick Douglass, *My Bondage and My Freedom* (New York: Miller, Orton & Mulligan, 1855), p. 319.

8. New York State Department of Education, press release, October 15, 1979.

9. Lawrence Cremin, "Family-Community Linkages in American Education: Some Comments on the Recent Historiography," *Teachers College Record*, vol. 79, no. 4 (1978), p. 689 (later published in Leichter, *Families and Communities as Educators*, p. 125).

10. Charles W. Anderson, Fred R. von de Mehdon, and Crawford Young, *Issues of Political Development* (Englewood Cliffs, N.J.: Prentice-Hall, 1967), pp. 4–5; see also Robin M. Williams, Jr., *Strangers Next Door:*

Ethnic Relations in American Communities (Englewood Cliffs, N.J.: (Prentice-Hall, 1964), p. 356.

11. Josiah Royce, *Basic Writings of Josiah Royce*, ed., John J. McDermott, (Chicago: University of Chicago Press, 1969); Josiah Royce, *The Hope of the Great Community* (Freeport, N.Y.: Books for Libraries Press, 1967).

12. Alexis de Tocqueville, *Democracy in America*, trans. Henry Reeves (New York: Schocken Books, 1961), pp. 54–55.

13. John H. Schaar, *Loyalty in America* (Berkeley and Los Angeles: University of California Press, 1957), p. 103.

14. Wilson Carey McWilliams argues that choice has been a significant element in determining family membership since ancient times. See his *The Idea of Fraternity in America* (Berkeley and Los Angeles: University of California Press, 1973), p. 11.

CHAPTER 19: REDEFINING THE ROLE OF GOVERNMENT, BUREAUCRACY, AND PROFESSIONALISM

Epigraph from Christopher Jencks et al., *Inequality* (New York: Basic Books, 1972), p. 256.

1. Leonard J. Fein, *The Ecology of the Public Schools: An Inquiry into Community Control* (New York: Pegasus, 1971). See my discussion in Chapter 13 on community control.

2. Peter L. Berger and Richard John Neuhaus, *To Empower People: The Role Of Mediating Structures in Public Policy* (Washington, D.C.: American Enterprise Institute, 1977).

3. Ibid., p. 3.

4. Stanley M. Elam, ed., *A Decade of Gallup Polls of Attitudes toward Education, 1969–1978* (Bloomington, Ind.: Phi Delta Kappan, 1978). The preference parents express for local control throughout the ten years covered in this book have apparently not changed. See George Gallup, "The Twelfth Annual Gallup Poll of the Public's Attitudes toward the Public Schools," *Phi Delta Kappan*, vol. 62, no. 1 (1980).

5. Evans Clinchy and Elisabeth A. Cody, "If Not Public Choice, Then Private Escape," *Phi Delta Kappan*, vol. 60, no. 4 (1978), pp. 271ff.

6. Albert Shanker, quoted in *New York Times*, December 30, 1979, p. 16E.

7. Albert N. Keim, *Compulsory Education and the Amish: The Right Not to Be Modern* (Boston: Beacon Press, 1975). See Wisconsin v. Yoder 406 US205, 32LEd2d15, 92 S Ct. 1526.

8. Talcott Parsons, as quoted by Samuel Bowles and Herbert Gintis, "I.Q. in the U.S. Class Structure," in Jerome Karabel and A.H. Halsey, eds. (New York: Oxford University Press, 1977), *Power and Ideology in Edu-*

cation, p. 228; originally from Talcott Parsons, "Evolutionary Universals in Society," *American Sociological Review,* vol. 29, no. 3 (1964), p. 507.

9. An interesting perspective on this is the recent judicial conclusion that faculty members of at least private universities are not "employees." See National Labor Relations Board v. Yeshiva University, 63LEd 2nd 115, 100 S Ct. 856 (1980).

10. Jencks et al., *Inequality,* p. 256.

11. Joseph Featherstone, "Rousseau and Modernity," *Daedalus,* vol. 107, no. 3 (1978), p. 186.

12. Hope Jensen Leichter, "Families and Communities as Educators: Some Concepts of Relationship," in Leichter, ed., *Families and Communities as Educators, Teachers College Record,* vol. 79, no. 4 (1978), pp. 596 ff.

13. "Teacher Burnout (How to Cope When Your World Goes Black)," *Instructor Special Report, Instructor,* January 1979.

14. Ronald Corwin, *Militant Professionalism* (New York: Appleton-Century-Crofts, 1970). Corwin explains teacher militancy as a response to bureaucratization.

15. John H. Marvin, "What Comes after Collective Bargaining," Maine Education Seminars, Maine Teachers Association, September 14, 1979; Myron Lieberman, *Public Sector Bargaining: A Policy Reappraisal* (Lexington, Mass.: Lexington Books, 1980); Mario Fantini, *What's Best for the Children* (Garden City, N.Y.: Doubleday, Anchor Press, 1974).

16. Urie Bronfenbrenner, *Two Worlds of Childhood* (New York: Russell Sage Foundation, 1970), p. 154.

17. Peter Berger, Brigitte Berger, and Hansfried Kellner, *The Homeless Mind* (New York: Vintage Books, 1974), chap. 2., p. 47. Berger et al. draw heavily on Weber.

18. Dan C. Lortie, *Schoolteacher* (Chicago: University of Chicago Press, 1975), p. 27.

CHAPTER 20: LEARNING PARTNERSHIPS

Epigraph from Malcolm Provus, "In Search of Community," *Phi Delta Kappan,* vol. 54, no. 10 (1973), p. 658.

1. Lawrence C. Pierce, "School Site Management," Occasional Paper, Aspen Institute for Humanistic Studies; Don Davies et al., *Sharing the Power? A Report on the Status of School Councils in the 1970's* (Boston: Institute for Responsive Education, n.d.).

2. "Improving Education in Florida: A Reassessment," summary of the consultant's report prepared for the Select Joint Committee on Public Schools of the Florida Legislature, February 1978.

3. Ross Zerchykov, Don Davies, and Janet Chrispeels, *State Mandates for*

school Advisory Councils in California, Florida, and South Carolina (Boston: Institute for Responsive Education, 1980).

4. New York Urban Coalition, *Options in Learning*, vol. 7, no. 3 (1978).

5. James P. Comer, *School Power: Implications of an Intervention Project* (New York: Free Press, 1980), pp. 66, 229.

6. See also Leonard J. Fein, "Community Schools and Social Theory: The Limits of Universalism," in Henry M. Levin, ed., *Community Control of Schools* (Washington, D.C.: Brookings Institution, 1970), pp. 76–99.

7. Don Davies, ed., *Schools Where Parents Make a Difference* (Boston: Institute for Responsive Education, 1976), pp. 158–59.

8. Ibid., p. 159.

9. Ibid., p. 158.

10. Evans Clinchy and Elisabeth A. Cody, "If Not Public Choice, Then Private Escape," *Phi Delta Kappan*, vol. 60, no. 4 (1978), pp. 272, 273. See also Anthony J. Morley, *Southeast Alternatives: Final Report—1971-1976*, Minneapolis Public Schools, July 1976.

11. Clinchy and Cody, "If Not Public Choice," p. 273. For another school system that has used family choice in connection with integration, see Margery Thompson, "Milwaukee's Specialty School Plan Promotes Learning and Integration," *American School Board Journal*, vol. 166, no. 5 (1979), pp. 30-33.

12. Diane Divoky, "Pluralism goes Public: How Lagunitas, California, Did It," in Davies, *Schools Where Parents Make a Difference*, pp. 22, 28.

13. Mario D. Fantini, *Public Schools of Choice: A Plan for the Reform of American Education* (New York: Simon & Schuster, 1973), and *What's Best for the Children? Resolving the Power Struggle between Parents and Teachers* (Garden City, N.Y.: Doubleday, Anchor Press, 1974).

14. *Education Vouchers: The Experience at Alum Rock* (Santa Monica, Calif.: Rand Corporation for the National Institute of Education, Department of Health, Education, and Welfare, December 1973).

15. John Grossman, "Tough Teachers Who Care," *The American Way*, September, 1978, pp. 57, 58, 60, 63.

16. Ibid., pp. 58, 60.

17. Ibid., p. 59.

18. Joseph C. Grannis, *Bedford-Stuyvesant Street Academy Evaluation, Phase I, Spring 1979* (New York: Public Education Association, 1979). Quotations in following paragraphs found on p. 79 and in "Summary," pp. vii, viii.

19. G.J. Anderson and H.J. Walberg, "Learning Environments," in Walberg, ed., *Evaluating Educational Performance* (Berkeley; McCutchan Publishing Corp., 1974); W.B. Brookover, et al., "Elementary School Social Climate and School Achievement," *American Educational Research Journal*, vol. 15, no. 2 (1978); J.L. Epstein and J.M. McPartland, "Classroom Organization and the Quality of School Life" (Baltimore: Johns

Hopkins University, Social Organization of Schools, Report No. 215, August 1976); R.H. Moos, *Evaluating Educational Environments* (San Francisco: Jossey-Bass, 1979); and Sarane Boocock, *Sociology of Learning; An Introduction,* 2d ed. (Boston: Houghton Mifflin Co., 1980).

20. William Glasser, *Schools without Failure* (New York: Harper & Row, 1969).

21. Urie Bronfenbrenner, *Two Worlds of Childhood* (New York: Russell Sage Foundation, 1970), p. 155.

22. Robert E. Slavin, *Using Student Team Learning* (Baltimore: Johns Hopkins University, Center for Social Organization of Schools, 1978).

23. Education Amendments of 1978 (P.L. 95-561; 20 U.S.C. 2701ff., Title II, §206).

24. Public Education Association, *Annual Report, 1979.*

25. Robert Cloward, "Studies in Tutoring," *Journal of Experimental Education,* vol. 36, no. 1 (1967), pp. 14-25.

26. National Commission on Resources for Youth, *The Youth Tutoring Youth Model; An Evaluation* (New York, 1972), pp. 11-15.

27. Public Education Association, "Evaluation of One Plus One Summer Peer Tutoring Program, 1980" (Evaluation by Bank Street College of Education, Janet Kane, principal investigator).

28. National Commission for Resources for Youth, *New Roles for Youth in the School and the Community* (New York: Citation Press, 1974), ix.

29. Bronfenbrenner, *Two Worlds of Childhood,* p. 156.

30. James S. Coleman, "Academic Achievement and the Structure of Competition," in A.H. Halsey et al., eds. *Education, Economy, and Society* (New York: Free Press, 1961), p. 367. William Spady reports evidence that small schools tend to create an environment in which everyone is needed to run programs, especially extracurricular programs, with the result that students tend to be more engaged in school activities. See William G. Spady, "Status, Achievement, and Motivation in the American High School," in Donald A. Erickson, ed., *Educational Organization and Administration* (Berkeley, Calif.: McCutchan Publishing Corp., 1977), pp. 88-109.

31. *New York Times,* December 22, 1979, p. 27.

32. Public Education Association, "Evaluation of One Plus One Summer Peer Tutoring Program."

33. Jonathan P. Sher, ed., *Education in Rural America: A Reassessment of Conventional Wisdom* (Boulder, Colo.: Westview Press, 1977), pp. 75-76.

34. *New York Times,* December 16, 1979, p. 69.

35. Interview by author with James H.K. Norton, member of school board of West Tisbury, Massachusetts, 1978.

36. *New York Times,* December 16, 1979, p. 69.

37. John E. Coons and Stephen D. Sugarman, *Education by Choice: The Case for Family Control* (Berkeley and Los Angeles: University of California Press, 1978), p. 49, 50.

38.   *New York Times,* December 16, 1979, p. 69.

39.   Edward McDill and Leo C. Rigsby, *Structure and Process in Secondary Schools: The Academic Impact of Educational Climates* (Baltimore: Johns Hopkins University Press, 1973), pp. 122, 123.

40.   Thomas Good, Bruce Biddle, and Jere Brophy. *Teachers Make a Difference* (New York: Holt, Rinehart & Winston, 1975).

41.   Nicholas Hobbs, "Families, Schools, and Communities: An Ecosystem for Children," *Teachers College Record,* vol. 79, no. 4 (1978), pp. 756ff.

42.   *New York Times,* September 4, 1979, p. B2.

43.   Cf. *Teachers College Record,* vol. 79, no. 4 (1978), pp. 600ff, 785–88.

44.   Eugene Litwak and Henry J. Meyer, *School, Family, and Neighborhood: The Theory and Practice of School-Community Relations* (New York: Columbia University Press, 1974).

CHAPTER 21: BUSING, BOOK BANNING, AND BILINGUALISM

Epigraph from James William Noll, *Taking Sides: Clashing Views on Controversial Educational Issues* (Guilford, Conn.: Dushkin Publishing Group, 1980), p. v.

1.   Meyer Weinberg, *A Chance to Learn: A History of Race and Education in the United States* (Cambridge: Cambridge University Press, 1977) esp. pp. 9–80; and C. Vann Woodward, *The Strange Career of Jim Crow* (New York: Oxford University Press, 1957).

2.   Judith R. Porter and Robert E. Washington, "Black Identity and Self-Esteem: A Review of Studies of Black Self-Concept, 1968–1978," *Annual Review of Sociology,* vol. 5, no. 57 (1979).

3.   See, generally, Stanley M. Elam, ed., *A Decade of Gallup Polls of Attitudes toward Education, 1969-1978* (Bloomington, Ind.: Phi Delta Kappan, 1978), pp. 199, 343–44.

4.   John E. Coons and Stephen D. Sugarman, *Education by Choice: The Case for Family Control* (Berkeley and Los Angeles: University of California Press, 1978), pp. 109–30; and Nancy St. John, *School Desegregation: Outcomes for Children* (New York: John Wiley & Son, 1975).

5.   See, generally, on the controversy, Alan Pifer, "Bilingual Education and the Hispanic Challenge," *1979 Annual Report,* Carnegie Corporation of New York; and Francesca Cordasco, *Bilingual Schooling in the United States* (New York: McGraw-Hill, 1976).

6.   Department of Education Office of Civil Rights, "Civil Rights Language Minority Hearings," September 1980; Noel Epstein, *Language, Ethnicity, and the Schools: Policy Alternatives for Bilingual-Bicultural Education* (Washington, D.C.: Institution for Educational Leadership, George Wash-

ington University, 1977); Nathan Glazer, "Public Education and American Pluralism," in *Parents, Teachers, and Children: Prospects for Choice in American Education* (San Francisco: Institute for Contemporary Studies, 1977), pp. 85–110; and Edgar G. Epps, *Cultural Pluralism* (Chicago: National Society for the Study of Education; Berkeley: McCutchan Publishing Corp., 1974).

7. Lau v. Nichols, 414 U.S. 563 (1974). Some argue that the *Lau* decision does not require any bilingual instruction at all, as long as alternate means are provided to ensure that non-English-speaking students can benefit from the instruction.

8. U.S. v. Texas Civ. No. 5281 Eastern Dist. Texas (Tyler Div.), decided January 9, 1981.

9. National Advisory Council for Bilingual Education, Department of Education, Fifth Annual Report, 1980–81. *The Prospects for Bilingual Education in the Nation*; U.S. Commission on Civil Rights, *A Better Chance to Learn: Bilingual-Bicultural Education* (Washington, D.C.: Clearinghouse Publication No. 51, May 1975), pp. 69ff.

10. Education Commission of the States, "Summary of the Tenth Annual Meeting, 1976," p. 30; and Arthur E. Wise, *Legislated Learning: The Bureaucratization of the American Classroom* (Berkeley and Los Angeles: University of California Press, 1979), p. 111.

11. Education Commission of the States, "Update VIII: Minimum Competency Testing," Report no. 124, July 1979.

12. Wise, *Legislated Learning*, p. 65.

13. See, for instance, The California policy for encouraging local initiative through school councils that can request waivers of state regulations. Cf. Cal. Statutes § § 52000–52038 (Assembly Bill 65).

14. Wise, *Legislated Learning*, p. 22.

15. Constance Horner, "Is The New Sex Education Going Too Far?," *New York Times Magazine*, December 7, 1980, p. 144.

16. James L. Collier, "What Ever Happened to Sex Education?" *Reader's Digest*, Vol. 118, no. 709 (May 1981), p. 131.

17. Ibid., and Elam, *A Decade of Gallup Polls*, pp. 315–17.

18. Collier, "What Ever Happened to Sex Education?" p. 129.

19. Horner, "Is The New Sex Education Going Too Far?," p. 138.

20. George Hillocks, Jr., "Books and Bombs: Ideological Conflict and the Schools—a Case Study of the Kanawha County Book Protest," *School Review*, vol. 86, no. 4 (1978), pp. 632–54.

21. Stephen Arons, "Book Burning in the Heartland," *Saturday Review*, July 21, 1979.

22. Brief of National Council of Teachers of English et al., in Pico v. Island Trees, U.S. Court of Appeals, 24d Circ., Docket No. 79–7690, Cahill, Gordon & Reindel, counsel.

23. Pico v. Board of Education, Island Trees Union Free School District No. 26, U.S.C.A. 2nd Circ. No. 619, Sept. 1979. Docket No. 79-7690.

24. Nat Hentoff, *The First Freedom* (New York: Delacorte Press, 1980), pp. 28, 29.

25. Ibid., pp. 32-34.

26. Ibid., p. 28, citing Minarcini v. Strongsville City School District 541 F. 2d 577 (6th Cir. 1976).

27. Ibid., p. 24.

28. Keyishian v. Board of Regents, 385 U.S. 589, 603 (1967).

29. Cf., however, Justice Brennan in Keyishian: "The classroom is peculiarly the 'marketplace of ideas.'" This is a worthy educational principle but a dubious constitutional law, since teachers inevitably must select materials for class use and thus control free speech in ways that should be absolutely prohibited by First Amendment rights governing the public marketplace.

30. Brief of National Council of Teachers of English, p. 16.

31. Donald Erickson, Richard Nault, and Bruce Cooper, "Recent Enrollment Trends in U.S. Nonpublic Schools," in S. Abromowitz and Stuart Rosenfeld, eds. *Declining Enrollments: The Challenge of the Coming Decade* (Washington, D.C.: National Institute of Education, March 1978); and Gene I. Maeroff, "Private Schools Look to Bright Futures," *New York Times,* January 14, 1981, Sec. 12, pp. 1ff. On governmental regulation of private schools, see Russell Kirk, "Tentative Victories from the Academy," *National Review,* January 1979, and "For Private Schools That Value Privacy," *American School Board Journal,* July 1978, pp. 16-17. See Religious News Service bulletins generally, or see specifically "Kentucky Decision Heartens N.C. Christian Academies," October 9, 1978; "Private Schools Object to Proposed IRS Guidelines on Discrimination," October 23, 1978; and "IRS Feeding Our Children to Lions, Christian School Demonstrators Say." See, generally, Jay Mechling, ed., *Church, State, and Public Policy: The New Shape of the Church-State Debate* (Washington, D.C.: American Enterprise Institute, 1978). State of North Carolina, et al., v. Columbus Christian Academy, et al., in the General Court of Justice Superior Court Division #78 CVS 1678. Reverend C.C. Hinton, Jr., et al. v. Kentucky State Board of Education, et al., memo opinion and judgment, Franklin Circuit Court Civil Action No. 88314 Division 1.

32. Hinton v. Kentucky State Board of Education.

33. Peter Skerry, "Christian Schools versus the IRS," *The Public Interest* 61 (Fall 1980), p. 19.

34. Ibid.

INDEX

305

ABOUT THE AUTHOR

David Seeley has for over twenty years wrestled with the policy problems of American public education, first as an attorney for the federal Department of Health, Education and Welfare, then as Assistant Commissioner of Education for Equal Educational Opportunity, later as education adviser to New York City's Mayor John Lindsay, and from 1969 to 1980 as the Director of the prestigious Public Education Association in New York. He has written on a variety of educational issues such as school productivity, equal educational opportunity, collective bargaining, and teacher accountability. He has served on numerous commissions, study panels, and consulting assignments, trying to find answers to the perplexing problems facing our public school systems. In addition to bachelors and law degrees from Yale, he has received his doctorate in educational administration from Harvard in 1970. He currently teaches at the College of Staten Island and serves as an educational consultant.

SELECTED AEI PUBLICATIONS

Excellence in Education: The States Take Charge, Denis P. Doyle and Terry W. Hartle (1985, approx. 70 pp., $4.95)

The Private Sector in the Public School: Can It Improve Education? Marsha Levine, ed. (1985, 77 pp., $4.95)

Aliteracy: People Who Can Read But Won't, Nick Thimmesch, ed. (1984, 59 pp., $3.95)

Debating National Education Policy: The Question of Standards (1981, 152 pp., $6.25)

Meeting Human Needs: Toward a New Public Philosophy, Jack A. Meyer, ed. (1982, 469 pp., cloth $34.95, paper $13.95)

Church, State, and Public Policy: The New Shape of the Church-State Debate, Jay Mechling, ed. (1978, 119 pp., cloth $12.95, paper $5.25)

To Empower People: The Role of Mediating Structures in Public Policy, Peter L. Berger and Richard John Neuhaus (1977, 45 pp., $3.25)

AEI ASSOCIATES PROGRAM

The American Enterprise Institute invites your participation in the competition of ideas through its AEI Associates Program. This program has two objectives: (1) to extend public familiarity with contemporary issues; and (2) to increase research on these issues and disseminate the results to policy makers, the academic community, journalists, and others who help shape public policies. The areas studied by AEI include Economic Policy, Education Policy, Energy Policy, Fiscal Policy, Government Regulation, Health Policy, International Programs, Legal Policy, National Defense Studies, Political and Social Processes, and Religion, Philosophy, and Public Policy. For the $49 annual fee, Associates receive

- a subscription to *Memorandum,* the newsletter on all AEI activities
- the AEI publications catalog and all supplements
- a 30 percent discount on all AEI books
- a 40 percent discount for certain seminars on key issues
- subscriptions to any two of the following publications: *Public Opinion,* a bimonthly magazine exploring trends and implications of public opinion on social and public policy questions; *Regulation,* a bimonthly journal examining all aspects of government regulation of society; and *AEI Economist,* a monthly newsletter analyzing current economic issues and evaluating future trends (or for all three publications, send an additional $12).

Call 202/862-6446 or write: AMERICAN ENTERPRISE INSTITUTE
1150 Seventeenth Street, N.W., Suite 301, Washington, D.C. 20036